Scooch!

Edging into a Friendly Universe

Published by fun & gains productions
101 E. State St., #133
Ithaca, NY 14850

ISBN: 978-0-9977401-0-3

Typeset in Adobe Garamond Pro
Manufactured in the United States

Scooch!

Edging into a Friendly Universe

JAYA THE TRUST COACH

To Rik Holman,
my inspiring brother-in-law,
because when life asked you to surrender so much of your power to choose, you found how to harness your power of interpretation and keep showing up with goodwill.

CONTENTS

acknowledgments

Thank you to all the clients plus a few random people who gave permission to have their stories used and worked with me to get them just so, with all kinds of facts changed to protect privacy while the integrity of the stories and what they illustrate remains intact. Thank you to all the clients whose stories aren't explicitly told here but who provided me the ample opportunities to articulate (and learn more deeply) all that's in these pages and to support real human beings in applying it. It's a profound privilege for me to get to hold others in this way—I don't lose sight of that.

Byron Katie, nothing I've got to give would be givable without you.

David A, thank you for sending me Florence's book for no reason (and for amazing coaching adventures).

Denise H, if the birthing of this book had a midwife, it was surely you. Your emotional support, easy willingness to give time to this project (with intelligence and intuition fully engaged), clear and specific feedback, editorial tweaks and typo-catching, prevailing belief in me and the whole endeavor—all were invaluable.

Ellen C, thank you for sending me Tosha's book for no reason.

Jennifer I, you've been a light beam to me, to the part of my family that managed to land in your city, and to this project.

Jude S, I would be neither the person nor the coach that I am without our long talks. This book, in many more ways than explicitly stated in the text, has been informed by your wisdom, your clarity, your holding me in the highest light.

Kelli Y, when you sat me down to offer your responses—and paid me to hear them, crazy/sane Two that you are—something important happened. Thank you for offering me the beautiful Kelliscope.

Laura B, your loving and fun-stirring presence in my life and bouilla-baisse dish, in the very fishy-water I swim in, is somehow fundamental.

Liana B, a mermaid told me, "Only you would hire a professional artist to draw a stick figure." Well, I'm in love with the stick figures you made me. May any number of good people look you up and learn about the gorgeous, complex, sophisticated art that you make.

Lise A, your selfless gift got me to Katie's School, and Katie's School got me here. Je te remercie de tout mon cœur.

Lorraine F, thank you for cultivating the magic with me and for contrib-uting your story to this book—absolutely the clearest example I had of the journey from vague vision to super-specific form.

Louise K, it gives me such joy to have you in my book and somehow an abiding, unshakable, and certainly brilliant presence in my life. I embedded a bad baby into this book for you. Consider it a treasure hunt.

Megan P, every good story needs the hero who swoops in at the end to make it all come out right. You're the one.

Nydia B, I'm in awe of the gold you keep spinning, girl, in both your evolving talent and personal evolution.

Sharron T, I love that you gave me your story to share here before you left it. You were a big, beautiful, quietly radiant badass.

Stephen M, thank you, thank you, thank you. You're worth a good three without my overstating it.

Steve H, that singular conversation with you was epic, in my little world, and ended up rippling out to many others. Some ideas in chapter 26 first took conscious form for me that day. That's not the only way you informed my coaching, and my effectiveness as a coach. It's because of you that I listen so carefully to my clients, and trust that listening.

Sy S, it was a few eras back when you saved my life, but you did, and took me seriously as a writer at a time I took nothing about myself seriously except my tempestuous feelings. With deep gratitude, I honor your place in my life story, in all that led up to this writing.

Tosha S, thank you for your unwavering insistence on divine order above all else, for all you add to these pages, and for giving your consent to be included here.

Tyi M, thank you for being such a proponent of my work, and for reminding me of the magic when I was birthing this book and needed, apparently, the very report you sent of how the Universe brought it all together for you, effortlessly and through unexpected channels.

Yael S, you named me Jaya the Trust Coach with such conviction ("That's who you are!") that it seemed kind of irrefutable.

Yheva, oh my goddess, without you this book would have the word *land* or some form of it on every other page. Still in there plenty, but I'm pretty happy with how it all landed.

Yvonne L, that such a remarkable human being would trust me with so much kind of boggles the mind. Thank you for enriching my practice and this book, and for letting me climb into the ELF.

Thank you to the Michigan Womyn's Music Festival as an entity in itself, and to Lisa Vogel who created it and bravely put it to bed when it was time, and to the amazing womyn I met there, and to all who attended my workshops and intensives there, and to those who became clients, invited me to their towns to give workshops, or came and keep coming back around to let me know how they've benefited from my work. Thanks especially to Julieta who first pointed me that way; Jess D, who has been and keeps being a blessing on so many levels, and who made it possible for me to be there the last year of Fest; Brandy for being my partner in crime in that last adventure; Leanne and Janice, who kept coming closer and just won't go away; Marcie the nutrition goddess (marciegoldman-dot-com) and the others in the Womb, who supported me every time I was on the Land with no-nonsense magic herbs, pure kindness, and wacky wit (though I only ever caught one pubic cervix announcement); Fabi, who more than once translated one of my posts on Facebook into Spanish, somehow magnifying their beauty and worth in the process; and Nisey, the specific sister-my-sister who reminds me in her very being that crazy, amazing, stunningly beautiful gifts can always come in unexpectedly, at the last minute, after the fact, at any moment.

Thank you to all retreat and workshop participants I've ever gotten to work with. It's a delicious experience to gather with others in that way. The specific individuals who have lent their marvelous energies to these events and to the processes we move through together have showered me (and one another!) with blessings just by bringing along their best and most vulnerable selves. The programs that allowed me to go so deeply and at varying levels of depth into the self-honoring, personal-power, and visioning materials, in particular, contributed to my solid grasp of the concepts and tools presented in these pages. Here's my vote for more and new client and workshop adventures of all kinds.

Thanks to the clients and people on my mailing list who received bits of this book along the way and treated them as wonderful gifts. Thanks to those following my Facebook page who get my coaching in little bites and still seem to be nourished by it, and who asked after my book and actually purchased it at the first announcement of its coming. Every time someone wrote to say they couldn't wait to read the whole thing, it was so bolstering, so affirming.

Finally, I hardly know how to acknowledge the three people I seem to think of as my children. They're all in this book because there's just no way around that. My heart has grown at least three times bigger for their shiny-funny-wondrous presences in my world. (Last and most certainly least, fredlyn, you reduce everything to, um, you cloak everything in, such as, by which I mean, from the bottom of my eye, words fail me.)

Scooch!

I just plain love the word *scooch*. I'm pretty sure people should sit around at parties and in coffee shops telling their history with *scooch* (and perhaps a few other great humble words). Here's mine. My grandmother was an Arkansas lady (not *woman*: those didn't really exist in Arkansas till Hillary got big, certainly never existed for my grandmother) who hardly ever bothered speaking without infusing a lot of *tone* and sometimes a fair amount of screeching into her words. She used to deliver a one-word command if she was plopping her hard-working self onto a car seat or couch cushion that one of her kin might be currently occupying without having left sufficient room for her. "Scooch!" she'd cry in her high-pitched, good-humored Southern-speak, and scooch we did, with no thought of talking back.

I started working with the concept of scooching to counter my clients' sense of overwhelm, discouragement, and sometimes defeat when they felt they had too far to reach. Finding themselves, for example, so far from love that it felt like hate (you know, the dreaded ex making one more thing unnecessarily caustic), they wanted to propel themselves straight to love (or thought they should or wished they could)—and it's just too far a trip to take in one leap. It's too far not only because it's on the other end of the spectrum, but because they were contemplating the journey from a low spot, with a sense of being off-kilter and unequal to the challenge.

So what if, in such a moment, you didn't need to get all the way to love? What if you could just point yourself in that direction, and feel good about any movement aimed roughly the right way? What if, instead of somehow mustering or conjuring some huge burst of fuel to get you all the way from here to there, you could simply ... scooch?

Soon after I started articulating this, I discovered Abraham—that is, I finally listened to an audio clip featuring Esther Hicks, a nice, playful Southern lady from Texas (not *woman*: Texas) who channels a playful consciousness (not a single entity) named Abraham who specializes in teaching the law of attraction (LOA). May I just say that I had a self-diagnosed allergy to channels before I fell in love with Abraham? (I wasn't thrilled with LOA either, and still don't appreciate how most anyone else talks about it.) For almost two decades, people had been telling me to listen to Abraham-Hicks and I would have none of it. Then one day, the title of one of their talks caught my attention on YouTube and I tuned in to the first of many, many talks I would give my attention to through many a dishwashing or qigong session.

I didn't have to sample too many talks before hearing Abraham articulate my scooching idea. I got so excited. I was hollering "Yes!" at my computer. *Scooch* actually sounds like a word Esther would use in her translations (she receives a message as wordless impressions, then puts Southern-American English to it so the rest of us can more or less get the message too), but I haven't heard *scooch* from Abraham/Esther. They do talk about the process of moving incrementally from one feeling state to another.

For example, they love to explain that, if you're depressed, you can't go straight to joy, but you might do well to get angry—which feels better than depressed because now you're not just shut down, you're moving—and then you can tone that down to frustration, which feels better still, and from there you could gradually get closer and closer to full-blown joy. Abraham on scooching!

I believe I held myself back in the personal-growth department for years (as do many human beings) by making my process unkind. It was full of guilt, shame, *should*, harsh self-admonitions, and self-evaluations that came when it wasn't time to evaluate (as in before the event even happened or while it was happening or instantly afterward, with no time for breath or for locating what actually felt good—or even fine). My process was lacking in forgiveness and full of multiple beliefs about what I did or didn't deserve and could or couldn't have, all of which finally got shaken up and scattered to the winds when I discovered The Work of Byron Katie.

A decade in, it's still astonishing to me how often I remember to live in ease and joy and kindness and love. It's amazing that I can be light and present and connected so very often. The fact that I used to be a moody, depressive, overwhelmed victim accounts for the if-I-can-change-anyone-can mentality I bring to my life-coaching work. I honestly wasn't sure I could change. And the thing that accelerated the improvements most was to stop judging myself or my process or how long things took or what I found myself doing *again* and so on. (What if you didn't judge yourself, ever?) I learned to drop judgments (not stay out of judgments) and question my thoughts about everything (not be without thoughts) thanks to The Work of Byron Katie. When I started applying all of that to my judgments about myself and the things I believed I could or couldn't be, do, or have—that's when life started getting really good.

This book will urge you repeatedly to make your process kind. Be gentle with yourself. Quit treating yourself like you'd treat no other human being, or like you treat your familiars in your worst moments (a pretty accurate gauge of how you treat yourself most anytime). I'm all about personal power, so I won't be advocating wimpiness or letting yourself off the hook. I'm not into gushy or sloppy self-love, but I'm supremely interested in self-love that's unrelenting and gives at least equal time to knowing and cultivating your magnificence as it does to ferreting out and fixing your flaws. Honestly, if you're being truly kind to yourself, it gets much easier to look at yourself realistically and course-correct when you find yourself standing where you don't want to be or heading in the wrong direction. (And note that you're not being realistic when you fail to notice where you're amazing.)

If you want to get somewhere, and the way isn't clear, the resources aren't apparent, and you're just not sure you can do it, quit striving, quit judging yourself, quit believing anything should be other than it is: just point yourself in the right direction, and scooch.

The thing about scooching is, it works. It keeps you from getting stuck. It does away with all-or-nothing. It does away with timelines or expectations of any sort, being more in the realm of "Let's just see how far I get, here" than "I'm supposed to be way over there already and I have no clue how to take the journey"—otherwise stated, "Cain't get there from here" (with a dash of "what-the-hell-is-wrong-with-me?" thrown in). Perhaps most important, scooching is kind, it's reasonable, it's realistic. What's not to like?

The first time I wrote the word *scooch* myself was in a Facebook post on my Jaya the Trust Coach page on Valentine's day of 2013:

A day for love! See, hear, feel, smell, taste your vision of love; remove or post a profile, get off a fence and land on your feet, catch the spark & kindle the flame; take the right dose of chocolate; light candles with a dear one or no one; gaze into her eyes, his eyes, a cat's eyes, everyone's eyes; give hugs, roses, smiles, winks, words of true praise & appreciation; laugh & create levity all day; love yourself & count the ways. Valentine's Day is a human construct, so don't use it to make yourself feel bad about relationship, romance, or sex. It's just a good excuse to scooch in closer to love.

There it is again: the kindness of scooching. Notice, too, what's special with this wording, as this is *scooch* with a twist: *scooch in*. To scooch in is to come even closer, as when cousin Buddy and Aunt Goob showed up next, and then the imperative was to make room on the couch for them too.

So c'mon, y'all—scooch in!

Scooch toward a Friendly Universe

Now a good decade ago, I snarled a frustrated comment about someone I loved but didn't live with well, and a woman used my statement to guide me through an inquiry process. I had such an instant experience of seeing another in a new, kinder light (and of liking myself a whole lot better) that I paid this woman to help me understand how to question my thoughts on an ongoing basis. This was Jude Spacks of Truth and Dare creative inquiry coaching, who later became my friend and colleague. The inquiry process was The Work of Byron Katie.

Katie (she doesn't go by Byron!) works from the premise that nothing that happens is inherently stressful. Pain, anger, sadness, frustration—all come from our thoughts about what's happening. These thoughts can be questioned. She also advocates finding the benefits in anything that happens to you, and looking for all that supports you to get through it. (She starts in the concrete here and now: this chair, the floor, the working phone within reach.)

After some months of fruitful inquiry, I attended the nine-day School for The Work (inner excavation—get out your worst fears, your greatest shame, your most painful love story) then made inquiry a daily habit. I changed. I changed in a way that even your children notice. I changed in the way that makes your spouse sign up for the same program. Within two years, things with my then-husband drastically improved, then we divorced. The short version is: we'd gotten the lessons and we were done.

Soon after this split, I drove through the desert to sit with a life coach named Steve Hardison for two hours, someone I met at the School for The Work. He told me this: treat everything like good news. Whatever comes to you, whatever doors open or shut, whatever happens even if it would look like failure and rejection to most intelligent life, believe that it's the best thing that could happen to you. This took what I'd learned from Katie to another level. Or perhaps it helped me to give more attention to that thing she teaches about looking for the benefits in

12

everything. This is what it is to live in a friendly Universe.

Since then, I've been experimenting with radical trust: seeing everything (everything) as the Universe conspiring in my favor. This was a phrase I'd heard before, and liked the sound of, but had no relationship with whatsoever. I've developed a day-to-day, moment-to-moment intimacy with this idea. I scooched in close, and I keep scooching. Whenever I've strayed from believing it's a friendly Universe, I turn again to The Work. I put my stressful thoughts on paper and launch another round of inquiry. I did The Work almost daily for three years after the School. Now I do it rarely, when something big comes up, but not because I'm done with it. It lives inside me. Hardly a stressful thought comes up without the simultaneous awareness arising that this thought just can't be all true. Stressful thoughts are jarring, so I pay attention to them: like the stranger who walks into the living room uninvited—why would I just pretend he's not there, even though my whole body bristles at his presence?

The first couple of years post-divorce brought plenty of thoughts to question. I moved to a town where I didn't want to be (so I thought) and didn't know anyone, simply because my ex moved there, so we could still co-parent together. (Can I just mention I was a lesbian before and again after this nuclear family detour? The place we all moved to, the college town of Ithaca in upstate New York, is about as queer-friendly as a town can get.) I arrived with little money, scant possessions, and no job. Suddenly, my decade-long source of freelance editorial work ran dry. This was a book publisher I was used to going to anytime I needed money, and they always had something for me. Now nothing. I cried over this during a memorable thunderstorm, used The Work to question my scary thoughts of abandonment, and recovered my courage by next sunrise. I found a low-paying job with a start-up and kept that for nine months (the boss-people systematically got rid of all their staff, each time making it about what was wrong with the employee), still had no savings, and figured if it wasn't time to panic—if everything is good news—it must be time to do what I love.

With four years' experience facilitating The Work, I expanded into life coaching. Here's one of the miracles that got me there, and a gorgeous example of the friendly Universe: A man named Brian Whetten had asked me to edit his book a few months earlier, and I'd said no because of my over-full-time job (yeah, the one that paid badly). I wrote to ask if he still needed an editor and still wanted me. Yes and yes. Then he paid me some money (rent!) and also created a trade with me. What does Brian do? He (very skillfully) teaches people with soul-centered practices how to get clients, how to dissolve their conflicts over charging money for helping people heal and grow, how to set up business structures that work—in short, how to make a living pursuing their true calling. I assure you I couldn't have come up with something so perfect all by myself.

While I learned from Brian (plus anyone I could find on the internet offering tips for free), persisted in looking for all that supported me, gave coaching away (sometimes unasked-for, ay), I fed my little family with food stamps and cleaned houses on the side. I got just enough jobs to patch it together, but not so many that I was starting a housecleaning business instead of a coaching business! I stopped buying most things I ran out of (who needs aluminum foil or Scotch tape?), buzz-cut my hair so I didn't have to pay for styling (great for reestablishing that lesbian identity), patched our clothes, and traded the old family minivan for another month's rent and bus passes. I held doggedly to the conviction that coaching—being the Trust Coach—was my calling. My first paying client was an old acquaintance who phoned me in crisis (divorce!) just because she found my number in a drawer and followed the impulse to call. Most of my first round of clients came from a chain of referrals that started with her, and some current clients actually still trace back to that beginning.

Proceeding through these challenges, I made constant use of a simple Byron Katie trick: list the benefits in whatever's happening. (Or ask, How could this be good news?) With enough boldness and courage, you can apply this to anything: when you've spilled the milk or been spurned by the lover, when your loss feels unspeakable, when your last best hope for help says no.

By choice and happenstance, I've started over in nearly every realm of life. Uncertainty has ruled. And far more often than not, I've been happy, connected, confident, reliable as a parent, quick to land on my feet, solid in my dignity, and shockingly kind to myself. I won't try to muster a sufficiently messy description of how I would've handled all this before The Work. Don't get me wrong: the uglies strike me sometimes. But they never pull me under or hold me down for long, because I can question any thought that isn't loving and serene, and come back to sanity. My coaching business is seven years old now, and thriving.

Sometimes Byron Katie invites people to look at a situation in their life and ask, "If it's a friendly Universe, how is this perfect?" It's a great question: If it's a friendly Universe, how is this perfect? I've come to ask this in a number of ways when I sit with people seeking to disconnect their suffering from their circumstances—whether they've lost or can't make money, don't know whether to stay or go in a job or relationship, can't help the helpless around and near them and aren't sure how to help themselves, can't get healthy, can't find meaning in their work despite trainings and promotions and following all the right paths, can't truly love and accept these people stimieing them at work or home. So here are your circumstances and here's the cast of characters playing on Earth-stage with you: How is it all perfect? How is it growing the muscles you lack? What's the invitation here? What healing is possible right in the midst of it—not despite it, but because of it? What is this situation teaching you that you need to learn? And my favorite, if you think in terms of meeting everything as consciousness, every face as the face of God: why would the face of God show up for you this way?

Would you like to experiment with the possibility of living in a friendly Universe? I invite you to this experiment. I invite you to scooch: just edge into a friendly Universe. In all my work, this is what I'm inviting people to do, whether I speak the invitation or not.

I do love to say, if you're going to experiment with the friendly Universe, or with scooching—if you're going to bother with any experiment at all—you may as well make it a grand experiment.

PART 1

Scooch In Closer to Your Pain and Suffering

Why begin the book with pain and suffering—especially the potentially odious idea of bringing them closer? Well, I figure what gets most people involved in personal growth and reading self-help books is this suffering thing. We all feel pain, we all suffer, and most of us tend to move away from pain and suffering. The initial impulse is to take note of what hurts and shove it down, push it away, make it stop. I invite you to bring it close, feel it fully, and thus go through it and out to the other side. Slow down when pain strikes—don't run. Paradoxically enough, I believe anything that feels bad moves along much faster when you slow ... way ... down the moment of meeting it.

Perhaps most important, in handling pain and suffering with presence, you won't abandon yourself. Presence is all I'm really proposing here. Get present to what you're feeling that feels bad: it has a gift for you. It may be showing you beliefs you have that aren't true (so you may want to clear them out). It may reveal what you're attached to that isn't serving you (so you may want to let it go). If it's a friendly Universe, even the things that initially feel bad are here to bring only your highest good.

chapter 1

The Pure Relief of Nonresistance

Of course it's never all about any one thing, but I've still given way to the temptation to begin with these words: *It's all about nonresistance.* Honestly, what most gets us in trouble are crazy beliefs along the lines of *This can't be happening* (when it is) or *This shouldn't be happening* (oh but look, here it is).

Byron Katie based her whole inquiry system on nonresistance and called her first book *Loving What Is.* Abraham-Hicks (that teacher from the Nether Realms I avoided for years out of a self-diagnosed allergy to channeling) loves the topic of nonresistance and urges people to notice when they're in resistance and to scooch toward acceptance and allowing. Deepak Chopra placidly harps on the law of least effort. Mihály Csíkszentmihályi first primed the concept of flow, and any number of people have eased themselves into that current, and they're going with it. Don't push the river. Let go. My favorite latest discovery in the spiritual-guidance department, Tosha Silver (whose book *Outrageous Openness* I own in tenplicate to lend out all over the place), stresses yielding to divine order—which means, among other things, letting what wants to come, come, letting what wants to go, go.

Nonresistance is a great concept, as it creates a bridge where people can't go directly to acceptance. It's a lot to ask, sometimes, that we accept what feels like the unacceptable, the ugly (especially in ourselves), the things that are really hard for us to do or show up for or let go of. Some of these, however, are things we must reckon with to save ourselves or at least to stop harming ourselves and others. So forget acceptance, never mind loving what is: how about nonresistance? That's doable. There's a striving in acceptance that releases in nonresistance.

Of course, it was Byron Katie who got my forty-two-year-old self onto the idea of letting life show me what's happening instead of telling life what should be happening. What matters, ultimately, is reality (what's

19

actually happening), not your preconceived notions and fantasies, or even your best-laid plans. I've come to say, *Show up for what's actually happening—not what you thought should happen, not what you wanted to have happen.*

Here's a hot-off-the-press (and very low-stakes) illustration of that, the story du jour. I'm writing this in a coffee shop during a longer block of writing time than I can typically work into my schedule. To maximize this coveted time, I called in a sandwich order to the deli at my nearby food co-op so I could jump on my bike, get lunch quickly and effortlessly, and power-pedal back to *Gimme! Coffee* to keep working while I eat. Ah, the luxury of modern-day efficiency.

I am, in fact, licking my fingers as I write, but I didn't get my sandwich in a hurry. I got to the co-op and announced myself and the adorable one behind the counter, a tall gangly twenty-something with hair like Shaggy's (of *Scooby-Doo* fame), said, "You're just the person we wanted to see." Ah, but not for love, only because they were out of some ingredient I'd asked for and had not even begun to fill my carefully called-in order. Somehow my vision of jogging up to the counter and grabbing my sandwich relay-style as I tossed money backward out of my pocket and sprinted back to the bike rack—vanished. I paused with the first sign of irritation that came (right) up. I gave it a nod (*Hey, there you are old friend—I know you*) and a breath, then brought myself back to a theory I like to keep coming back to: that I'm not entitled to have everything go my way all the time; that, in all likelihood, such a thing wouldn't be to my advantage.

So I stood there asking myself, *What if there's some inspiration I could open to now that could serve me when I go back to write?* I thought, *This is letting life show me what happens. I thought I was getting the most efficient lunch on the planet. Turned out to be something else. Let life show you. ...* Then Shaggy handed me my ticket and suggested I go get the paying part over with. It wasn't that long till I was back in my seat at the coffee shop, typing away. Truly, no problem.

Here's a higher-stakes example. One morning, when I was working at home, I noticed my refrigerator was making strange noises. It had indigestion, or it was cracking up—some undiagnosed, indefinite something was most definitely underway, and I was pretty sure it was not pretty. I did walk over and peer in quizzically at some point, but this gave me no new information. My fridge has two long doors in front that run parallel to each other, top to bottom, the freezer door on the left being skinnier. I lingered there. Something up with the ice maker? I'm really not a fix-it kind of gal. I went back to my comfort zone, which was also my scheduled work. Then I left the house for some hours and returned around suppertime to a small pond in my kitchen. (No frogs or beavers yet, so that was good.)

I opened the freezer door again and more water gushed out from the pond's source inside. Everything in there was soggy and sagging, and I gave the contents the once-over with that grown-up head-of-household eye that calculates in a flash money thrown out and resources wasted. The floor looked okay, just really (really) wet. I opened the refrigerator side and not even a wee gasp of cold breath issued from there. To be sure: not pretty.

I can't count how many times I've heard Byron Katie ask, "Where's the problem?" So, very often, when I catch myself reacting, alarmed, or in any way freaking out, I come to and say, "Jaya! You're thinking there's a problem!" Katie also admonishes us to think of stress as the temple bell calling us back to truth—or, if I may amend her words, just calling us back, from wherever we went, to wherever we actually are.

I used to participate in intensive programs that included long meditations, much longer than I practiced on my own, and when we were supposed to come back from our altered states (as opposed to when I actually did, if I ever got there at all), a lovely bell chimed. I loved the sound of that bell. Oh, how my mind and hips and back and legs and mind all twinkled to that bell.

At some point in my self-observations, I came to understand that the F-word is my temple bell. It really is. That's the word that flies out of my mouth when the computer won't turn on, the jug of milk slips out of my hand with the lid off, or the refrigerator has emptied its ample liquids onto my floor. *F**k!* It's part of my mission to help spiritual types understand that it's really okay to have reactions: as long as you still have them, they're still okay. We keep them going much longer with the idea they shouldn't be here. (We're not in nonresistance when we believe we shouldn't react!) When I'm reacting I *know* I'm reacting because my temple bell goes off. And this calls me back. *Oh. I'm thinking there's a problem. Where's the problem?*

There really wasn't one in this instance, as I could clearly see as soon as the F-bell alerted me to look again. It did take hours to clean up the mess. I didn't try to salvage the freezer foods, as I take the threat of botulism seriously. So with no urgency to rescue freezer foods, I prioritized cleaning the floor. It happened that I was taking care of cats across the street for vacationing lesbian neighbors, so once the floor was relatively dry, I boxed and bagged up the stuff worth moving—veggies and nuts and meats and eggs and oils and dairy products and condiments. I drew some firm lines and left behind anything whose origins weren't obvious or remembered. I read some expiration dates for the first time in a couple of years, purging things that might have been moved along a good while back.

It took a few trips across the street. As I walked back and forth in the dark on a lovely pre-spring evening, breathing the fresh air, feeling capable and strong, I was taken by a thought that I very likely first heard from Katie: *I've gotta be doing something on planet Earth tonight—it may as well be this.*

Everything didn't fit into my neighbors' already pretty full refrigerator, so I went next door to the other lesbians on my block (hey, you, too, could live in Ithaca), and they made room for the rest. Now all my salvageable fridge foods had somewhere to chill. I came back and filled trash bags with what had so recently and randomly become trash, including all the contents of my freezer except for bags of flour and those hard freezer packs that could be frozen again when conditions were right, to do their job another time.

I really, really dislike waste. It was somewhat appalling to throw out food, food that had been paid for and in a few cases had cost a life. All of it would have been perfectly good to eat without this seemingly pointless refrigerator meltdown. But thanks to Katie, I could say to myself, *Sometimes waste happens on this planet.* That's just a fact. If you're trying to line up with reality, that's actually truer than *Nothing should ever get wasted.* Nonresistance means lining up with reality.

I'm not sure when it occurred to me that night that, in the not-so-distant past, this whole episode would have ruined my day, and the internal spoilage would have carried on well beyond. It certainly wouldn't have occurred to me to let life show me what I was doing that evening. I would have been furious to spend my time cleaning up and carting food about, knowing I was setting myself up Sisyphus-style to reverse the process and bring it all home again once the fridge was back in working order. I would have done the required tasks with angry, nervous energy, mulling over my gripes the whole time. I would have been devastated by the waste, and that feeling would have dropped into the pit of my stomach and fermented there into despair and the not-so-vague feeling that I was a bad person and, really, the whole planet was a hopeless case. I would have been anxious about the outcome, when, how long, how much, whose fault. ...

None of that was with me. I simply sent my landlord an e-mail and she wrote back that she'd be in touch in the morning, hopefully with the news someone was on the way. A nice man came over the very next day and cheerfully did his job, and my landlord (not I) paid the bill. And I did take the time required for all the food's return trips, which gave me more fun moments with the good-humored women next door and another rumbly purring moment with Sadie, the cat across the way, who is *the* official flirty cat of the neighborhood.

Before I brought the food back, I washed my emptied freezer and fridge, a task that was sorely overdue and that I just breezed through after life's brilliant set-up for that task. When the food was back in place, I don't believe my fridge had ever looked so tidy. It felt great. I'm sure some huge galactic feng-shui tectonic-plates-in-the-cosmos alignment thing happened right then. And since I did really have to be doing something on planet Earth at that moment, it may as well have been that.

Nonresistance. There really is no problem. It really is all good.

Shortly after I wrote the section above, I had a session with a client whose daughter uses a wheelchair and seems to have been doled out an inordinate share of procedures and surgeries to show up for. Aubrey described a two-hour trip to another city the day before a recently scheduled surgery, the travails of setting up an overnight hotel life, getting up the next day at the crack of dawn, and getting to the hospital only to be told the surgery was off—they didn't have some gizmo they needed to make it happen.

After exploring various possibilities and scenarios, Aubrey decided the smartest way to proceed was to drive home (it was still quite early in the day) and drive back the following morning. She was actively playing with nonresistance at the time and found that she was able to allow an initial small meltdown and then simply locate her best choice and take it. There was really no problem. In the scheme of things that could get derailed and go crazily askew in her daughter's life, this was no more than a blip.

But honestly, it sounds like a big pain. I stand in awe of her application of nonresistance and am struck by the perspective her story puts on what most of us deal with. Life inconveniences us, that's for sure, in small and large ways. Why huff and puff over any of it? What if we remembered to ask, *Where's the problem?*—and kept finding that there isn't one?

chapter 2

Show Up for What's Actually Happening …

… not what you thought should happen; not what you wanted to have happen. I began to talk about this in the last chapter on nonresistance and am now scooching in closer. It's such a helpful phrase to apply in all realms of life and every present moment. It's good for helping you stay grounded in the world instead of lifting off into fantasy. It's a way to live in the *now* instead of rushing to a future.

On the most basic level, this is what I meant when I used to tell my son to look before crossing, even if the stoplight did just turn red and the little white-light pedestrian-crossing dude did just start glowing. Show up for what's actually happening: yeah, the car approaching is supposed to stop; more to the point, is it stopping? There could be folks turning right on red, too—did you check that they actually saw you before even sticking a toe in the crosswalk? If you walk out into the road just because they *should* stop, just because you *wanted* them to stop, things really won't go well for you if in fact they don't stop.

Let's zoom in to the realm of dating to look at this more closely, then we'll pan out again for you to apply to other realms of life. (If dating doesn't apply to you, even better—you'll be able to see the concept clearly.) Ay, the romance thing. It's just so exciting to meet someone new who's attractive and interesting. Oh, never mind exciting: it's a relief, sometimes, after weeding through some frightful specimens of ill-health (stick a *mental* somewhere in there), to connect with someone wonderful—or even wonderfully normal. He can string together three grammatically functional sentences! She doesn't sound like an ax murderer when she talks about her ex! No reference to a live-in mother! (Or, in the case of lesbians, a live-in ex.) We get intoxicated. We stop showing up for what's happening, because with very little information, we decide we want this to take. We want it to last. Coming back to *now*, can you remotely know you want such a thing? Not likely. You need a whole lot more information, even if that date looks really good on paper—even more if that date looks really good, period.

25

Consider the sanity of staying present to what's actually happening in each new moment and scenario as you come to know another human being. You might actually notice the red flags without being scared of them, or even seeing them as great disappointments. They're just information—very handy information for what you're considering. Go ahead, have fun; be excited, glow in the sparks. And at the same time, show up for what's actually happening. You'll make more reality-based decisions that actually serve you better.

My client Sandra went through some harsh pain in a breakup because she got involved with Ted too quickly. There was so much to like about him initially that she dove in and got swept away—swept herself away—in the fantasy of coupling. He was so attentive, so verbal about his appreciation of her, such fun to be with. Why would she say no to great sex and a kind, open face turned her way? Well, because he didn't want kids, and she wanted nothing more.

There's nothing stupid or dull about Sandra, but the realm of sex and love is tricky territory, isn't it? Somewhere in her mind, the two of them were already three. Tonight's restaurant meant tomorrow's strollers and diaper bags. For him, while tonight's restaurant didn't mean disappearing the next morning, it had more to do with hanging out tomorrow afternoon drinking beer and seeing a great show later on. It didn't take long for Sandra to get that he wasn't remotely suited to the life she was after.

It would have been less painful for her if she hadn't gotten so deeply involved sexually and emotionally—which she could have avoided by showing up for what was actually happening instead of what she wanted to have happen. She could have lingered in the information-gathering stage. She could have waited longer to get in bed—not because of any right or wrong, but because she knows about herself that her clarity goes all topsy-turvy in the horizontal realm. She could have walked away more quickly and easily if she'd simply taken in that, however dreamy it felt to look into those eyes, this guy just didn't want what she wanted: they—and their dreams—actually weren't compatible.

Please note that it's not the fact Ted didn't want kids that created a problem for Sandra. This is in fact the thing that let her know what she most needed to know—that he wasn't the man for her. The problem was the agenda she carried in that kept her from showing up for what was actually happening. Notice that when you're (in delusion) focusing on what you want to have happen or what you believe should be happening, you see anything that would keep it from happening as somehow working against you! Actually, when the signs show up to reroute you, this is a good thing. It's your guidance system working on your behalf, with your best interests in view. Ultimately, it's more evidence of the Universe conspiring in your favor—pointing you to what you do need to see (not thwarting or depriving you).

I've invited any number of clients to look for a time they were dating the wrong person when they didn't get all the red flags they needed pointing them to get out early on (and again a bit later, and again after that). I've yet to talk to anyone who can find that no-flags scenario. People got the red flags and disregarded them, minimized them, pushed them to the background, and focused on the compelling factors that kept them pretending that this was the one, or even just insisting that they wanted to keep going when it was in fact time to stop.

The dating game offers potent and easy application of this principle of showing up for what's actually happening. Now apply it to everything in life. You thought this was going to be a really fun and special event with your kid (who's all mopey and droopy through no fault of yours)? Just show up for what's happening—then you may be able to keep from getting mopey too, or snappy and threatening. ... This was supposed to be the job of your dreams, not a constant battle of the wills with your boss? Well, show up for what's happening. It may very well prove to be that job after all or lead you right to it, especially if you use this custom-made opportunity to develop skills you were lacking—like the ability to hold your ground without going into attack or defense. ... The shopping trip was supposed to be quick and uneventful so you could knock out another hour or two of work? Apparently not. Show up for what's happening and let life show you when the religion of efficiency and optimum output needs to be shed for something else: breathing, patience, looking into whatever eyes show up without any agenda but meeting consciousness.

Ever hear yourself ask, "Who am I kidding?" (If you weren't being rhetorical, wouldn't you answer, "Myself" every time?) Here's how not to kid yourself, about anything: show up for what's actually happening—not what you thought should happen, and not what you wanted to have happen.

My client Dana told me to tack on this addendum: *and not what you fear will happen*. She told me about feeling like she was always reacting to all the imagined scenarios in her head—the scary things that *could* happen. In particular, she was looking at the way she shut down in relationships when she succumbed to fear that the current conflict or misunderstanding would result in various painful ends, all culminating in total abandonment. I love her addition. Sometimes (often) there's little to do with your fears except notice that they have nothing to do with what's happening now—and come back to reality.

You might also remember the power of intention. When people tell me their entirely valid fears (most fears fall under this category), I tell them this: Turn your fears and worries into intentions, because fears and worries tell you exactly what you do and don't want to come into being. You're scared the new baby will create a rift between you and your toddler? Set the intention that you'll stay close. Scared the young, sharp one just hired will oust you from your role in the office? Set the intention that you two will collaborate, that you'll learn from her, that you'll find your proper place for the greater good—and imagine her doing the same. Worried that you'll lose your cool while speaking and stop making sense? Set some intentions around your preparedness, your connection to the audience, your ability to roll with anything, with sense of humor intact.

And ... show up for what's actually happening.

chapter 3

Mind the Pain Body, Tend the Mind

When you're suffering, you're simply carrying around thoughts that make you suffer and feeling (perhaps intensifying) emotions that confirm the sense of suffering. When you're suffering, notice all you disconnect from: you cannot be here now, practice nonresistance, believe there's no problem, trust that a friendly Universe supports you, or keep moving toward what you're seeking to create in your life. In short, whatever spiritual concepts or good-life ethics and practices you aspire to all become tricky to hold firm to or slip out of reach altogether.

In my coaching practice, I invite clients to practice a two-part process in response to their suffering: mind the pain body and tend the mind. Whatever they're going through that feels too hard or too much, whatever they write me to say they don't know how to face, whatever has them confuzzled this time, I point them again and again to minding the pain body and tending the mind. Think of it as a practice, never done, just something to keep coming back to: mind the pain body, tend the mind.

Mind the Pain Body

I was sort of struck upside the head the first time I heard Eckhart Tolle talk about the pain body. This was also the first time I gazed into the face (on film) of this adorable toad-eyed creature with a goatee. (I sat riffling through possibilities: modern-day German hobbit? Über-actualized alien? Ever notice his initials?) Listening to his words, I felt he was articulating what began to set right some chronic imbalance in me. Now, years later, without having particularly gotten into Eckhart Tolle's work in any significant way, I've changed my relationship with the pain body drastically. At some point, I began guiding my coaching clients more and more into being with the pain body as an entirely separate process from meeting and working with their thoughts—especially since working with thoughts doesn't necessarily (and rarely immediately) make pain go away.

At the simplest level of explanation, the pain body describes that place in your body where emotional pain lodges. It's the beast that clamps your throat or rubs raw the inside of your chest or settles weightily on your gut and won't get off. The pain body isn't personal. Every human being will experience its flare-ups at various points in life throughout a lifetime—part of the package deal of being human. But we tend to take the pain body very personally, especially when we believe the thoughts that show up when it's active. I like to depersonalize it and give it its full generic due by simply telling myself (based on how I heard ET describe it), "The pain body's active." This allows me to create distance from the story while still coming close to the pain itself.

When you think of it this way, then, little does it matter what events—what story—actually activated the pain body this time. We're so conditioned to get involved with the story that got the pain body going, and the telling, retelling, and believing the story as we retell it again and one more time (or ten). ... If you know that life will get the pain body going at some point or another over some point or another, you can actually step back from the latest story that revved it up. It really makes no difference what it was. Someone will diss you or betray you or grossly misunderstand you or drop their end of an agreement or get sick and die on you. You'll get injured or hear about a natural disaster or scary political situation, or you'll suffer a costly technological snafu. In the greater scheme of things, the current story doesn't matter. How you meet the pain body matters very much.

Think of meeting the pain body as you might respond to a child who runs in crying with a skinned knee. Let's say you're working at the computer. To risk stating the obvious (call this next bit "Advice to a Clueless Parent"), don't keep typing. Don't glance over and say, "Aw, bummer," and crank out the next paragraph. Instead, drop what you're doing because, even with that deadline coming up, your work has just been temporarily usurped by something more important. Stop and give the child your full attention (full awareness). Cleanse the wound, apply a balm; give kindness, give love.

So you know what to do with a child—but are you a clueless parent to yourself? With the pain body, you can simply place your hand there once you locate it. More important, think of the breath as a balm, the only balm you can apply from within. Breathe into the pain body for a few breaths, gently expanding into it then beyond to make space around it. (Don't breathe deep or hard, don't force anything, just gently direct the breath to soothe the pain body.) Give this a minute; give it a few. We love to rush through these moments, as if the to-do list were more important. When the kid runs in crying, nothing else matters—just for a bit. It all shakes back down pretty quickly—really just a minute or two, most of the time, for the kid to feel tended to and run back out for the next bit of fun—so just be still awhile. The truth is, if your child is distressed, you'll give it however long it takes: you're willing.

When the pain body gets all raw and hurting, or heavy and oppressive, it's time to stop what you're doing and take care of that. Please don't plow through the next e-mail and throw it an "Aw, bummer." Don't do that because it doesn't work.

The other thing not to do is to believe whatever thoughts are running alongside the pain. Just because we *feel* something, we take this as evidence that our thoughts around the feeling are true. They're not. They're certainly not, to use Byron Katie's phrase, *absolutely true*. Thoughts need to be met, questioned, looked at from different angles. That's what the inquiry process called The Work of Byron Katie does so brilliantly. Katie's process offers the *how* for disentangling from thoughts. We'll look at this more deeply when we turn to tending the mind.

But minding the pain body is a separate process that you can attend to with no reference to what you're thinking—especially if you know not to believe your thoughts. If they're a strong presence, you can write them down—that's what Katie urges people to do. The writing fixes your thoughts to the page (or screen) so they can be still there, and you've got half a chance of seeing them clearly. It leaves you with a finite list of thoughts to work with (when you get to it) and sometimes the thoughts, once visible in ink on paper, fairly scream at you, "Not true!" Write down the thoughts, put them aside—acknowledging to yourself as clearly as you can that they're just thoughts, so they can't be absolutely true—and turn your attention to the pain body. ("Remember," I re-remind my clients when they're really distressed and caught up in their thoughts and fears of the moment, "mind the pain body! The story that activated it doesn't even matter.")

The process of meeting the pain body is almost absurdly simple, because the pain body wants two things from you: awareness and breath. More than anything, what's required is to bring your full, focused awareness to the place that hurts. For even a brief moment, give it your undivided attention. Be one-pointed, even for a few seconds, if that's all you've got. I tell my clients to just go to the restroom if that's all you can manage, and attend to your pain body for the time a potty break usually takes. The duration isn't what counts: what counts is full awareness, or total immersion. Drop into your pain body as deeply as you can, as you might get into a jacuzzi, right up to your chin.

From here, be your own soothing parent. Apply that balm from within by breathing into the place that hurts. Breathe the pain body for several breath cycles, watching the breath go in and out, watching for any ease or release that comes of this—without forcing anything. Your job here is giving awareness and breath, not making it all better or fixing it.

As you breathe into the pain body, seek to fully feel what hurts. Get curious about it. Go into scientist mode, finding details beyond the pain body's general location: What are the parameters of the area affected? How far out does it go? Does it go beyond the limits of the body? How deep inward does it go? What's the pitch and timbre of it? How dense is it? Could you give it a color?

Now you're not just immersed in the pain body—you're witnessing it. I always find it useful to consciously locate the witness and notice that a part of you can separate from the pain body and watch you hurting; a part of you can even watch you attending to your hurting. It's like layers of awareness you can access and check in with. I remember being taken through an exercise once during a meditation intensive that involved locating the witness, then the one watching that one, then the one watching that one, in potentially endless succession as when two mirrors face each other so that a ricochet of reflections ensues.

To my mind, what's most useful in that with reference to the pain body is that you can always find some part of yourself that's outside of the pain, or beyond it. Ultimately the pain body is not who you are, no matter how much space it's taking up or how loudly it's screaming; you're always bigger than that. It's weirdly counterintuitive: when you enter into the deep end of the pain body by giving it your full awareness, you start to distance yourself from it at once, because you release identification with it and become its observer instead.

Note that if you become conscious of the witness, you can also notice the quality of the witnessing. If you find you're witnessing with distaste, aversion, or judgment of any kind, call in the compassionate, dispassionate witness. The compassionate one will feel truly caring toward you, bringing some modicum of warmth to the observing. The compassionate one is gentle and nonjudgmental. The dispassionate one won't get sucked into the drama, always stands on neutral ground, may not even believe any attendant story that the mind fairly insists on hooking into. So once you're aware of witnessing, access the compassionate, dispassionate witness—or scooch that way.

Having given the pain body that full-on, one-pointed attention, even briefly, having applied the balm of breath, then carry on with what you need to do without losing track of the pain body. You know those infant carriers that allow you to strap a baby onto your chest and keep it close as you go about your business? Carry your pain body around like that. When you've got a baby in one of those things, you can do just about anything: work at the computer, talk on the phone, wash the dishes, walk, shop, teach—no turning cartwheels, but most things work. Some part of you, though, will remain aware of the baby. You'll do little check-ins, monitoring noises, giving a sniff, applying touch. You might even move your body a little, providing a subtle rocking.

Likewise, carry on with the business at hand, giving it the majority of your focus, but don't lose track of that pain body as long as it's active in any way. Give it some part of your awareness, send some breath its way. Keep it gently, tenderly on your radar, like the baby in the carrier. You can even use a rating scale, if you're that type: *now it's a 6; it's dropped to 3; spiking again at 9*—no judgment in it, just a way to check in.

I have a client who's taken to saying "the pain baby" for the pain body. Another was struck by this image of carrying the baby around and had a tender epiphany around her own failure to be sufficiently gentle with herself when she's feeling painful emotions. I'm always in favor of increasing the kindness and gentleness you bring to your own process. This metaphor (with its good-parent mindset) promotes just that.

If you're scooching toward consciousness, you must show up for meeting the pain body one way or another. Think of it this way: sometimes, you'll have an appointment with the pain body. It's a date that won't show up on your calendar ahead of time (though sometimes it will—as when you know you're signed up for something pretty much guaranteed to set it off, like the visit with your family of origin or the high-stakes interview

33

or court date or whatever). When it's time for the meeting, don't avoid it. Drop anything else, or incorporate it all: there's room for the pain body no matter what life requires of you.

The pain body must be met—it's part of your job as a human being. Ignoring it, shoving it down, buffering it with food, alcohol, your drug of choice—this is what brings you ongoing harm. The pain body itself won't harm you. Neither will the particular story that got it going this time, however painful most people would agree the story to be. Something has to activate the pain body: look dispassionately at the story and think, *This is as good a trigger as any*. I do recommend meeting your thoughts about the story, covered in the next section just below. I also recommend meeting the pain body as a separate and crucially important process in your growth and healing.

Tend the Mind

The first step in tending the mind is so important that I've already given it to you: write down your thoughts. Since I cannot stress this enough, let me overstress it. I usually tell my clients to write down their thoughts many times over before they actually try it in a moment of distress, anger, sorrow, or emotion of any kind. Either they forget or they decide in that unclear moment that this is some bullshit, not-truly-relevant thing I said that has little bearing on this very real occurrence happening right now and their actual capacity to meet it. Nothing could be more relevant in a moment of mental confusion than to empty the contents of your mind onto paper. (Note that you're mentally confused when you're angry, outraged, ashamed, alarmed, appalled, sorrowful, disappointed. I'm not saying that these emotions aren't valid—just that they take you out of clarity in your thinking.)

It's a mucky, murky, slippery morass up there, and when you get the swirling, seemingly endless mess organized in list form—which simply requires spewing it out on paper—the first thing that's apparent is that you're working with a finite list. It's even often surprisingly short, much shorter than it seemed to be when it was swirling redundantly round that hamster wheel of the mind. As part of her inquiry system, Byron Katie offers a form for capturing thoughts called the Judge-Your-Neighbor Worksheet. Katie likes to say, "All war belongs on paper," and the point of this worksheet is to expose your vile thoughts about someone to yourself so you can explore them (she says, "meet them with understanding") instead of using them to clobber people (even if plenty of us agree that they deserve it). But you can also simply write down your thoughts, and I always follow and point clients to Katie's directive to use short, simple, sentences, one thought per line.

She also offers an insanely simple trick of adding the words "and that means that …" after a general prompt related to your upset so that you can generate your list from there. For example, you might hear yourself think or say, "I'm completely overwhelmed." Noticing that your pain body is screaming as you walk around under the influence of this unexamined thought, you might want to first mind the pain body for a moment. Then after you sit with that—or even as you sit, if the story won't stop asserting itself while you do—take a blank sheet of paper or open a blank screen and write it down. It may look something like this:

I'm completely overwhelmed, and that means that …

- There's way too much going on.
- I can't possibly meet this deadline.
- I can't take care of Corey *and* get my work done.
- I need more help.
- My computer can't be acting up now.
- I can't be late with this project.
- I can't do this well if I get it done on time.
- I don't have time to eat.
- I'm sick of being the only grown-up around here.
- It's all up to me.
- This job is too much for one person.
- I can't love what I do when there's so much of it.
- I'm missing the joy of living.
- I'm losing track of gratitude.
- I'm not sleeping enough.
- I wake up haggard and pinched and horrid.
- I'm aging too quickly.
- I can't do this.

Don't stop till you feel you've gotten it all down. If it feels like it's getting repetitive (and it will), you can call it done. It's worth sitting still a moment: pause and wait and maybe watch your breath for a couple of in-out cycles. See what else wants to come. Invite it. And then notice you've got a finite list.

There's a whole spectrum of possibility for how to then put your list to work for you, and I invite you to find the right level of attention to give it in the moment. The most basic level, which I invite you to do every time, is to simply look at the list and tell yourself that it's just that, a list of thoughts. Byron Katie made it crystal clear to me that thoughts may present themselves as if they're narrating reality inside your head, but they're really just thoughts. Every time. This means they're never true— or never *absolutely* true. So look at your list and simply say, out loud if you want to make sure you really hear it, "These are just thoughts. They're not true, at least not absolutely true." You might add, "They do explain why I feel so bad. Anyone believing this set of thoughts would probably feel pretty rotten."

On the other end of the spectrum is the possibility of looking closely at every single thought you've recorded. And, as always, there are multiple possibilities between the polarities, which we'll briefly consider after I take you through an example of The Work of Byron Katie, the best way I know to question the thoughts on your list. This is an inquiry system that consists of four questions (with plenty of possible subquestions, especially for question 3), and what Katie calls the turnaround, which is a recasting of the thought in a few ways to consider it from other angles, noticing that even the direct opposite may be as true as or truer than the original thought.

If this inquiry process is interesting to you as I've laid it out here, I invite you to read Katie's book *Loving What Is: Four Questions That Can Change Your Life* (co-written with Stephen Mitchell), in which she demonstrates The Work over and over again on any number of topics. The audio version is lovely, because you get to hear the voices of the people she facilitates as well. Finally, Katie's official website, TheWork-dot-com, is full of free resources, including numerous videos that allow you to watch her in action.

A side trip into The Work of Byron Katie

The four questions of Katie's inquiry process are as follows:

1. Is it true?
2. Can you absolutely know that it's true?
3. How do you react, what happens, when you believe the thought?
4. Who would you be without the thought?

Let's take one thought from the sample list above, *I can't possibly meet this deadline,* and walk it through what the Q-and-A process could look like.

Q: *You can't possibly meet this deadline.* Is that true?

A: Yes! Well, I don't know.

Q: *You can't possibly meet this deadline.* Can you absolutely know that it's true?

A: No. Meeting the deadline is actually within the realm of possibility.

[The following few questions, until we get to question 4 (*Who would you be without the thought?*), are all subquestions for #3 (*How do you react, what happens, when you believe this thought?*), all designed to explore cause-and-effect. Notice what it gets you—what kind of life you give yourself—when you believe this thought. Take your time exploring this. I don't tend to ask the overarching question for #3 but simply proceed through the subquestions, usually beginning with what emotion the thought produces and where it strikes in the body. You don't have to ask all the subquestions (in fact, please don't!). For me, it's a very intuitive process to choose what to ask and in what order. Ultimately, it just doesn't matter. All you're doing here is exploring the so-called reality you see when you look through the lens of this particular thought.]

Q: When you believe this thought, *You can't possibly meet this deadline,* what emotion do you feel, and where do you feel it in your body?

A: I feel heavy all over. I feel scared and irritable and irritated. The scared part sits in my gut. Then it's like I have these waves of sensation that move through my head. I feel incompetent, defeated. Tired, overwhelmed, *heavy*.

Q: How do you treat other people when you believe this thought, *You can't possibly meet this deadline?*

A: I have no patience. I snap. I made a big deal last night of who should do the dishes, when a simple conversation was all we needed. I start getting into everything everybody does *all the time* (and exaggerate that) instead of just dealing with what's up in the moment.

Q: How do you treat your boss (including in your mind) when you believe *You can't possibly meet this deadline.*

A: I can actually hate her. I feel she wants too much of me and pays too little attention to all that's on my plate. Or I start begging her in my mind. I've had pathetic, embarrassing conversations with her in my mind.

Q: Does this thought, *You can't possibly meet this deadline*, make you feel connected or separate?

A: Separate. So alone.

Q: Does it give you peace or stress?

A: Stress!

Q: Does it put you in or out of your power?

A: Out.

[Katie doesn't do much with the concept of personal power, but I do. This is my question (not that I'm saying no one else ever thought of it—I'm betting they did and do). I just love it, and I use it a lot. I personally don't wish to hold on to thoughts that make me feel I have no power, no agency, no choice.]

Q: Whose business are you in when you're believing *You can't possibly meet this deadline*? [Katie's three kinds of business are yours, someone else's (hers, his, theirs), and God's (as defined by you). For the latter, I prefer to say the Universe's.]

A: The Universe's. I'm declaring what is and isn't possible, and that's not mine to determine. I'm also declaring something about my innate capability, and I don't have the last word on that. Oh, I'm also in the concept of time with this deadline thing, so that's always the Universe's domain. Ay, I'm completely out of my business with this thought.

[When I facilitate people in The Work, I love to remind them that the point of the three kinds of business as Katie explains it is that there's a self-abandonment in leaving your business. You leave yourself—you're no longer here to take care of yourself, or to tend what's actually yours to tend—when you're minding someone else's business or the Universe's.]

Q: What is it you fail to notice or lose track of completely when you believe *You can't possibly meet this deadline*?

A: I lose track of the fact I almost always meet deadlines. And when I don't, there's a very good reason and the deadline gets moved. I notice I'm scared this time because I don't see this one getting moved. But I've never gotten in trouble with this boss for not making a deadline. I used to get in trouble with that when I was younger, but not now, and never in this job. I also completely lose track of the idea that you can do jobs at different levels, and I need to quit trying to hold a standard of perfection when I'm up against a deadline. I just need to complete it and let it be as good as it is.

Q: How's your relationship with the present moment when you're believing this thought?

A: I'm not in the present moment. I'm jumping to a future where everything's not okay. I guess I go to the past, too—at least the immediate past, to review how hard it's been. Wow, this thought doesn't allow me to get totally present to the time I've got and make the most of that.

39

Q: Are there any addictions or addictive processes you go to when you're believing the thought *You can't possibly meet this deadline?*

A: I go over old victimy thought patterns about how hard life is. That whole list of thoughts I wrote from the prompt pretty much sums it up, plus a few more thoughts specific to the single-mom thing.

Q: Can you think of one peaceful reason for holding on to the thought *You can't possibly meet this deadline?*

A: No.

Q: Close your eyes and watch scenes of what it's actually like to move through the days and hours leading up to this deadline. Who would you be (in this reality) without the thought *You can't possibly meet this deadline?*

A: Okay, I think I'd be the competent, good worker that I am. I'd stand in the truth of how good I am at this, and allow what I can do in this time frame to be enough even if it's not my best. I'd be less frazzled and freaked out. I could maybe even relax a bit, or at least be focused and stay steadfast with the work—really give myself to it when it's time to do it and breathe a little when it's time to pause for food or to do something with my kid. Amazing: I can breathe more right now just thinking in these terms.

Q: Let's turn the thought around. Find an opposite for *I can't possibly meet this deadline.*

A: I *can* possibly meet this deadline.

[Note that the turnarounds ask that you change as little of the original phrasing as possible. Thus, the simplest turnaround is to make a negative statement positive or a positive, negative.]

Q: Does that seem as true as or truer than the original thought?

A: It could be at least as true. I mean, it's interesting to me to notice that it's true at all!

Q: Give a concrete example of how it could be true that you can in fact meet this deadline.

A: It's possible. I can meet it because I could go for the bare minimum and simply make sure that the beginning, middle, and end are in place. It'll be done, just not with all the bells and whistles. And if I get the bare bones in place, there could still be time to go in and flesh it out a bit here and there—a very good chance of that, in fact.

Q: Find another example of why it's true you *can* meet the deadline.

A: Well, there is some time left. I don't have to turn it in right this second, which would be a fiasco.

Q: Find one more example.

A: I can meet the deadline because I'm smart and capable and know the priorities and have done this enough times to know what I'm doing, even with the specific unknowns of this specific project factored in.

Q: Do you still want to believe that you can't possibly meet the deadline?

A: No. It's really not true, and it really messes me up to believe it's true. I choose to believe that I can.

[This completes Byron Katie's inquiry process for the statement *I can't possibly meet the deadline*. Note that the situation in which you might believe such a thought would likely also have you believe there's no time to question it. Can you imagine the upgrade in efficiency once this thought is questioned and countered? My experience has been that self-inquiry is always worth the time it takes—even, and perhaps especially, in time-sensitive situations.]

Note that there are often several turnarounds. The most basic is the one we did here, going from positive to negative, or vice versa. When you do just one turnaround, that direct opposite is a good one to explore. It may be worth going another direction with a different kind of statement in which you're strongly accusing someone of something or calling them something, especially if you're very focused on what's wrong with them or how maddening they are. In that case, you might benefit even more from turning it around to yourself.

The turnaround to the self simply entails saying about yourself what you're saying about another. Thus, "She can't see past her own nose" would become "I can't see past my own nose." You take the other person out of the sentence altogether and make it all about you. "He's so pigheaded" becomes "I'm so pigheaded." Then you'd find three examples of how you are or do what you accuse another of being or doing.

Spiritual teachers from any number of traditions emphasize seeing others as the mirror. What drives you crazy in them is what drives you crazy in you, so it behooves you to check out how you do what you're faulting them for doing. You may balk at this when the other has that quality or does that thing way more than you have or do. But really, that doesn't matter. What matters—what truly serves you—is to find how it plays out in you and clean that up. So if their version of some flaw outdoes yours by a long shot, just think of the other as the funhouse mirror: to stay with *pigheaded* as our example, your father may be a grotesque, squashed, stretched, ridiculously exaggerated version of *pigheaded*, while you get that way only a wee-little hardly-ever bit. Perhaps you get pigheaded especially in relation to him when you dig in your heels to oppose him. Seeing it so blatantly in him—the magic of the funhouse mirror—may be just the thing that makes you serious about clearing up whatever vestige of *pigheaded* remains in you (but not to be righteous, or more righteous than he is—only for your freedom).

You may also find, by turning around *pigheaded* (or whatever) to yourself, that you're willing to give yourself permission to be that way on occasion—for example, to make sure you bolster yourself to keep him from manipulating you. It actually makes sense for you to make space for that. This will help you to give another permission to do the same. He's in charge of when he allows himself to be pigheaded; you're in charge of you.

This is a good one for you if you still believe self-care is selfish (if you have what I call a false equal sign between self-care and selfishness). Maybe when you're mad at someone else for being selfish, you can turn it around to yourself and find how you're selfish—even if the other is the Queen of Selfishness and you just dabble, and that with a good measure

42

of guilt. Maybe you could give yourself permission to prioritize thinking about yourself sometimes, calling that *selfish* if you must, and leave the other to her selfish ways as well.

For the record, the third classic turnaround, when there are two people in the sentence, is to do what I call switching the characters. So "They drive me crazy" becomes "I drive them crazy." You may find it useful to acknowledge that it goes or may go both ways.

Can I just say that the turnarounds are brilliant?

There's an interesting misunderstanding that happens with turnarounds that I'd love to clear up. Because The Work begins with looking for how a thought isn't true then finishes with looking for truth in opposite thoughts, people get the idea that they're supposed to see the original thought as having no truth and the turnaround as embodying truth. Not so.

The original thought very likely does have some truth in it, or you wouldn't be thinking it at all. But when we think stressful thoughts, we tend to get hyperfocused on them and see nothing else. Believing he's pigheaded, focusing on that, you're not going to see where he's open and flexible. You're not going to see how you can be that way too. The turnarounds simply allow you to walk over to the other polarity way across from your thought and check out what's true over there too. Since you've reviewed any amount of evidence to validate the truth of the original thought, Katie asks you to stay with each turnaround long enough to find at least three concrete examples for how this new thought may be true as well—perhaps even truer than the original thought.

In no way does this mean you need to reject the original thought categorically or set up camp in the other polarity. It's more like stepping back far enough that now you get a wide-angle view on reality that encompasses both the thought and its opposite, and everything in between. Katie suggests that you use the turnaround as your prescription for how to be with a situation differently. But this doesn't mean you'll never find truth in the original thought again—and you don't have to feel crazy when the original thought does seem true. Still, it's not the whole truth, and you don't have to take it so seriously. You can visit the turnarounds again, if you need to, to remember what else is true. Once you've done The Work, the turnarounds may revisit you on their own and provide spontaneous perspective.

This inquiry process is a fabulous way to get free of a thought and not be ruled by it as if it dictated reality—it most certainly does not. But don't expect inquiry to make a thought go away, and don't expect the associated pain-body sensations to dissolve at once just because you can mentally stretch your perspective. Let the pain body catch up when it will, keep minding the pain body, and keep questioning your thoughts as needed.

Let's go back to that list of stressful thoughts. In between the two extremes of simply noticing your thoughts aren't true and doing full-blown inquiry on each thought, you've got any number of options. You might go through the four questions and turnaround for one thought (choose the zinger, or the one you'd feel most relieved to shed) then do a simple turnaround for the others or even for one or two others. Or you might go through the whole list and just ask, "Is it true?" about each list item. You might go through and quickly turn each thought around—though, remember, the task associated with the turnaround is always to find at least three concrete examples of how the new opposite statement could be true, and it behooves you to do just that.

Let's say you're turning around the thought *I'm missing out on the joy of living*. Don't stop at saying, *I'm NOT missing out on the joy of living*, but add at least three reasons this could be true:

1. I had my favorite breakfast this morning, and it worked fine to eat at the computer—I tasted it and enjoyed it.
2. Even though I didn't get much time with Corey last night, we laughed really hard about his shoes-in-the-pond story at bedtime.
3. When I finished the proposal part of the project, I had a huge sense of satisfaction. I really felt bolstered by how nicely that turned out and remembered why I love this work. That helped me move right on to the next part.
4. I keep noticing the vase of flowers in the kitchen when I go through there. It's such good timing that those landed here while this is going on—they really do brighten things up.

Other methods for tending the mind

There are any number of ways to tend the mind that don't require any inquiry process. I use The Work of Byron Katie in my life and my practice because it's far and away the most potent thing I've come upon that can truly address and clear out the thoughts that keep you from your joy, peace, well-being, loving essence, or personal power. Not only does it move along specific thoughts that aren't serving you, but with repeated use it actually changes your relationship with your thinking. You come to know that any thought can be questioned. You learn not to take your own thoughts so personally, because the very same thoughts are a lot of other people's own thoughts too—they're really not that personal.

I was fascinated when my thoughts started showing up hand-in-hand with *Is it true?* Or they showed up with their turnaround already pointing me to more possibilities and greater kindness. Some thoughts are tough, stubborn, deep-seated ones that aren't so willing to cozy up to their own undoing. For those, I found that at the very least I stopped simply swallowing them whole as truth just because I felt something strong when they showed up.

So while The Work of Byron Katie is a great way to tend the mind and offers the added bonus of changing your relationship with your thinking, you might also write in a journal, talk to wise friends, take it to a therapy or coaching session, work with positive affirmations or otherwise choose your mental focus, make gratitude lists, consider the worst-case scenario and notice how far you are from that and whether you could handle it if that's where you ended up, think of other people in other places who'd love to trade in their problems for yours, and so on. See what else you can come up with.

However you do it, do tend the mind. Otherwise, it will have its way with you, and you'll walk around unconsciously believing any number of things and choosing (or failing to choose) your life based on those thoughts.

Mind the pain body, tend the mind. They'll both be active whether you give them good attention or not. You may as well bring it all to consciousness. You may find a whole lot of pain and confusion gets dislodged and released when you do.

chapter 4

(Quit Telling Me to) Breathe

In my defense, when I first noticed it was *a thing* for people to exhort each other to *Breeeaaaathe*—wasn't that in the eighties?—I was properly irritated. *What is this New-Age bullshit? Obviously, I'm breathing already or the reminder to breathe would fall on deaf—no, dead—ears. Take your vapid rainbow unicorn advice telling me to do what I'm already doing and ...* So how did I become someone who keeps telling people to breathe?

Well, I didn't. I actually tell people to bring consciousness to the breath. That's different. I even sometimes explicitly acknowledge: You're breathing anyway. So breathe with awareness, watching the breath go in and out, all the way in, all the way out, and insofar as you can with no straining, direct that breath to the place in your body that hurts while you're thinking what you're thinking and feeling what you're feeling. That is, direct it to the pain body. And as you do this, you may well notice that this conscious breathing translates to slightly longer, fuller breaths, and that therefore, a) you quickly find this to be calming and anchoring, and b) you become the witness of your pain body and slip out of identification with all that messy stuff going on in there.

Is breath the way to freedom?

In case you're already bored with breath, let me amp up the entertainment factor. This paragraph is brought to you by *Star Wars*. My son recently had a helper ask him to take long, loud breaths that no self-respecting seventh grader would ever go along with. He calls them Darth Vader breaths and, when no one else is looking, imitates for me (with what I can only call puke-face) what it would look and sound like if he actually went along with Darth Vader breathing. Which, as a self-respecting seventh grader, he most certainly does not. Please know that I'm not asking you to take Darth Vader breaths. Just breathe consciously—you're breathing anyway—directing the breath to the place of pain, and let the breath expand if it will. But don't force it. No puke-face.

I just got interrupted from this writing by Dana, calling from an airport to talk about the tantruming toddler that's taken over her currently activated pain body. With the aim of disentangling the inner child from the pain body while acknowledging their obvious kinship, I asked her to hold the pain body (awareness and breath) while she holds the tantrumming child (awareness, maybe visualization) to teach her small self that this pain is containable, it's bearable; this situation is manageable, and her adult self is managing it. But Dana, don't put the child in charge of your relationship (or Reader, your whatever), or even in charge of the next step in that realm. Do breathe.

Why bring consciousness to the breath—never mind talk about it, write or read about it, remind people to breathe? Breath is (far) more powerful than we give it credit for. I once had the pleasure and privilege of attending a workshop on the psychic structures of the nine personality types taught by Russ Hudson, a (I want to say *the*) preeminent elucidator of the Enneagram. I was fascinated to find that Russ kept bringing his discussion back to the breath as he moved through the types and explained how we can trump the tendencies of our particular personality style. Connecting to breath allows you to witness yourself. It can assist you to choose more consciously where you go next in mind and body.

Let me digress for two paragraphs here to note that the Enneagram is a personality typology system that I use in my coaching practice because it's such a gorgeous, complex, elegant system. Unlike other models, it's not a listing of separate types, but draws clear interconnections among the types. It therefore makes sense that the Enneagram is depicted by a round diagram with nine points and lines that connect the types to one another (the more detailed reasons for which I won't get into here). We're all ultimately all the types, but one particular type with a neighboring wing explains our personality strategy for managing life. (By "neighboring wing" I mean the number right next door: I'm a Four with a Three wing, while a friend of mine is a Four with a Five wing. We share core issues and tendencies, but because of our differing wings, for starters, she's far more reclusive and her image consciousness is less overt. The time I suggested we do a radio show together, she laughed—basically told me to take my Three wing and go fly solo.)

You don't need to know a thing about the Enneagram to understand what I write about in what follows. If you're curious about your type, there are free tests on the internet or in any number of books. I'm a particular fan of the Enneagram Institute (put it together and add dot-com and you've got their website address). Besides a free short test, they also offer a longer test of higher validity for only 10 bucks as of this writing. (Note that you're the purest version of your type in your mid-twenties, so if in doubt, answer the questions as you would have then.)

Back to the breath. For the sensitive types—though all types have their own sensitivities—the emotions can be supported and contained through grounding with the breath. The problem isn't being too sensitive, Russ explained. The problem is the fact of not being grounded in the body. The heart's sensitivity must be contained by the body, and we facilitate this through feeling our feet on the ground, embodying our hips, and bringing consciousness to (you've got it) the breath.

Thus, groundedness gives Fours the capacity to contain their alarming emotions without getting sucked into despair or believing that all of life boils down to what they're feeling in the moment. It gives Nines the confidence to meet life's problems instead of shoving them down and shutting them out. It gives Sixes the ability to get out of the mind's futurizing *what-if*s and make a good choice for right now. All the types benefit from grounding through the breath. Whatever your type, the breath is your ally in grounding so that you can bring yourself back from your habitual tendencies—whatever unhealthy tactics you default to when the going gets rough.

Why is that? Russ helped me more clearly connect the dots between breath and presence. (Hmm, didn't the phrase *Be here now* come into vogue round-about the same time everyone started saying *Breathe*?) To stay with the examples given above, the Four isn't present when sucked into those compelling emotions; the Nine isn't present when pushing out the inconvenient, intrusive world; the Six isn't present when mentally spinning all the options and their terrifying potential outcomes.

Shall I go through the other types, too? Please skip ahead to the next paragraph if you don't care to consider each one. The Two isn't present when reaching outward to take care of others without first checking inward for self-care needs or personal wants. The Three isn't present when pushing through all barriers to the glorious finish of a project that every red flag in the vicinity is waving to call a stop to. The Five isn't present when ducking back inward because, once again, relating with the beings who populate the world out there turns out to be less than obvious. The Seven isn't present when jumping mentally to the next activity, the next encounter, the next rush. And Eights and Ones just aren't present when requiring others to get behind what they want (8) or what they consider to be right and good (1).

Is breath the way to freedom? Maybe. I'm pretty sure you can get free only here and now (not irrevocably into forever as fans of enlightenment often strive for), and you can't get free here and now if you're not here, here and now.

Do you want to be present? Do you want to bring consciousness to all you do—or even to some of it sometimes? You need to be grounded to be present. Like a good writer, you need to connect to the senses and the sensory details of the moment. You need to be aware of your body and breath.

If you want to roll your eyes when someone says *Breathe*, go ahead and roll away. Plenty of us will join you. And then—since you're breathing anyway, and only if you want to get grounded or be present or scooch toward a bit more freedom from your habitual tendencies, only for right now—do nothing with your breathing but to give it your awareness (all the way in, all the way out).

chapter 5

Managing Pain by Bringing It Closer

Some years ago, life gave me the most amazing teaching through a harsh kitchen burn. It taught me a new way to be with physical pain. Eventually (this bit took me a while), I learned how to apply the technique to emotional pain—which, like physical pain, expresses as sensation in the body. The pain-body work that's become so central to both my personal process and what I walk others through really began for me that night.

I don't remember what I was cooking or how I burned my finger, but the memory of the ramifications is vivid. It wasn't sufficiently serious to warrant a trip to the emergency room, but bad enough that no amount of ice or aloe eased the pain. I couldn't sleep. I was so tired, and kept dozing off, but this screaming event in my hand kept jolting me back to being fully awake. Then I was miserable and distressed and dreading the rest of the night and the next sleep-deprived day. (I was not present.) Finally, the hour got late enough and the misery great enough that I came to and decided something else needed to happen here. Somehow, I understood that I needed to meet the pain more directly. I needed to be present with it, and see what gift it might have for me.

I have no idea what, beyond the pain, prompted me to do such a thing. This was well before I began to habitually meet everything in life as a gift. But I found the gift, and with it a three-part formula that I've come back to again and again: Let it sear, let it fade, let it go.

First, it came to my attention that I was adding to my discomfort by avoiding the pain. All my muscles were tightened up with dread, and the pain that I dreaded was already here anyway. I relaxed, as best as I could. I decided not to ward off the pain but to welcome it. I decided, in fact, to move into the pain, drop right in. I brought all my awareness to the burning sensation in my hand and gave myself over to feeling it.

Initially, the pain got bigger. I somehow managed to notice that it wasn't so big I couldn't bear it. I actually got curious about its parameters, or its potential: how big could it get? I decided to expand it further. I focused my awareness and let the pain climb as high as it could possibly go. I stayed with it. Because it was a burning pain, this allowing and expanding phase phrased itself in my mind as *Let it sear*.

At some point, in much less time than I might have expected (though this wasn't what I'd expected), the pain began to shrink. It was dying down! Finally! It was moving back out! I was so amazed and caught off-guard that joy slipped right in. I felt a bit elated, maybe just to be in this process of discovery. And it made so much sense: Where else can pain go once it reaches its peak? Nowhere for it to go but down.

Again, it baffles me that I even thought of this next thing (*grace*, anyone?), but the moment came when it struck me that I was still trying to maximize the pain, and that this was no longer called for. That part was over. Now was the time to notice the pain was dissipating, and to bring my attention to that. The right action at this stage was to *Let it fade*.

Here, memory fails me as to my actual process that night. I don't know when I came up with the final piece, *Let it go*. What I came to understand was that pain fades, but I find myself still telling the story of the pain, thus keeping it present mentally. (Who knows how I phrased it to myself then. Those are Katie-like words, and I hadn't yet encountered The Work of Byron Katie and her talk of telling and dropping a story.) What's needed, once I've let the pain fade, is to let it go completely. It has no intention of being permanent unless I make it so with my mind.

The memory of the kitchen burn came to me one day as I was coaching a client in meeting her moments of big emotional pain—as she moved through an important and sometimes terrifying life transition. I notice again and again that we human types don't like to be still with our pain. We don't like to meet it fully. We seldom invite it to sit down and stay awhile. I believe this is because we fear it'll move in forever. But truly, it never does. Pain never has the intention of coming to stay. Only the mind can try to pin it down in permanence.

We also fear pain when we expect it to get so big it will take us over. It will engulf us. It may even be the end of us. One of my memorable takeaways from Byron Katie's nine-day School for The Work is that pain is never more than I can bear. If it ever were, then I'd be unconscious, or I'd be dead—and something's going to kill this body one day, I'm certain. Until it comes to that, I can take whatever comes. And I can take it much better if I meet it fully, let it be exactly what it is, invite it in to bring its gifts. Then, more likely than not, after it sears, it will fade, and it will go.

My purpose in this chapter is to help you look at pain-body work from another angle and to consider again that physical pain and emotional pain are much more alike than they are different. Mentally, you can pretty much treat them the same way. So let me close by offering a way you can accelerate your work with the pain body through a practice of tuning in regularly to what's happening in your body. If it's easier for you to tune in to what you perceive as physical pain unrelated to emotion, then create a habit of scanning your body and bringing direct awareness and breath to any place that hurts. There's usually something.

As you do this, you'll find the line blurs pretty quickly between physical pain and emotional pain, as your scan might alert you to some disturbance in the belly that will turn out to be anxiety or dread or that spoonful of shame that went down with that weird little encounter with You-Know-Who, and—ah—it still hasn't been fully digested. Scan at bedtime, for starters, or before you get up in the morning. Take a break to check in during the day. Tune in on the bus, since you're just sitting there. Watch for what's happening in your body and, even briefly, give it your awareness and breath.

This will help you work more effectively and more immediately with the pain body when it activates, because the disturbance will feel odd (you'll be used to feeling more clear as an ongoing way of being), and will therefore come quickly to your awareness. When pain is normal, it's hard to notice it, never mind respond to it appropriately. This practice of noticing pain and momentarily expanding it, strangely enough, denormalizes it. Pain becomes something you no longer unconsciously carry around, like excess weight, but an intrusion that gets your attention and invites a proper response.

Let it sear, let it fade, let it go.

chapter 6

Good Tears versus Bad Tears

What is a good cry, anyway? Can crying be bad? At some point, for myself, I came to understand a distinction between good tears and bad tears. It sounds absurd to put those labels on tears, but there's actually a distinction worth making here. It's important, because it parallels the distinction between pain and suffering—pain being something you can simply allow, that runs its course and moves along, and suffering being something that takes you over, or feels like it will, and that you inflate and get stuck in by believing it means you're not okay.

Good tears are free-flowing. They move through, and they move on, like the rain. Once they're gone, you feel relieved. It's like the calm after the storm: everything just smells better, and the colors are resplendent. A natural pause comes in, and you breathe into that, and it's over. Something has been washed clean: good tears.

Bad tears don't have this flow or this effect. They take hold and churn you around—it's more like being trapped in a malevolent washing machine. Pauses happen, but then you reach for the story and crying takes right up again, with a vengeance. Whatever the tears are expressing—that life is against you, that there's something terribly wrong with you, that no one will ever love you the way you want to be loved—whatever it is reasserts itself, grabs you and shakes you and whispers it won't ever let go. When you're done crying bad tears, you don't feel done—you feel toxic.

What makes the difference between good tears (or pain) and bad tears (or suffering)? Story. There's plenty you can do to work with that story thing, and the first tactic is so simple that its power is vastly underrated: just notice the story as story. Notice the fact that you're in a story. I'm not even talking about true or false, here. Even if the story were 100 percent accurate, it would still be a story. You need to move away from the story making you cry in order to cry cleansing, clearing tears.

The noticing itself is enough to pull you one degree out of total immersion. You can step further out by moving consciously into witness mode. (Remember, go for accessing the compassionate, dispassionate witness.) This simply involves watching—watching your feelings, your thoughts, your behaviors, even your hands—so that you feel less identified with it all. If you can watch a story, you can know you're separate from it, even if it brings you to tears. You can tell yourself, *I am not this story*.

Watch the story. Hear the words that tell it, catch the repeating themes. I'm a great fan of writing thoughts down: this diminishes the threat that they'll engulf you; it lets you see clearly what the mind is up to; and with your thoughts spelled out and clearly visible, you can begin to question them. At the very least you can recognize them as thoughts (you can tell yourself, *They're just thoughts*), instead of believing that your mind is narrating objective reality.

When you believe and hold on to a sad, self-defeating story while you're crying; when you grasp for the story and call the tears back in after they subside into natural pauses—that's when the tears are bad. The word *wallow* comes to mind. Wallowing isn't inherently wrong—but it will make you suffer. Otherwise stated, it's a way you perpetuate your own suffering.

Start noticing when the feelings flow through as needed and do their marvelous stormy job of rebalancing your emotional electrons. Notice in an approving way: good tears are so good.

Start noticing, too, when the crying feels off, and let that *off* feeling be your cue to check out whether you're in a story. If you catch yourself there, no need for self-flagellation. You're doing nothing wrong—only being human. Would you like to be human in a more conscious way? Just begin by noticing the story. Look for the story and, if you're brave enough in that particular moment, get it down on paper. (Again, best to work with short, simple sentences in list form.)

All of this supports you in minding the pain body and tending the mind when you need to cry. All of this allows you to kindly give yourself a hand up when distress tries to take you down.

As a certified (I used to think *certifiable*) Enneagram Four type, I used to have a dark relationship with crying bitter tears. I would give myself over to weeping copiously, and it gave me a weird satisfaction to suffer so deeply. Then there came a point in my life when my body wouldn't have it anymore. I'd wake up the next day with horrible dark puffiness around my eyes and a sick headache as if I'd been on a drinking binge. A twelve-step type I knew dubbed it an emotional hangover, and there was no denying that's just what it felt like. At the time, I was learning how to take responsibility for anything I was feeling (learning to stop being a victim, in other words), and the consequences of crying the toxic kind of tears made it really clear to me that this indulgence wasn't worth whatever I thought it did for me.

Now, when I cry, I've got this very helpful piece: I look away from story. I allow the crying fully but only for as long as it wants to move through as a cleansing phenomenon. I'm fascinated and amazed by how quickly it passes. Every once in a while, I've been disappointed by the brevity: *Aw, is that all?* But I like it much better this way, and the next morning, I'm fine. In fact, right after crying, I'm fine. When you let crying be what it's supposed to be, it's very cleansing indeed.

chapter 7

Getting Out of Overwhelm

Overwhelm is not a given, ever. Not when there's a lot going on and you have no clue how you're going to manage it all; not when you're up against a deadline with one task lined up after the other and not a moment to spare; not when you're in an emotional pressure cooker and life feels frightening and out of control. In such moments, things may indeed be inarguably full. You may benefit from being very diligent or focused, or both. You may choose to accept some discomforts (less sleep than feels good, less peace or leisure than you typically enjoy) to get what you're after (maybe to simply keep your job or take care of your children, or both and then some …). You may have some strong emotions to field. Still, in all of that, overwhelm is optional.

So how do you get out of overwhelm when you find yourself in it? How do you learn not to go there when it all feels like too much?

I've found a grand solution to overwhelm in Byron Katie's three kinds of business (which she presents in *Loving What Is*). This is quite relevant to me personally. My two most often repeated declarations used to be "I'm overwhelmed" and its close cousin, "I'm exhausted." After The Work of Byron Katie came into my life, it dawned on me at some point that anytime I felt overwhelmed, I was out of my business. I started checking for whose business I was in whenever I felt overwhelmed or heard myself say I was. Invariably, I was out of mine—truly, every single time. I started wondering: Could it be there's no such thing as overwhelm if you live in your own business?

Let me go over Katie's three-part model. (I touched on it in "Mind the Pain Body, Tend the Mind.") In your thinking, there are three kinds of business she posits for you to be in: yours, theirs (anyone else's), or the Universe's (she says *God's*; I have a client who calls it *the world's*, which seems to amuse me no end, probably because he managed to get every last drop of *woo* out of it). When Katie talks about the three kinds of business, her emphasis is on self-abandonment: when you're out of your business, you abandon yourself. This is important—crucial—because people tend to correlate the concept of leaving their business with a harsh admonition or that rap on the knuckles: *Bad girl! Bad boy! Mind your own business! Get out of my business! That's not your business!* Katie's approach is meant to be kind: Come back to yourself. If you're not in your business, you've left yourself; you're no longer here to attend to yourself.

I find that people are often struck hard when they realize the self-abandonment of it. Noticing how far afield they habitually go, they get very serious about getting back to their own business. The way Katie speaks it, when you're out of your business, you've absented yourself to go tell God how to run things or tell other people how to live their lives, so no one's here for you. (Katie's conceptualization of God, by the way, is very open-ended, non-patriarchal, and not based on a human image—certainly not the white bearded guy in the sky. For her, God is reality. Reality rules: what is, is.)

The best metaphor I've got for being out of your business is treading water. You exert yourself trying to apply agency where you don't have it, so nothing happens. At best, you keep your head above the surface. You exert, exert, exert until you exhaust yourself (*I'm overwhelmed, I'm exhausted*), and at some point you may well feel like you're drowning. When you're in your business, taking care of what's yours to take care of, applying agency where you've actually got it, your efforts are productive: swimming!

A premed student gearing up for MCATs, for example (somehow I've talked to more than one of these, living as I do in an Ivy League college town), could slip out of her business in any number of compelling and torturous ways. If she brings to her test preparation how much time she's got to prepare (is it enough?); the score she needs (what if a *good* school doesn't want her?); the actual score she'll get (outcome!); the competition (horrendous in the med-school world); the steps yet to follow the dreaded test (including potentially terrifying interviews—and what will they think of her? ... she gets so weirdly inarticulate in such moments); how she'll cope as a resident functioning on interrupted sleep while absorbing crazy amounts of life-and-death information; and how in the blazes she'll manage to cultivate a solid and juicy relationship so she can somehow gracefully juggle family and work one day—holy hell! Is this manageable?

If she comes back to her business, she's down to one thing: prepare as best she can for the test in the time she's got left for preparing. That much is manageable.

Let me ask an obvious question because it bears asking. Which maximizes the chance of a good outcome? Staying in her business and simply preparing as thoroughly as she can, or going out of her business to theirs and the Universe's, then carrying and processing (in her poor, overtaxed pain body) all the anxiety this produces? And while I'm asking the obvious, one more: which is more likely to keep her out of overwhelm?

It's mostly pretty clear when and where you go into other people's business, but there are any number of times you might go there without quite realizing you're not where you belong. This may happen with your *should* concepts, your wonderful ethics and great ideas (I mean truly wonderful and great ethics and ideas) about how people ought to treat one another, drive safely, talk to their children or siblings, get out of codependence, run meetings more efficiently, buy local, calm down—you name it. But if you're not the one doing the treating, driving, talking, getting out, running, buying, or calming, you're in someone else's business, visiting your sacred concepts, as Katie calls them, on others.

And are you clear about staying out of their thoughts of you? It's common, perhaps universal, for people to very much want to manage what others think of them. The idea that doing so takes you out of your business isn't Katie's brainchild. Folks in the 12-step world love to declare some version of, "What other people think of me is none of my business." So are you clear? Are you willing to come back to approving of yourself when you're concerned about the approval of others?

I've found that the their-business-my-business line blurs for people most where their children are concerned, with spouses or primary partners coming in a close second. The argument for children usually includes some refrain about being responsible for them. I agree that there's no inarguable black-and-white demarcation, and the line, wherever it is, changes pretty drastically from one year to the next as kids keep growing up. I acknowledge that people have varying parental philosophies that would yield a variety of calls as to whose business this or that may be. Let me venture briefly to propose that there may be a lot more room for calling it their business than parents typically call it. Children have their own journeys and paths, they have their own personality types and tendencies, they are a product of their generation, not their parents'. The things parents do in the name of keeping their kids safe and supporting their growth as good human beings often amount to too much control or to getting involved with more of the kids' business than need be.

This whole topic is a book in itself (and if I were the writer, there'd be a hefty confessional component about my grossly overcontrolling early parental misadventures), so the short version might be this: I invite you, parents, to consider more often whether you might let go of the thing you're trying to control. I invite you to take the long view and trust that the kid will work out the thing you're concerned about over time, and that perhaps you didn't have that one worked out by that age either, and you didn't need to. I invite you to trust the tremendous power of your own modeling (whether kids acknowledge valuing what they see you do or not). I invite you to keep the lines of communication open, because if they're talking to you about their choices and messes and thoughts about what they're moving through, and you're not seeking to control their perspective (their business) but listening to it and offering yours when it's wanted, you get to have a lot more influence than when you're angry at them for not being you, or for not being fully formed, or for experimenting with some of the multitudinous arenas for exploration on planet Earth.

Let me add a final word about worry where your children are concerned. You're most certainly out of your business when you worry about your kids, and you do them no good whatsoever in sending angst their way. As Tosha Silver describes worry, "Imagine a black Express Mail envelope marked 'Thinking of You' filled with muck, mildew and a few skull bones." Bad idea! Allow your children to go through pain, sorrow, failure, disappointment, feeling bad about their lives—because anything that could happen in a human journey just may happen to your children. Don't teach them they're not equipped to handle life. I especially like saying such things to parents contemplating divorce, or agonizing over a split that's already done. Your kids will deal with their own hard decisions and relationship troubles. Throughout their lives, they'll go through sorrow and loss and having to let go of what changes in this impermanent reality through no fault of their own. They may as well have some serious practice runs with you still there, loving them through it, talking about it, allowing whatever emotions come up, and persisting in believing in their resilience and their ability to heal and grow.

Give up worry (move away from it when you catch yourself there) and give your energy to believing in them, holding up positive mirrors for them, predicting good ends, telling them you trust them to work it out over time, asking angels to keep them safe (if you're into that), having real conversations with them about safety issues and (ideally, without being moralistic) about the consequences of choices. You're definitely in your business as a parent doing any of those things. I love Abraham's emphasis on pointing our kids inward, to their own guidance systems. Because my kids talk to me, I'm able to point out to them when the way they're telling it indicates something feels off *to them*. This is very different from telling them they're out of line with my values! Do you hold the exact same values and set of experiences (thoughts, emotions, sensibilities) your parents had? Neither will your kids. Leave them to their business.

The argument for spouse types is more about how we're undeniably impacted by what that significant other does—and isn't there something called *our business*? Well, sure, and maybe you and your partner want to work out some agreed-upon territory about what constitutes your shared business. I'm not sure how much energy I'd put into that, but this could be useful for a recurring issue. Better, you might engage in loose dialogue over time about how you as individuals have an impact on each other and on that greater you, the couple. You might stay open *not* to nailing down all the various pieces that don't need to be perfectly in place for a relationship to stay on solid ground as two people move around and make space for each other's differences. (Next chapter is on getting comfortable with your discomfort!)

Let's look at the Universe's business. In short, this is whatever no one can control, certainly not you. I like to flag outcomes and time as the two classic categories here that are likely to get most anyone in trouble.

The concept of outcomes is pretty self-explanatory: how it all turns out. You can't know until it's revealed at the end of the story. What you can do is locate the ways you can appropriately influence the end result, or cast your vote toward a certain end. Ask yourself what's actually yours to do to move toward your desired outcome (or your vision, as we'll conceive it in part 4). That action-toward-desired-outcome is your business. Beyond where you have power to influence outcome, let go. Give it to the Universe (put it in the God box, if you will).

Your sphere of influence may be a big fat chunk or a tiny sliver: identify what that actually is, focus your efforts there, and see about cultivating detachment for the rest. This could look like catching yourself in a worry or prediction about outcome and coming back to *now*: *now* is always your business. What's yours to do here and now? Come back to that, and remind yourself that the Universe holds the rest.

Time includes timing—that is, how long it'll take, when you'll get there, how quickly all the pieces not yours to manage come together. Any facet of timing that's out of your control just isn't your business. When emotion will ease up is a great and unexpected example, because you can't control that: it's the Universe's business when rage, sorrow, or grieving will release its grip on you. (But you can certainly mind the pain body, for as long as it's active, from the perspective of the compassionate, dispassionate witness. You can tend the mind, questioning the thoughts associated with your strong feelings. Minding the pain body and tending the mind—under the rubric of self-care—are always your business.)

Time also includes the past and the future, as, again, most of your business happens here and now. Note that in-your-business time travel (such as going to the future in order to plan and prepare, to troubleshoot, to coordinate efforts with someone else, or reviewing the past to rectify something) won't land you in stress. If you're stressed out while mentally visiting past or future, and if there's no action required on your part, you're almost certainly out of your business. If you're imagining a future you'd like to create or usher in (visioning!), revving up the good emotions you'd feel if this were your reality, there's no problem whatsoever, and no need to check in with the three kinds of business.

People love to make much of planning to argue that the future is in fact their business. Well, consider how much of your time spent in the future is to plan and how much is to worry, make bleak predictions, declare what will never happen, hash over various outcomes and worst-case scenarios, and so on: that productive-planning part (your actual business in the future) usually entails a pretty slim slice of the pie. And by the way, you could be in your business looking at worst-case scenario if you're doing that to get clear about whether you could handle it—to assess risk factors for clear decision-making. You know the difference between valid ventures into the future and pointless forays—the kind that scare the bejesus out of you. Again, stress is your reminder that you're out of your business.

Where the past is concerned, you're out of your business there when you're going over it in ways that aren't useful, revisiting what just doesn't need to be revisited *again*. A useless foray into the past is often characterized by blame, regret, sorrow, longing, or believing that what's over and done should still be happening, that whatever happened shouldn't have happened (or at least not the way it did), that anything or anyone gone should still be here, or that you'd somehow be better off now if that thing hadn't gone down or if this moment still held what is no more. If you're visiting the past in therapy, for example, in a way that yields ease, insight, forgiveness, letting go—you're in your business. If you're reviewing the same scenes with your shrink five, ten, twenty years later ("Please," a new client said to me, "not one more word about my father!"), you're out of your business again and may well benefit from another modality or a different therapist. If you're visiting the past with joy and gratitude, you don't even need to wonder whose business you're in (nothing to fix in that scenario).

Finally, I want to flag that you're in the Universe's business when you declare limitations or character flaws as if they were universal laws. I especially find myself pointing this out to people when they're in self-judgments, which for many people are far more harsh than anything they direct toward others. You can't do that, you won't get there, you don't get to, you're not capable, you're too flawed? Who are you to declare that about anyone, even yourself? There's no universal law that says you can't create, thrive, and fulfill your potential alongside every other human being. Come back to your business, which is to determine where you want to go and head that way; let the Universe show you what you can and can't get to.

In terms of overwhelm, it's crucial that you stay out of the Universe's business. Do I need to tell you that you're not equipped to do the job of the Universe? If you'll excuse the G-word here, must I remind you that you're not God? (In parenting, sometimes, I feel relief when I remember I'm not God—just the mama figure.) How could anyone be anything but overwhelmed seeking to take care of the turning of the planets or the hands on the clock, the weather, the unexpected natural disasters, and most anything to do with life and death, war and peace, what is or isn't possible, and the way it ultimately will or did turn out?

So when you're overwhelmed—whether you feel trapped in your car in the midst of gridlock or you're in a wretched hospital environment waiting to learn if a beloved will live or die—ask yourself two simple questions. First, "Whose business am I in right now?" Find where you're out of your business—in theirs or the Universe's: you will surely be in one or the other, if not both. Then ask this follow-up question: "So what is my business here?" Once you locate your business, go there. You'll be right where you belong. You might feel instant relief. Even if your actual business isn't a comfortable place to be for the moment, you'll still be equipped to manage it. You can calm yourself in traffic. You can be with the sensations of grief taking over your body and look into whatever set of eyes shows up to meet yours. A premed student is entirely capable of spending an evening preparing for a test. She isn't capable, that same evening, to manage her entire schooling and career while coming to grips with how to manage the balance of work and home life in such a demanding profession.

Two questions: "Whose business am I in right now?" and, if you're not fully in yours, "So what is my business here?"

Sometimes your first order of rightful business, when you come back to it, is simply to mind the pain body that got activated when you left. Be with yourself kindly and gently. Access that compassionate, dispassionate witness. Soothe yourself. And from there, take care of anything else that's yours to take care of, carrying that pain baby with you.

It's certainly possible for what's actually your business to be quite sizable and daunting. If that's the case, trying to manage all of it at once puts you right out of your business again. You can't swallow the whole ocean. You can, however, pull out one bucketful and do something with that. (I don't actually recommend swallowing it.) So take large tasks or situations and make it your business to break them down into bite-sized, manageable bits, then show up now and now and now for each task before you. You can only do one at a time anyway—whatever's up right here and now. (Okay, sometimes you can multitask. Do that if it makes the most sense and keeps you in your business. And note that you can only multitask so much. Let's get Zen about it: When you multitask, just multitask.)

66

If there's a long string of tasks with a deadline looming, be clear about how much time you can allot to each one. This may mean relaxing your standards a bit. Is your mind going to what your boss or client will think of what you present, or whether you'll get done on time or not? You're out of your business, unless you're reevaluating how you want to proceed. Worry (or any stressful emotion) is a clear sign—use it as a reminder—that you're out of your business.

Then there's the phenomenon I call straightening the button drawer. Don't order and color-code the button drawer when it's time to move through the whole of a project. Somehow this idea came from living with a kid who for years loved to let a room get to alarming levels of chaos before dealing with it. She'd then declare a day of cleaning, and when I checked on her three hours later, she would show me some painstaking task she'd conquered in the realm of minutia (*Look, all the buttons in this drawer are arranged by size and color!*) while chaos reigned all around. It's a good idea to move through any momentous task in an unpolished way from start to finish, then go back in and tweak toward perfection as time allows. This, too, helps with overwhelm.

There's no *staying*, in life. As with everything else, you can't stay in your business. You can't stay out of overwhelm. You can, however, hold the intention to live in your business, free of the idea that it's all more than you can bear, free of the sensations related to that idea coursing through or lodging somewhere in your body. With the intention in place to live without overwhelm, catch yourself there. (You'll land there again, so be willing to catch yourself kindly.) Check out again whose business you're in. Having found that you're out of your business, you can then simply come back to what's actually yours to mind. That's as good as it gets, and it's plenty good enough.

chapter 8

Get Comfortable with Your Discomfort

Discomfort is here to stay. Or rather, it's here to pass through periodically, and you must step through it on your journey, sometimes daily. Are you willing?

You'd better be. When you set up your life to avoid discomfort, there's so much that has to be shut down, so much to be denied, dreaded, warded off. You're also likely to have an irritation response, anger, or a sense of something gone wrong anytime discomfort shows up. In other words, in failing to embrace discomfort, you increase it.

It's not that you need to go looking for it—discomfort gladly comes to you. Nor do you need to make an ascetic religion of never setting things up for comfort: creating comforts and minimizing discomforts is part of self-care and care of loved ones. Hyperpreparing, though, to be ready for any eventuality, makes you a slave to avoiding discomfort. Believing it shouldn't happen and being upset when it does puts your focus in the wrong place. The trick is to trust that plenty of comfort comes to you, and be willing and able to meet discomfort whenever it passes through.

And pass through, it will: a chill wind, a sheet of wet rain, a season of heavy pollen; the food that sits wrong in your belly (and more, ugh, how much did you eat?); the shameful memory, out of the blue; the mom being horrible to her kids at the store (and you think, *I'm never that bad*, but the problem is she's just an exaggerated version of your most exaggerated fear about your worst self); the outfit that never came together (but you're no longer home when you notice); the niggling thing that you don't deal with, and it won't shut up; the person whose rolling glance in your direction and away tells you, with utter clarity and no actual rudeness, that you just don't make the grade; that overbearing tendency of yours that just took over again, with the volume turned up in that precise moment when some oddly universal lull in conversation descended; those sudden false insights that tell you you'll never have the

X, Y, or Z to get through this life gracefully; the tiresome, compulsive second-guessing; the thing happening to your kid that you just can't prevent and can't even see how to address; the realization you're outside of the group, even though everyone's being lovely; the financial predicament you're in, again (or worse, still); those 10 pounds you're so tired of gaining and losing again you're thinking of throwing out the juicer and just succumbing to fat, sick, & nearly dead. Got discomfort? A human being can only answer yes.

So how do you get comfortable with discomfort? Start with allowing it; embrace that it's part of life. When any thought moves through that would suggest it's a problem, notice the thought. Notice the absurdity, the lie of it. If you're in the right space, it could even make you laugh. Your sock shouldn't be twisting into an imprecise ball inside your boot? That's a good one. Your kid shouldn't be using that tone or that volume or that urgency to express those woes? Another good lie to throw you off and keep you from getting present. ...

Be still with it. Pause when discomfort strikes, instead of moving away from it. Bring it close; expand it. Turn the light back on if you just extinguished it to keep from seeing what's there. Someone recently told me about shutting off the light to keep from seeing her body since she's gained weight. This is as good a metaphor as any and, for plenty, there's nothing metaphorical about it. Maybe the body idea still works for you with something other than weight: for me it's the one more varicose vein that just pushed through to the surface or the next squiggly purple capillary that ruptured there—and Goddess knows I already had a religion of keeping anyone and everyone's eyes off my legs. What if you allowed the light? What if you looked directly toward what you want to look away from? Can you gaze at what you find ugly, right on your own person? Can you find the beauty in it and the beauty in spite of it?

If you tell me I have truly ugly veins in my legs, I'll agree with you. Tell me they're beautiful rivers that flow through my body's terrain murmuring a woman's story of ... okay, I'm getting queasy, and I don't believe you. But if you tell me those veins make me ugly, I won't believe that either. I know they don't, though I still need to work with this in some moments. I can sit with them and walk myself through from *hideous* to *human body doing something human bodies do*. I can pan away from them, with my legs still in the picture, and see *beautiful human being, imperfections included.*

I can scooch toward getting okay with what I used to consider categorically unacceptable, that made me seriously uncomfortable.

How else to get comfortable with discomfort? Again, tend the mind: work with your thoughts. Does fat keep you from creativity or love? Are varicose veins a liability for a single woman who's hit fifty? Only if she's a commodity. Working with my thoughts, I can remind myself that in all my life these legs haven't kept me from love—or sex, for that matter. Why would they suddenly do that now?

This paragraph is brought to you by my love of The Work of Byron Katie. Sometimes I remind clients, Just take a blank sheet of paper and write down every thought you have about whatever the current discomfort is. ("Ah, yes, it's *so helpful* when I remember to do that.") Remember, when you've got the list of thoughts before you, you can see that your painful thoughts on the topic at hand are finite. You can take in that they're thoughts—just thoughts—not a narration of reality; not truth. You can notice how universal they are (as Katie says, they're recycled). You can imagine how any human being sitting with the same discomfort may have a nearly identical list of thoughts. If you don't have time to question those thoughts or turn them around (i.e., look for how the opposite could be just as true, and find concrete examples of that perspective), then at least you've begun to tame the dragon by naming it: Just Thoughts. Thoughts, Byron Katie says, are the source of all the suffering in the world. They're certainly the culprit that brings on any suffering related to discomfort.

Another way to get comfortable with your discomfort is to take action. The action we most often take in response to discomfort is either to move away from it or to (try to) make it go away. Either one of these may be just fine as a workable response, but another possibility is to look for the invitation. What's my discomfort inviting me to do? If I'm uncomfortable about clutter, instead of telling myself I don't have time to deal with it, I might take ten minutes to file things away or make two phone calls on the to-do list or consolidate several lists into one, shrinking it as I go by simply dashing off the e-mail instead of making a note about it.

My parents—who have some quaint forms of speech that, like them, originate in Dixie—often use a number we don't have in the Northlands: the fascinatingly imprecise number *toorthree*, which itself has precisely two syllables. They use this number all the time. In their world, hardly anything happens in twos or threes, and innumerable things happen in toorthrees. And truly, there's hardly anything calling for you to deal with it that you couldn't give toorthree moments to in order to do toorthree things to move them along—thus clearing or at least alleviating your discomfort.

Wait—may I speak to procrastination? Let me address this phenomenon directly, as it's the ultimate discomfort that thinks it's keeping you from discomfort. And doesn't it only compound it?

I counseled someone who avoids her art to stop when the discomfort of procrastination shows up. Welcome it; be still with it. Go sit in front of your canvas with no thought of doing art (or in front of your computer with no thought of writing, or next to your phone with no thought of calling). In that space, fully allow the discomfort of *not* doing to take you over. Locate it in your body. Connect to the sensation and give it your breath (the balm you apply from within). Ask yourself, *Is this any harder to face than the discomfort of the blank canvas?* Notice that you can stand the discomfort, even if you don't like it. (It's not bigger than you. It won't take you over.) Being willing to meet the discomfort of procrastination, you may find yourself willing to meet the canvas, page, e-mail, phone call, clutter, financial reckoning, yoga session, or that thing you told someone you'd do that you don't do and don't do and don't do.

The discomfort of procrastination is always (at least somewhat) appeased when you face directly the thing you don't want to face. It's really that simple. When you let something niggle and gnaw at you and vaguely react or protest but don't really put a stop to the thing, I call that swatting the fruit flies.

Let me tell you about a puppy who was starting to gnaw on a colorful, green-minded reusable grocery bag while a woman (my client Molly) was working on a computer and harboring a strong preference to stay focused on the screen. She didn't want to get up and deal with the puppy. And that fuzzy wiggle-worm of a dog-child, with all that adorable cutlery in its mouth, had gotten its paws on that bag and was all over it. But the computer task … But the puppy, the bag …

Add to this that Molly was working hard on not being irritated by things in her day-to-day life, with the greater goal of not feeling victimized by all the small and large challenges she came upon while navigating what anyone would agree was a tricky set of circumstances.

72

She wanted, in fact, to stop living a struggle.

That's why—since change happens only now, and now, and now—she decided to make a decision in the moment. She stopped typing just long enough to say to herself, *What matters more to me now is completing this task and feeling good about that. I'm going to sacrifice the bag to that endeavor. While I know this officially makes it a no-longer-reusable bag, it also cost something like a dollar, and I'll get another one. The puppy will be blissfully busy destroying it and lying around in the rubble for probably just enough time that I can do what I want to do.* And that was that.

Before that moment, she was trapped in a swarm of fruit flies, and there was little to do in that scene but feel irritated and victimized (by a cute little puppy—oh, the jailers we choose!).

Note that truly eradicating fruit flies, as opposed to swatting them, requires presence (actually attend to the discomfort at hand) and choice (make a clear decision about how to respond to it). When you let things hover untended like fruit flies, you're not choosing. You're not choosing what you want to do, or what you want to give your energy to. You're not choosing to take action in response to what's calling you. What is it? Pause when you notice some buzzy little pest in your emotional field and make a choice. Your fruit flies could be pertinent to that moment or day, or they might point to ongoing pests like clutter or taxes or that gizmo that doesn't work—you might actually fix the thing or throw it out. Ah, but the fruit flies could also be in your face about the cherished dream you keep not getting to. Whatever it is, pay attention. Attend. Quit swatting the fruit flies.

Please note that I'm still not promoting getting rid of discomfort. I'm not suggesting that it's possible or even desirable to do any such thing. But I do invite you to meet it. Where your tendency may be to push discomfort away or numb yourself to it, instead, come closer. Scooch in.

I used to dread winter. I hated what felt like cruel and relentless cold. Still, I spent a decade on the coast of Maine, and here I am in upstate New York. One winter, I started noticing how much I tensed up against the cold—as if that would make it feel better. I started allowing it instead: nonresistance. I let it feel exactly as bitter and biting as it felt. As I relaxed into the sensation of sharp cold, I started to find it more interesting than uncomfortable. Whenever I caught myself resisting it again—as if I could somehow push it away by squeezing my muscles together—I shifted to feeling it fully. I let go of any physical tension and came back to witnessing like a scientist what this precise cold felt like here and now.

The result has been that winter feels much kinder to me. I keep practicing this (I'm currently writing in February, with the temperatures dipping below zero), and it keeps working for me. Note that I haven't come to find frigid cold comfortable. I simply keep getting more and more comfortable with the discomfort. I also notice, embrace, and deeply appreciate the contrast when I step from the cold into a warm room.

Sometimes when my clients and I have covered their thinking and their emotions and their action plans, it seems that what's left, if a bit of a furrowed brow remains, is this simple, can't-get-away-from-it truth: just get comfortable with your discomfort. It's okay.

chapter 9

Why Joy Now?

As a matter of course in my work, I listen to people tell me about how unhappy they are. I hear about how much they hate their job, or how pinched off and dried up they feel in their relationship, or what an impossible financial corner life has backed them into, or how dreadful it feels to be in their body, or what a thankless, joyless, frustrating task it is to parent their particular child or children, or how they would love to create the life they want—of course they would—if only they knew what they really wanted or had any clue how to get that information. ... I assure you there's hope.

No matter how harsh the story or how hard the row before them to hoe, I hold a firm conviction that they, you, anyone can be happy (or happier still). You can move from the life you have now into a life that's most fulfilling to you and offers your highest service to others, because all of life wants to support you in this. We're supposed to feel good and—it's really quite miraculous—life guides us by what feels good.

There's not that much mystery in it: if in doubt or baffled by choices, go for what brings you joy. If you don't see much choice anywhere, find where you have any choice at all and love it. You could do this if you were in prison or in a wheelchair, and you probably aren't. Choose to stay alive for the experiment of it and love the fact that you keep showing up, even if you can't (yet) actively love your life. What about that shade of azure in the sky, or the mix of grays and mauves with that tinge of cornflower blue? Find what you love, and love it. Find the joy, even if it's the thin margin set against a long narrative of woes. Focus on what brings you joy.

If you go over all the compelling, grisly details of what's wrong, you'll have a very hard time getting to what's right. It may in fact become quite true that you cain't get there from here.

They're *really* good, aren't they, all those marvelous details about the thing that broke the camel's back and the proof you'll never get out of here alive and the truth-is-stranger-than-fiction did-that-really-happen(?!)

moment when, of all things, just when you thought it couldn't get any worse. … The price of going over these details again and again, repeating them to friends and to yourself, and to anyone who'll listen, and to yourself, is that you get stuck in them. That, in a nutshell, is what the law of attraction is all about, but in simple pop-psych-talk (nothing New Agey about it), you keep reinforcing that reality, so you get entrenched in that reality. You keep believing that's what's true, that's all there is, that's all that's possible. The details reviewed become the stakes you pound down, deeper and deeper, that ensure you won't budge from where you are.

Okay, we can all see your point about the perils of getting another degree. Quit swirling around the same eddy that reiterates them. Sign up and invest if it makes your heart sing to get that Master's. Decide not to if it's just not right at this point in your life, but don't review it, regret it, and tell the story of what you don't get. Whatever that choice represented that you long for and wish to create, the Universe is more than capable of bringing to you in a form that actually fits with your current life. Let go of what you're not choosing. (This requires some trust, or experimenting with trust, in a friendly Universe.)

In reviewing and believing the details of why you're stuck, you believe (and also reinforce) all the underlying thoughts that support those details you choose to tell. I mean the ones you're not even (or mostly not) aware of, which, if you listed them, would go something like this:

- This shouldn't be happening.
- Life is treating me unfairly.
- I'm a victim [of the economy, the insurance mess, my boss's megalomania].
- I still think I am who my parents [or my siblings or my ex or the popular girls/football jocks in high school] thought I was.
- I'm rattling around on my own in a random Universe that doesn't give a shit about me.
- I'll never be okay.
- What works for others to heal and succeed doesn't ultimately work for me.

And so on … If all of this subtext weren't along for the ride, all those other details, however compelling, just wouldn't matter. They're just the stuff of life. They're the stuff of a good story.

(A practical aside, at the risk of repeating myself: It really helps to use Byron Katie's trick of simply getting out a pad of paper when you're distressed about your life and to write down everything you're believing. Just give yourself a super-simple prompt, like "I hate living in this house and that means that ..." and make a list of short, simple sentences, one thought per line, that gets on paper what's swarming around in your consciousness. All of the resulting thoughts—or even one of them—can be questioned.)

If you feel bad, just find any small thing that might make you feel better. Whatever you feel bad about, scooch toward feeling good about it. *Please keep reading.* I'm not talking about that old and tired put-on-fake-cheerfulness-positive-thinking thing. (I'm with you. I hate it too.)

Sometimes people tell me that they *try* to tell themselves all kinds of good things, but ... Stop right there. No *try*, no *but*. The moment you move (again) toward misery in your focus, the second you permit yourself to rehearse your woes—right there, that's when and where you veered away from joy; and from there, you could equally head that way again. Just a little bit—whatever you can muster. If a cup of tea is all you can think of to make it all feel even a little better, that's the ticket. Celebrate even a centimeter in the right direction. This is the art of scooching.

Get out of all-or-nothing. Don't try to turn the whole thing around. Bring it to *now*. Don't fix your finances, just notice that right now you actually have all you need to survive—and then some. Don't fix your relationship, or your single status, but tell yourself (without the words *at least* in it) whatever you see that's good about the partner you have, or about being single. Don't get a whole exercise regime in place, just get to the pool this very morning because you can and you honestly love a good swim and the smell of chlorine. Just right here, right now, point yourself in the direction of what feels good. Life will get you to a better place if you let it—that is, if you keep stringing together one *now* moment after another in which you scooch a bit closer to joy.

If your maddening teenager is doing and saying any number of crazy, infuriating things, it's hopeless between you if that's what you keep reviewing and talking about, to yourself, to your kid, to your confidantes, to anyone. You'll go nuts if you make it your mission to get them shipshape academicallysociallyfinanciallyhealthfully. Can you find

77

what you love about this person? Right now, in the midst of messes and dysfunction and procrastination, can you find one thing you love and admire and hold up a mirror to your teen reflecting that? (This may be the very thing that gets them through, or that rises to the surface and most informs their life when they're out of this insane passage.) Can you articulate what you admire about them? Can you laugh with them about any topic? Can you find one song they listen to that you actually like? Can you listen carefully when they're willing to talk to you about anything, grateful for the opportunity even if you don't get to be wise or appreciated or as carefully listened to in return? All of this requires letting go of controlling, letting go of the future, letting go of thinking you're the one responsible for whether it all turns out okay. It requires letting go of all-or-nothing and finding just one little something to feel good about right now.

Again (apparently I can't say this enough), don't try to correct the whole picture when it looks like everything's wrong. Bring it to *now*. Don't project a future where it stays wrong. Don't set up a timeline that declares it'll take a very long time to set things right. None of these things is your business. Your business is simple: How can I make myself feel better about this right now? How can I move just a bit closer to joy?

I have a client who stopped going over all the details of what's wrong with her husband and why he's such a disappointment. Life conspired with her by shifting her focus onto some other things in another realm of life that she was excited to learn about and create. She started living in more joy because she was doing what she really cared about. She no longer needed to obsess about what he didn't provide because she was providing her own joy. (Personal responsibility! Victim no more! Gotta love it!) She recently sat across from me with this amazed expression on her beautiful face as she told me the stunning news that it turns out he's the perfect partner for her, and listed all the inarguable, specific evidence for why this is true. We weren't meeting to talk about that. I hadn't asked her to turn her thoughts around. She simply offered all that was being revealed to her now that she'd stopped reviewing the old story of his failings and started looking for joy—all the ways she was already happy with him (and despite him!). What's funny and fascinating is that all the details of why he's perfect are no more or less vivid, compelling, or convincing than the old details of the utter mismatch.

This is why I laugh when people worry about fooling themselves with positivity. Good Goddess, you do it with negativity all the time, where's the problem? If fooling yourself is all you're doing (and I seriously doubt that), then at least fool yourself in a direction that feels good. Just move toward feeling good. Move toward joy. Not toward fixing your life, not toward making it all better, not toward being sure you're doing the right thing or being a good person. Just scooch toward joy however you see to do that, right here, right now.

You'll move. Guaranteed. You may even stumble, drop, or flow right into the life of your dreams.

chapter 10

Oh, the Messy Process of Applying It All

When people get excited about clear new concepts and perspectives, about new ways to approach things in life, for some strange, entirely unfathomable reason, they believe they're going to love trying out these new principles. Love it! Somehow, it's going to feel fabulous to face heartbreak next time. They'll have some kind of chill fest when they next run out of gas or trip onstage. Whatever life category they're putting this to, they're going to do it right, and they'll feel righteous and proud of themselves as they show up differently, and just plain show up, for their life.

So right here and now, let me be the one to tell you, you might not like it one bit. And you won't feel righteous, or proud, or possibly even good in any way, because, for example, to learn to come close to a sting requires that there be a sting, and a sting stings. And before you drop into nonresistance and land in total acceptance of the sting, you may have a first reaction of crying out, sobbing, cursing, or feeling that unshakable tail-twitching annoyance that it happened because if only you'd done this or that instead, it wouldn't have, so you blame yourself; and to add another layer, you're furious that you're reacting, and you may decide one more time that you're hopeless before you remember that's just a thought to question while you sit witnessing the pain of the sting and all it just brought up for you. All of which is to say, the application of anything in the preceding chapters and in what follows will not be fun. Sometimes you will in fact hate it.

Speaking of stings, let me tell you about the day after I made this post on my Jaya the Trust Coach Facebook page:

> When something stings, consider that it might be a false sting, a sign of something old that's really not here to sting anymore—like phantom pains for amputees. Pause with the sting and ask yourself relevant questions: Do I even care about this anymore? Did I really want this? Do I truly value that person's opinion?

Does this mean anything about my actual worth? Have I not gone over this one so many times that there can't possibly be much juice left in there? Could it be that their behavior (words, opinion) has nothing to do with me? What if I were simply gentle with myself and soothed the sting without getting sucked into some story?

Wise words, right? Reading this, you could imagine a lovely process of witnessing a sting from a lofty, safe, comfortably numb, humming distance and asking questions that have lovely answers and set you as straight as you like to be. Let me give you something else to imagine.

So I went to brunch with my friend Jenna who had invited her friend Marian, letting each of us know that the other was single. (It turns out we're both unwaveringly into butch women and, one nanosecond into the gathering, we both knew this would not be a romantically inclined connection.) Jenna (clueless to this) gave a careful introduction when we were seated, first putting forth all the things we had in common, which included, among a long list of positive attributes and accomplishments, a few negative points (thrown in for good measure?) (for the love of truth?). From the moment they came out of her mouth, I was never able to retrieve but one, because my mind got so tripped up on it: "You can both be high-strung," she said. I immediately reacted with a (quasi-playful) questioning look and gesture, and Marian immediately—dispassionate, unfazed—copped to it with some shrugging statement of where Jenna might in fact have seen such a thing in her. In other words, she did what Byron Katie says to do: Find it. Don't argue or defend, just find it. I did no such thing but I was able to (temporarily) let it go and be present for our encounter, we all had a lovely time, and later, in the aftermath, what kept rising to the surface was, *High-strung?*

So when I wrote Jenna about the brunch, I included, "I'm still trying to work out your initial description of me today. (Jenna sees me as high-strung and nervous and what else???)" To which she wrote back, "Not nervous [so that wasn't one of the descriptors I immediately lost track of] but can be high-strung. And what about all the positives?" Well, I couldn't deny all those positives, which I'd in fact already pointed out to myself.

But this did not dissolve the issue for me. As time went by, the feeling inside me of hating being introduced as high-strung kept growing. I realized it was growing. I sought to mind the pain body, and I even managed to do so in a slipshod sort of way, with my focus continually veering back to mental obsession. *What does* high-strung *mean anyway? I hate* high-strung. High-strung *sounds like what I was called growing up by the people who thought I was too sensitive and* weird. *It feels like when I was called* unstable *by people who had it all together when I was floundering through my twenties. It feels awful. Jenna sees me as high-strung? When has she seen me be high-strung?*

At some point, I remembered to just find it, and flashed again to how gracefully Marian had done just that right in the heat of the moment. There was a brief, subtle wave of shame for her apparently being ahead of me in that way in that moment, but I make it a habit to catch such waves and was able to hit the pause button, take a good look at that one, and shift to feeling bolstered by her example—*if she can do it, I can do it too.*

So I found it. I found some moments at various points in my life when I could have been called high-strung. It wasn't hard. That is, it was neither difficult to find examples nor did it feel too terrible to land in the truth of *high-strung* that they revealed. I didn't find them in the A-plus way, which would have involved a) writing them down and b) seeing if I could take my time looking at them without freaking out (the way high-strung people will totally freak). Nor did I pull this off in the A-minus way, which would have involved saying them out loud to make sure I really took in each example. I did go through mentally and locate some images, and I made up a few points by seeking to get okay with the scenes I visited. I extended compassion to my younger self who was pretty sure she wouldn't make it to thirty, and to my young mothering self who was pretty sure she was doing irreparable damage to other (smaller, cuter, worthier) human beings, and to my more recent mothering self who wasn't sure her daughter would make it to eighteen. That was useful. (It wasn't fun.)

It churned me right along to the next round of mental machinations, which involved the fact that whatever Jenna had seen in me that she might call *high-strung* must have come from her listening to me in my most distressed, most vulnerable moments, when I was entrusting her with my heart and my dignity and the harsh things happening in my household that year, all the while believing that she knew I was in a process and she knew I knew it was messy in the moment, and I never in a million years would have thought she was sitting there making an ugly label for me and sticking it on. *But we all do that. I've done that* (then I went on to find how I'd done that). And then, of all things, she'd gotten that label out to use while introducing me to someone she thought was a prospective romantic partner for me. *Here's Jaya, I'm sure you'll want to fall in love with her, because among her many sterling qualities that scare everybody off, you'll also find this adorable humanizing tendency toward being adorably high-strung.*

Note that in this story, minding the pain body and tending the mind took place over several hours and through many activities. I meandered through many instances of lying to myself then countering lies with truth. I got appalled by what Jenna had done wrong then remembered again and recounted again all she had done right and out of love and generosity (she even paid for the brunch) (she didn't even cancel it despite the fact someone she loved actually died the week before) (she's generous, generous, generous). Didn't she want only to support the well-being and pure happiness of all concerned?

Then, right on the heels of that, I'd find myself saying out loud, "Who introduces people by naming their bad points? Who gives balanced tell-all introductions? *Ever?* In any context?" then thinking *I would never do that to Jenna,* which would briefly tilt the balance to hoist me to a position of superiority, except that she was a vision of serenity and I was—obviously, right now, at least in my mind—nothing but high-strung. (Well, I *can* be.) I meanly tried to find something I might *not* say about her in some sort of (*insane, I would never!*) attempt at a balanced intro-duction *(that's not a thing),* and I found an adjective or two, but this felt so mean-spirited I stopped. I even tried to do the opposite. I sat there awhile focusing on beautiful and amazing and impressive scenes of her, which was really easy to do because she is truly an exemplary human being and I admire and love her. And as a devoted and tireless student of the Enneagram, I reminded myself that every type has negative traits and positive traits—and I think all the types are amazing—therefore every person has both negative and positive traits, including me, including Jenna, including every last human being on the planet, so how could it be a problem to have one of them pointed out?

I had toyed with this particular line of thinking early on in the process, when I was asking myself, *Why should it sting for someone to say I'm flawed when I know and embrace that we're all flawed? Where's the problem?* Actually, most of these thoughts cycled around redundantly, as thoughts do. I noticed and kept coming back to the fact that in no way had Jenna's introduction harmed my prospects for love: even if the very butch of my dreams had been sitting across the table from me next to Jenna, I knew it couldn't possibly have kept me from any form of love or joy that was mine to have. I also told myself in clear terms (and I believed myself) that if this stung so badly and required this much processing, some very painful button had been pushed, and it was my button—it had nothing to do with Jenna. Most important, perhaps some profound undoing was in the works, something that would lead to a new level of healing. (It's interesting to note here that the morning after this brunch, entirely oblivious to how it related to my own current process, I'd posted a reminder on Facebook that IT COMES UP TO CLEAR OUT, NOT TO SHOW YOU WHAT YOU'RE STUCK WITH. I wrote it just like that, in all-caps, which one of my page followers commented on, joking that she'd never seen me yell my message before. Was I yelling? What, to get through to myself?)

And at one point, not understanding why I was mad at Jenna at all, coming back again and again to the face of God thing (I'd uncovered many, many good reasons why the face of God would show up for me this way), I realized that I felt entirely dismissed by her pointing to the positives when I wrote to ask about *high-strung*, and then mentally accused her of evasion, because whether the positives are there or not, I don't want to be introduced to a new person with something negative thrown in that someone has decided about me, even if (*find it, find it, find it*) there is some truth in it. (*If and when we get close to people, won't all parts of who we are expose themselves in due time?*) And when I let someone know it didn't feel good that she'd done that (but I didn't really declare that in clear terms or let Jenna know its import, did I?), I want her not to tell me what she did right but to acknowledge at the very least that she didn't mean to make me feel this rotten (but then the responsibility for how I feel is all mine, isn't it, and ultimately not about her or this incident at all!) and she wasn't trying to humiliate me in front of a stranger (and in fact I never felt humiliated).

(I'm so good at talking back to my thoughts. I just want to take one parenthetical paragraph to speak to that. It's so helpful. Truly, despite the fact that in this harrowing example the talking-back didn't clear it right up for me, as it often does pretty quickly, it still helped in that I didn't just believe all those thoughts or get sucked into pure agony and possibly hatred. It's an acquired skill, to be sure. I didn't used to be good at this. I also want to emphasize that thoughts still do what they do no matter how good you become at meeting them. None of this is about trying never to have problematic thoughts. Thoughts happen. You can simply learn to notice them as thoughts and respond to them very differently. You will not be saved from having thoughts, but they will decrease immeasurably. The number of times I find myself in mental situations as I'm describing here are few and far between, and for that reason, they really get my attention—and I scooch in close and attend to my process, both the parts I'm managing well and the recalcitrant parts—and invariably something good comes of it. But first and foremost and all along the way, the point is, as I learned from the radical Work of Byron Katie, you don't have to believe your own thoughts. You don't have to take them personally.)

All of this led to looking again at how *high-strung* as a concept figures in my history, and to thinking (and I recognized this as a victim thought, which I love to ferret out, and am religious about not judging), *It's so strange that I just really, truly don't live that way now, and still someone (someone introducing me to a potential lover) describes me in that way.* I do insist on never seeing life as being against me (friendly Universe, all good news!), and I don't believe in being stuck with anything, so I clearly saw this couldn't mean those things. Which led me to look again at *high-strung* in the present—past five years, past year, really recently—and then, finally, I took a good look at the opposite. Katie's Gift of Criticism exercise asks you to agree, when you've been accused: find it. And once you've drummed up concrete evidence for how it's true, find how the opposite is true as well. This puts you much closer to truth than either defense or denial or even owning the negative trait as if it told the whole story.

I did this. It was comforting to think that my kids—who live with me day in and day out, who've seen me at my worst in moments of exhaustion or at the peak of minding and mitigating their dramas—don't think of me as high-strung. (Then, though it wasn't part of the exercise, I considered some negative things they might actually call me and sat with that, and sat with being okay with that.) I was so stuck on *high-strung* I could barely discipline myself to name its opposite. I flimsily settled on *calm* and saw, in my mind's eye, many scenes of calm—in fact, the predominance of calm in how I currently live my life and meet its challenges.

(Are you exhausted yet? Please remember that I was in the grips of one of those things that gets you and grabs you and has you. Anything I did to be with it and to respond to it was an effort to scooch toward truth, toward clarity, toward kindness to myself and to Jenna. I wanted to be with what was there anyway, to open to the possibility that there was some gift for me in the exploration. And while I was kicking and screaming at least some of the way, I was also okay with that. This confessional telling has one purpose: to help you be in a process that's both effective and kind; to urge you to get okay with yourself however you move through that process, even as you seek to try on the best tools you've got—perhaps those I offer in this book—even as you fail, even as you try again to come back to what feels kinder and truer, as you scooch, scooch, scooch at your own pace.)

So while I was washing dishes several hours into this no-fun no-I-did-not-love-it-or-feel-great-about-it process—in which, by the way, I continually reminded myself that I shouldn't be beyond this, because here I was—I somehow suddenly accessed the next level of total aversion to being called high-strung. And a huge breath came in. And I thought, *There it is.* And I saw Jenna's face and thought again, fully believing it this time, *the face of God.*

Here's what I found: Every day in my manifesto (you'll hear all about that in its own chapter in part 4), I recited at the time of this story something deeply important to me in considering the thus-far elusive partner I was mentally inviting into my world. Those words were, *I bask in her energy.* I won't explain the supreme importance of this, but it was and is supremely important to me—crucial, nonnegotiable—that I love what it feels like to be in the presence of my beloved, and the phrase *I bask in her energy* truly sings to me. And I saw that if you flipped that to her basking in mine, well, who basks in *high-strung*? The pain I'd been in for hours and hours (these were the evening dishes on day two) was the pain of believing myself to be ultimately unlovable, unpartnerable. Because I could heal, grow, evolve, transform; have my own sister start calling me my new name because, she declared, I had actually changed so profoundly that a name change was in order; have two kids who persist in loving me over years together even with all the minor blips and big bad bumps; heal my relationship with my stepdaughter and keep showing up to heal what next presents itself; have loads of clients who appreciate the power of our work together and send me thank-you notes and give me little gifties and speak highly of me and send people they love to me; move through my community fearless of anyone thinking ill of me and finding any number of faces turned my way with great goodwill—and still, it would all boil down to my being entirely unlovable if anyone came too close. I wanted to bask in someone's energy and what I had to offer in return was energy she might want to run away from as fast as her laid-back self would allow.

So I'd gotten to the bottom of it, that hideous, warped, pressurized thing in the deepest depths, and I knew already it wasn't true, and I could iron it out as I went along, minding the pain body, tending the mind. I cried good tears. I went to bed certain I'd wake up refreshed and ready to step again into this life I so love, and did one of my little healing rituals as I put myself to bed. (I have a good ton of them. What they all have in common is that they're deeply relaxing and calming and kind; they connect me to self and source and all manner of spiritual guidance; they firmly place my focus on all that supports me and all that is love. Thus, I drop into unconsciousness entirely caught and held by a friendly Universe.)

PART 2

Scooch In Closer to Yourself

I'm pretty sure I could write a whole book on the idea of living in the recognition of your own magnificence without getting weird or weirdly inflated. Hubris and narcissism are so far from my meaning that I may not mention those even once in that book—don't even want to give them enough weight to place them on the scale across from What I Really Mean.

The thing is, we're amazing, and we don't act like we're amazing because we don't remember we're amazing. We're certainly not taught or encouraged to place our focus there. If we connect to the marvel and magic and wonder of what it means to be on this planet (with red poppies and blue whales and bizarre bugs—ever notice you can keep encountering bugs you've never seen before?) ... then why not connect to the splendor of being human?

It's true that we can be as ugly as we are beautiful. It's true we can be awful, mean, small-minded, self-righteous, vindictive, criminal, and then some. What I notice is that people are much more concerned and fearful, even defensive, about negative traits they might embody than they are joyful about or aware of—never mind properly in awe of—how amazing they are. Many review their limitations in daily recitations, while failing to keep in view that sky-wide potential. "What you focus on expands," one of the most-repeated New-Age truisms, makes an important point— even if poster text irritates you. What if you spent much less time putting your flaws and weak spots under a microscope, gazing with dismay at the overblown version of some horrible aspect of your humanity?

What if you focused instead on your big-blue-sky all-things-possible crazy-gorgeous love essence? Could it be that you'd express that more often, know it better, bring it more fully and consistently into being?

This part of the book is aimed at pointing you toward your beauty, inviting you to hold it in your awareness. It's about being kinder to yourself, scooching toward ongoing, expanding kindness and lavish self-forgiveness. If your personal-growth process isn't kind—why bother? If growth doesn't make you feel better, more joyful, truly excited about the expansion, what's the point? Did you have the experience, growing up, of adults standing you up against that same place on the wall or door frame to periodically chart your growth? Didn't you love that next mark that took that line-with-your-name-on-it just a bit higher than last time? Didn't it help you take in that you were big, that you kept getting bigger?

I invite you to love your growth process, which begins with loving yourself.

chapter 11

Got Self-love?

American culture is a bit obsessed, especially in Hollywood and the music industry, with the highly mythologized phenomenon of romantic love. February is the worst, the month we're bombarded (or Cupid-arrowed) from every direction with the joys of romantic love: sunsets and candles, chocolate and wine—and more chocolate and, hey, got something stronger than wine? If you're single, it's easy to drift into the illusion that all loneliness and frustration would be resolved by the relationship thing. If you're in a couple, it's easy to imagine you should be with someone else who's better at this or has more of that or is less—something.

Whatever month you're reading this, it's a perfect time to get serious about your relationship with yourself. Have you committed yet? I'm not interested in self-care clichés from women's mags here—this isn't about taking yourself out to eat or treating yourself to an elegant pedicure or lavender bubble bath (though these may be lovely). I'm after self-love that involves consistently generous kindness to yourself. I mean self-forgiveness applied not only in big moments of cutting loose some monster from the past, but through ongoing, daily, moment-to-moment practice. I mean refusing to tolerate self-talk that puts you down, refusing to lie in bed at night obsessing over what's not done, what wasn't done right, what you shouldn't have said, what you'll never catch up to or make happen. By self-love, I mean supreme self-honoring.

How? You could begin by dropping your version of the perpetual negative self-talk most people practice and think nothing of practicing daily. It's the air too many people breathe. They take it—mistake it—as normal. Before your mind starts reaching back to source this with mother, society, or other culprits, let me assert that as a personal-growth coach working outside of a therapy model, I focus on the present. My interest is in how you operate, not where it came from: what are you doing right now that doesn't serve you—that in fact constitutes ongoing self-deprecation and ties you to false limitations? (Please note that I'm a fan of good therapy and have benefited from it myself. It's simply not my perspective in this writing or in my coaching.)

Most human beings tolerate a level of verbal harassment from themselves that they'd be outraged to receive from anyone else. What if they didn't tolerate this? What if you didn't?

My wish for humanity is that everyone be struck by the absurdity of what they say to themselves that's all about what's wrong, imperfect, incomplete, unattractive, unimpressive, lacking in social grace or ease, evidence of being permanently stuck, of being a total failure, and on and on. Would you talk to a growing child this way, or to a young person you were mentoring? Would you talk to anyone this way? Sometimes when I want clients to take in what they're doing to themselves, I ask, "If a child were put in your care, would you help her grow and thrive by following her around hissing in her ear all she's doing wrong, everything embarrassing everybody's thinking about her, and all the reasons she won't ever be able to get to where she's going?" I haven't gotten a *yes* on that one yet. Obviously, this would be a very poor child-rearing tactic, more likely to make the kid insecure and fearfully held-back instead of confident and joyfully spontaneous. You probably wouldn't treat a dog—or even a plant!—that way.

You are an evolving being. Believe this. Watch for it. Look for the evidence that you've grown, learned, improved, mellowed, blossomed. This could be your focus, or the lens you look through—and whatever lens you choose determines a whole lot about what you see and experience. When that lens is about shortcomings and failures, to put it mildly, you just won't be at your best.

This isn't the first time I've referred to thoughts as lenses. The metaphor is pretty self-evident, but allow me to expound on it a moment. Let's say you put on a pair of purple glasses. Looking through purple lenses, you can see only a purple world—no way around it. If you never took these glasses off, and wore them daily for the rest of your life, you might forget that the world isn't actually purple. You might remember intermittently, but you'd also actively behave, probably most of the time, the way anyone behaves in purple! You could go to the grave having become convinced this world is a purple world. Still, the world was never purple. That isn't and never was the reality.

You create a sense of reality, and an atmosphere to breathe and move around in, with the habitual thoughts you review inside your head and speak out loud. Are you habituated to an ongoing inner narration of your (perceived) (exaggerated) faults and failures? Somewhere in my personal journey, when I was doing The Work of Byron Katie daily to question my habitual negative thoughts, it was like a switch got pulled. Suddenly, it wasn't okay to think bad-loser-incompetent-inadequate-never-enough thoughts about myself. When these thoughts showed up, I noticed them with a jolt, because they were no longer the norm. I knew the second they formed that they were untrue, unkind, and unacceptable. Don't tolerate negative self-talk. It keeps you from truth, from peace, and from the knowledge of your own beauty. It keeps you stuck where you don't want to be.

Here's another twist on the topic: One night I got the gift of feeling self-hatred again. I almost never experience this thing anymore that I used to swim in for daily laps. It was a gift that night because I noticed it very quickly and gave myself entirely to the work of self-forgiveness and -love. It's not that hard. Just lie there allowing yourself to drop fully into the sensation and feel how *off* it is, how completely wrong. And tell yourself, *Sweetheart, you're a child of the Universe. There's nothing here but love.*

Let's talk about meditation—but only because it's my favorite metaphor for (not) sustaining things. Let's say your intention is to sit for twenty minutes in the pure clarity of your empty mind and that, to support this effort, you'll focus on the breath going in and out. I guarantee you won't spend that time sitting in a clear mental space of gorgeous silence. Far from it. Your focus will stray, probably within seconds, far, far away from the breath that's responsible for the rise and fall of your belly here and now: you'll be in other places and times, you'll even travel to the future, you may find yourself oceans away. So what? As soon as you catch yourself in a thought, you simply come back to the breath. That's all you have to do: come back, keep coming back, come back to the breath as often as you catch yourself off somewhere else.

If you start beating yourself up when you find you've strayed, you won't be meditating anymore. You'll in fact move even farther from the serenity you're after. Better, simply bring yourself back to the breath. Thus, for twenty minutes, you'll be in a constant process of catching yourself in a thought and coming back to the breath, catching yourself and coming back, catching yourself and coming back. You're mentally adding coconut butter to the grocery list, then you come back to the breath; watching that teacher who called you a pig in third grade, then back to the breath; drifting off into leather and lace, then back to the breath. This constitutes a valid meditation, and it actually does something. And eventually—no, really—you may get better at sustaining a focus on the breath, if only for a few more seconds, a bit more of the time. (I hear some people get really good at it.)

In the same way, should you decide to banish negative self-talk from your inner world, you won't clear it out once and for all just for saying you're done. More likely, you'll catch yourself predicting you won't cross the finish line then bring yourself back to kindness. You'll make up a mean reason why she didn't respond then bring yourself back. You'll catch yourself declaring where you're hopeless and bring yourself back. *Do not take a side-trip giving yourself a talking to about what a loser you are at quitting negative self-talk.* Just bring yourself back. This is a practice: will you bring yourself back as many times as you catch yourself? It actually does something.

As in romantic love, a good relationship with yourself can be cultivated in bed. Spoiler alert—this is rated G. It's such a tender, vulnerable, liminal time—that time when you're slipping in or out of consciousness. As you approach sleep, notice the anxiety or frustration that accompanies letting go of a day. Notice the parade of images that call up dissatisfaction, or anything negative, from the annoyance of that parking ticket right down to shame over your weird flare-up in response to the cashier's rudeness—which shame-memory could yank you in a heartbeat back to an ancient one that still makes you cringe (and that there's not one good reason to get out for review!). This is the stuff not to tolerate.

Will you consciously be kind to yourself instead? Will you put yourself to bed kindly, as you would the beloved, as you'd do for any child in your care? Will you deliberately forgive yourself for each thing your mind offers up as evidence of *failed* or *not-enough*? Will you systematically look for all you've handled well, all you feel good about? Will you catalog what's completed and good enough? Throw a little confetti in your mind to celebrate all that's done!

Strangely enough, if you came to me as a client, no matter what the general intention of our work together, I'd probably ask you at some point how you put yourself to bed. Why? Because it makes a difference in how you sleep, how you wake up, and how you live your life. At bedtime, connect to all that is love. Connect to what you love about yourself, to what you loved about your day. What if you told yourself you're amazing and beautiful, your day is complete, it's all good enough, and all of life is supporting you to keep healing and thriving? I can't say it strongly enough: drop into sleep from a place of love, kindness, gratitude, and sufficiency, and you'll wake up ready for more of that; you'll also then consciously create more of that throughout the day. (This idea is treated more deeply in "Blueprints for Your Personal Manifesto" in part 4.)

Now I'd like to push you a bit further, from basic self-honoring, in which you counter negative self-talk and speak sweetly to yourself, to supreme self-honoring, in which you actually hold an awareness of your own magnificence. You might start when you put on your clothes in the morning. Don't dress unconsciously: remember that you're dressing a magnificent being. In fact, in the act of putting on each article of clothing, simultaneously step into your own magnificence. You're not exactly putting on your magnificence in the same way you put on your clothing—because your magnificence is already intact and in place. But use the physical act of dressing as a way to remember, reclaim, re-embody your magnificence.

My friend Louise is a glorious model of self-praise. She loves to ask things like, "Do you wanna hear my latest brilliant idea?" Or she'll say, "I'm so amazing ..." and then offer recent evidence. She's a fascinating human being, who's made a career of being a storyteller (by the time she was an undergraduate, she'd set her sights on being a clown, then life honed the vision from there). She's also applied her marvelous creativity and her connections to other creative types to make things happen toward any number of good causes. For example, she created the Haw River festival, which travels for a few weeks along the river that ran at the time she conceived it behind her house (the river stayed there, but she moved). The program involves gathering cool grown-ups—artists, environmentalists, and just plain good folks—who volunteer for one week at a time to camp along the river and create for fourth-graders a sort of day-camp experience for one single singular school day.

What a day it is! The kids come by bus through the public schools and other educational groups and hold class on the banks of the river, learning through various creative games and songs and art projects how to be environmental stewards, making choices for the well-being of the water that supports their lives. Think guitars and ukeleles, puppets, paints, skits, flora-and-fauna finds among grasses and trees. Most of these kids have no prior concept of a watershed, and have never connected an actual river to their address or the tap water flowing there. Brilliant indeed.

I used to wonder how Louise got away with this self-congratulatory thing. She never sounds obnoxious. She's not a showy personality. She's actually one of the most humble achievers I know, though you wouldn't know it by this manner of talking. It took me a while to pinpoint why it works, but oh, brilliant one that I am, I nailed it: she talks this way about others too.

All she's doing, it turns out, is applying freely to herself what she dishes out for others. I don't know that she's ever introduced me to anyone without adding, "Isn't she beautiful?" after my name. When she talks to me about others, she tends to describe them in glowing terms, highlighting some marvelous thing they do or some special quality in how they move through life. We're all comfortable with someone speaking highly of other people, casting a beaming light on the best of all they are and do. But Louise departs from the norm by her ease in equally speaking this way about herself. And the fact is, she truly is brilliant and amazing, more so than she could ever say herself. Louise is quite literally an award-winning human being.

If this isn't how you perceive yourself, you're probably looking through the wrong lens. You probably don't put yourself to bed kindly, don't wake up wide-open to what you'll discover is possible today. You don't have a love affair with all of life, the whole universe, and you certainly don't have that with yourself. But you could. It takes intention, and practice. Would you like to scooch that way?

Since I started this chapter with romance, let me add that self-honoring is sexy. In or out of a relationship, you're more attractive when you love yourself. Just watch how people move and hold their bodies: you can tell without a doubt who's walking around thinking they're cow patties and who feels pretty good about what they've got to give. In self-honoring, you're less needy: you don't look for reassurance or approval (you're getting these from yourself). You're more compassionate and accepting, better able to see the beloved for who he/she/they are right now, not through tired stories and negative lenses. If you're single, you can practice to be a great partner by being a great partner to yourself. We tend to give those we're close to whatever we give to ourselves, so that fault-finding and dissatisfaction toward the self almost always gets extended to the other—have you noticed? Obviously, this doesn't promote thriving for anyone—neither the individual nor the couple.

Would you like to thrive? Honor yourself. Talk to yourself like you're worthy of love. And when you catch yourself speaking unkindly to yourself, just bring yourself back: back to the reality—the truth—of your magnificence, your beauty, your complete worthiness just for being here in a human body. This is the love I wish you every day of every month. I invite you to it. I dare you.

chapter 12

That Crazy Comparison Thing

I know a woman who has such a remarkable story to tell, and her impulse (inner imperative) is to write it. Terra is one strong woman. Whenever I'm in her presence, I find myself appreciating and admiring everything about her: her death-brushing and maybe death-defying experiences; her energy that's a mix of sweet, soulful, super smart, no-nonsense, and irreverent; her through-and-through beauty. Terra doesn't write her story, though, because she can barely get a few pages out before she starts obsessing over not being as good as (plug in here whoever's really good at creative nonfiction—Anne Lamott, Audre Lorde, Maggie Nelson?). Warped by this thought, her mind declares it ridiculous for her to write. She can just hear her imaginary critics ranting, *Who is she to waste all of our time with this pathetic effort?* Ay. Familiar?

In my coaching work, people tell me their thoughts that compare them to others. They often then rush in to assure me they know the comparison thing is a bad idea. Is this you? Do you know this? Do you know it vaguely or with crystal clarity? Do you know it like you know not to eat rat poison, or do you sit there sticking your finger in the stuff and sucking on it?

I invite you to crystal clarity: it's really, truly, absolutely a bad idea to compare yourself to others. Let's face it: you don't compare yourself to connect to the spiritual truth that we're all one, or even that all human beings are created equal. You compare to prove that some are more equal than others, usually from the angle that finds you less than.

It's absurd (and mean and rotten), considering there are billions of human beings on the planet, to isolate a few particular samples (or even one other) chosen as comparison models to highlight whatever you're lacking. You might have perfectly fine skin with the usual minor flaws, but you stare at the woman with such amazing complexion (Wait, she can't be air-brushed if I'm seeing her in the flesh, right?) that you may as well be the poster child for ravaged faces. You could be entirely skilled enough to start that cooking class you can see (feel, hear, taste, smell) in your mind, but you fixate on someone whose culinary brilliance so outshines yours that you become the kitchen idiot by comparison—and then what are your chances of acting with joy and confidence to get that class from vision to fruition?

When you compare yourself with others who outshine you, here's the rat poison of it: It takes you out of your power (that's why you'll find the concept of comparing in the "Power Zappers" chapter). It costs you your energy, sometimes plenty of it. It throws on the brakes right when it's time to go for something full-throttle. It makes it very hard for you to be a beginner, which is a necessary prerequisite for getting good at anything, never mind for becoming an expert. It keeps you from seeing (honoring, celebrating, focusing on) what you're doing right and doing well. It keeps you from assessing your skills and talents clearly, never mind shining as brightly as you can at your current point of personal evolution.

If, as a beginner, you compare yourself to the expert (as if the comparison were relevant!—let's compare how Baby Sally walks to how Johnny runs!), you may find yourself to be so lacking, you'll just give up, maybe before you even start. At any stage in a process, in fact, you can always choose to compare yourself to someone who's ahead of you in the game. Or you could choose not to, and simply measure your own progress as you walk on down the road. Anyone have a preference here?

Consider going for personal best, which is just about you beating your own best prior score or outdoing your own best prior effort. Go for being self-referential, which involves looking inside rather than out to determine your own standards of excellence or your criteria for self-evaluation. (There's a whole chapter in part 3 on "The Power of Self-referral.") Let go of both *better than* and *less than*. Neither seek out nor fear either: don't refer to such measurements at all.

And what about those compelling comparisons to family-of-origin members? To my mind, these are just as random as any other. I don't mean to negate the significance of those you grew up with. They're powerful characters, especially during those growing-up years. But I like to get "That was then, this is now" about it—especially if you've already reviewed it all in therapy or in late-night talks with lovers and pals. It's actually optional to keep sucking marrow from dry bones forevermore. It's optional to keep extracting I-dentity from it.

I hold a healthy respect for the fascinating characters each of us grows up with who bring into bold relief the themes we seem to be here to work through and master; and most of us, let's not forget, have instilled by those same people some positive traits and beliefs that bolster us along the way. Look, something had to lay down the plot line: why not your particular story with that particular wacky crew (their brand of cluelessness and unkindness included), and all the things they said, and all the ways you came to think you were, by comparison, incompetent, not smart enough, too big for your britches, too fat, too flimsy ... or whatever it was.

So you've found the pluses and minuses of your growing-up reality and can identify how it all left you poised for what you've set out to do, create, and become in the ensuing years. Great. Now drop your self-comparisons to the other characters in the story. You don't have to live in reference to them any more than to anyone else on the planet. You don't have to live in reference to what your sister did better than you or make your life a defense against something your brother decided about you or follow your parents' dreams instead of your own. You don't even have to be in contact with these people, but it's a fine choice if you want to be—especially if you hold the clear boundary that differentiates *me* from *them* or, even better, *what I think of me* and *what they think of me*—and resist those crazy comparisons. Resisting, by the way, can simply mean catching yourself when you indulge in comparing you and them and bringing yourself back to you and you.

All you're ever doing when you reach for someone specific to compare yourself to is locating proof for some painful thing you're believing about yourself that's either exaggerated or untrue. Ultimately, the whole comparison game is as insane and painfully poignant as the scene where the anorexic stands in front of the mirror hating the fat girl reflected there. All that's being reflected are her thoughts. Do we ever see ourselves clearly when we make random comparisons designed to show that we're wrong, we're not enough, we're not okay? Ultimately, the act of comparing keeps you from any prayer of achieving your full potential, or even from having all your energy available to move in that direction with any modicum of ease or efficiency.

Living in Ithaca, New York, I sometimes get the cool opportunity to offer a program at Cornell University. It's fascinating to me that the students there deal with thoughts of not being smart enough and struggle with confidence issues. If they're there at all, they've achieved a level of merit through excellent grades, high test scores, and other accomplishments; they've been accepted to a learning institution that turned away many other applicants. They then go from comparing themselves to the general populace—as in high school, where they obviously stood out as academically advanced—to sizing themselves up in reference to all the other crème-de-la-crème types. It's terrifying for many of these young adults to find their footing in such an atmosphere that everyone agrees to be highly competitive.

What if they didn't believe in competition? What if they knew that if the Cornell doors opened for them, they must be in the right place (until life shows them otherwise) (and then there would be another, better place for them)? What if instead of being concerned with how they measure up to others, they simply kept being engrossed in the process of learning and choosing to do whatever they needed to do to get the grades they wanted. If they didn't find this to be an expansive and rewarding process, couldn't (shouldn't) they choose something else?

There are so many paths to take in life. But how can people see the validity of different paths if they value only one way, one place, and feel they must fight and claw to make it there, forcing things to come out a certain way? If you trust life, you don't have to force a thing.

So will you take this comparison thing seriously? Will you stop sticking a finger in the stuff?

How are you like Terra? What's the thing you don't do—or you have to overexert yourself to do—just to push against the crosswinds you churn up with crazy comparisons from left and right field? There's so much writing (painting, playing, directing, teaching, organizing ...) out there of every kind and caliber. If you have something to write (paint, play, direct, teach, organize ...), isn't there a place for you in the greater scheme of things? I'm thinking there must be, because here you are and here's that urge (inner imperative) to express yourself in that particular way. Do you need to sit around comparing before or after you write, or comparing instead of writing (or whatever your thing is)? Could you, would you, just make it between you and you, and tell or do whatever comes up from inside you to tell or do? Go ahead: just say yes.

104

chapter 13

Harness Your Power of Interpretation
(Sometimes It's the Only Power You've Got)

There's so much we legitimately can't control in life. Weather happens, traffic thickens and clogs, deadlines come at us, sometimes in swift succession. Gravity pulls things from our grasp and makes messes. Time moves us along (ready or not), we fall in and out of love, accidents catch us off-guard and change the course of our lives. Other people fail to do their part or listen to our wise words, and the whole project is lost through no fault of our own. But in any situation where we have little or no agency—no power—there's one thing that's always in reach: that's our power of interpretation.

Very few things in life have inherent meaning. Meaning is assigned. In other words, you're interpreting all the time. If someone doesn't write or call back, you might imagine they don't like you or were annoyed by your message, or you might tell yourself they're busy or have a scary inbox—it's not about you. (Try them again if you still want to make contact.) If you're getting no action in the dating realm, you can decide you've lost your appeal and nobody wants you, or you can say you haven't yet met the right one. (So change your strategy in attraction/pursuit or make a joyful project of being single, for now.)

If illness strikes and you're down for longer than you ever expected, few would fault you for thinking that life sucks and that any speck of God-force you could believe in has withdrawn from the premises. But you could opt to declare you needed extended downtime, it's finally time to practice excellent self-care, something had to teach you to impose on others and ask for help; here's the overhaul your life needed from the inside out. (Now make your whole life about healing—for now.)

If you keep hitting dead ends in one attempt after another to get a job on your career path, you can say you're screwed, life has turned against you, you're one more victim of an abysmal economy—or call it a friendly universe giving you the nudge you needed to become the entrepreneur you see you could be (even if, at this point, you see it only vaguely).

There are countless ways to interpret everything that happens all the time. Stay alert to this fact and craft your interpretations consciously. Catch yourself making bad (sad, cynical, self-defeating) interpretations and reframe them. You could live a certain set of circumstances and declare yourself a loser and a failure; you could as easily take the exact same lot and declare yourself to be in a brilliant process of growth and discovery. The first interpretation will lead to more of the same—if that sounds New Agey, go back to psych 101: self-fulfilling prophecy, right? The second, conversely, will create a joyful, confident, connected way of moving through life.

Having lived both ways, I strongly prefer the second. (Don't you love your strong preferences?) But there's no clear line to cross for stepping into the realm of positive interpretations. It's not a once-and-for-all kind of thing. Instead, it happens over and over through a series of choices, now and now and now. If you just can't find a good interpretation, this isn't the moment to interpret. Get some sleep, eat some good food, breathe some fresh air, move your body, talk to someone who loves life and loves you, sniff a farm animal, clear some clutter, and come back to the drawing board refreshed. (Always treat sleep like the marvelous reset button that it is. Promise yourself *all things new, all things possible* in the morning and believe you'll wake up with your courage back.) Refuse to sit around telling yourself that whatever you're facing means *they* can do it but not you, life's against you, you're not fit for love, you don't have what it takes, it's too late, it won't work.

My client Liza was fifth in a line-up of people accepted to an MFA program in creative writing—a program that takes four people. I'd be beside myself if I'd almost gotten into that particular school. I would definitely interpret that as evidence of the validity of my writing and of myself as a writer. She was stuck seeing it as (more) evidence she didn't quite make the grade. (Meantime, other graduates from notably less prestigious programs, like me, walk around feeling perfectly legitimate as writers.) So we gathered, Byron-Katie-style, the evidence of her being a true writer: a known writer had taken her on in a mentoring capacity, she'd been accepted for a stint at a writer's colony, she'd gotten any amount of positive feedback on her writings from other writers. Liza opted to focus on all that and to let go of the not-good-enough interpretation. That doesn't mean it never suggested itself again. It did mean a commitment on her part to keep coming back to legitimatizing (and prioritizing!) her own value as a writer.

In a later session, she realized she was holding herself back with a typical writer's belief that there was no use writing unless she had a certain block of time to stretch into. This kept her from writing very often, then she easily slipped back into not-a-real-writer mode. Notice all the interpretation here: call 20 minutes not enough time or call it an opportunity to tweak even one paragraph in the manuscript—it really is your call. See yourself as a real writer or not—completely up to you.

Shortly after that session, Liza wrote me these words: "I successfully wrote every day last week. Why? I committed, and decided to take in one very important thing you said, which is that those people who write even 20 minutes a day feel more like writers than those who don't write at all and then judge themselves. And I decided I wanted to be the 20-minutes-a-day writer, not the person who did not sit down at her desk."

When you're not aware of this interpretation thing constantly at play, you won't even recognize your interpretations as such. You'll take your thoughts to be fact. You'll state them as fact. Notice you can always find people to agree with you and confirm these thoughts as facts. It's possible to end up bamboozled by a so-called reality with nothing real about it— not to mention that it's negative and self-defeating.

I've heard so many variations of, "But I'm afraid I'd just be tricking myself by finding all these positive interpretations." Well, yeah, exactly. We trick ourselves with our minds all the time. We usually do it in the self-defeating direction, looking at ourselves through the loser lens, or money through the not-enough lens, or life through the it's-so-hard lens. Go ahead and trick yourself—only do it in the direction of self-empowerment. Err on the side of overstating all you're capable of, how very much support you have, how connected you are no matter how you feel in the moment, how adorable and creative and smart you are. If you're making it all up anyway, make up that you're the winner and that the cards are stacked in your favor and that even if this looks like the next failure in an endless string, it just may be the next glorious lesson or piece of information that's going to get you where you're trying to go. I've written one book I (rightfully) burned and two more that were (rightfully) unpublished. Does that mean I'm not a writer? Not to me.

Do you know Thomas Edison's famous (perhaps tired) quote? The story goes, he tried some alarming number of times to crack the code for making a long-lasting, workable light bulb (he didn't actually invent the thing), and people kept telling him to give it up, Buddy—not working. Our intrepid inventor is said to have responded, "I haven't failed. I've just found 10,000 ways that won't work." I repeat the quote because it's such a great illustration of the power of interpretation.

Let's bring it to modern times. Remember what Ellen DeGeneres was up to before she got more famous than ever through her current talk show—which has run now for more than a decade? (The Ellen Show is in its thirteenth season as of this writing.) Back in 1997, she came out as a lesbian on her old TV sitcom, Ellen, which promptly got shut down. For a while no one would touch her, and the things she touched didn't exactly turn to gold. She had good reason to go for bleak interpretations. She could have decided she was washed up, would never regain sufficient public support to succeed, would only meet total humiliation going before the public again.

Those would not have been actual realities—they would've been interpretations. She sure could have made them real. She does talk about this era as being dark, but obviously she didn't destroy herself or give up entirely. She's mentioned being especially bolstered by young people writing her to express gratitude for her coming out (I wonder how many queer suicides she prevented?). She also reminded herself that she wasn't willing to hide who she was and live a lie. I find her an inspiring icon for carrying on even when things look pretty hopeless—and this requires not interpreting evidence and events in ways that stop forward movement.

Here's a real-person example, in case Ellen's current grandness makes her seem less than human. Bonnie came to me to work through a pervasive anxiety about job security that robbed her of daily joy. She had a good job as an engineer that honored her intelligence, but she never felt quite safe in it. Anytime she was challenged by a colleague or a superior, her mental default was to fear she'd lose her job—though no one else implied or threatened such a thing. It was as if, in her movie, some mean workplace raptor might swoop in at random and snatch it all away from her. This kept her in a mode of ongoing mild wariness that spiked sometimes into prickly hypervigilance. As Bonnie and I worked together to question her thoughts and examine her belief system, she decided to experiment with the idea of harnessing her power of interpretation.

One day, her supervisor made a comment that Bonnie might want to interview with other companies in order to have leverage in requesting a raise in a difficult economic environment. While she knew full well she already deserved a raise, this was just the sort of thing that might typically send her into an inner frenzy of anxiety and an outer scuffling—which could look like overly dedicated hard work at best, workaholism at worst. She watched herself, finding she could witness the inner reaction without a lot of judgment and without instantly acting on it. She saw that she was taking his words to be threatening, as if they threw into question her worthiness not only of a raise, but of her very position. He had stated no such thing. Recognizing that she was interpreting the actual words, she remembered she could choose any interpretation she wanted.

This pause led her to the clarity that it would violate her own personal ethics to force the company's hand in that way to get a raise. She also got even clearer that she was uncomfortable with the legal but not entirely ethical way her boss conducted his area of the business. It was starting to look like a great idea to interview with other companies, but she would do so with an open mind and the intent to take only a better position, should the right fit present itself.

Thus, she took her supervisor's comment as an invitation to check out whether there was another job for her out there even better suited to her gifts and experience. She was relaxed when she reached out to a prospective employer that was a particularly well-known and sought-after corporation, because no part of her needed a job (or had even been thinking of looking for one!). She was just scoping out what else was possible. Note that she wouldn't have followed such an impulse before, because she saw this bigger-better corporation as coveted in her field, which made her potentially not good enough to join.

But *not good enough* is an interpretation, isn't it? She armed herself with curiosity instead and, since they invited her to an interview, went to see what these people might have to offer her. They offered her a job. Bonnie ended up describing herself as "orders of magnitude happier" in her work, which continues to be a place of thriving for her. She loves that she's often asked to collaborate on various projects throughout the corporation beyond the scope of what she was hired to do. Her sense of job security is firmly intact, and she actively remembers and uses her power of interpretation.

Then there are those over-the-top applications of harnessing the power of interpretation, as we see in people like Nelson Mandela or Viktor Frankl or Harriet Tubman. Mandela was a political prisoner for twenty-seven years. Twenty-seven years. It's mind-boggling. He could so easily have become bitter and given way to despair, which surely visited him a time or two thousand. But he was able to frame his worldview in such a way that he ended up being president of South Africa for five years upon his release. I wonder what he told himself in his dark moments.

Frankl was an Austrian Jewish psychiatrist who spent three years in concentration camps during World War II. He doggedly persisted in interpreting his circumstances in such a way that allowed for the possibility of finding meaning under any circumstances, even these, and of experiencing the redemption of holding on to love. His book *Man's Search for Meaning*, with its 1946 copyright, had sold more than 10 million copies in two dozen languages by the time Frankl died fifty years later. The original German title contained the words *Say "Yes" to Life Nonetheless*.

Harriet Tubman was a five-foot-tall force to be reckoned with. Growing up as a slave, she was beaten so badly that she suffered brain damage and dealt with seizures and even hallucinations for the rest of her life. She was seriously ill more than once and somehow bounced back each time. By the time she escaped to New York State to live as a free woman, you'd think she might have said to herself that she'd been through enough and that someone mightier than she would be more qualified to take on helping others escape. Nope. Her interpretation was that if she could get free, others could too—and it was up to her to help them. Instead of staying where she was relatively safe, she headed back into hair-raising danger by choice.

As a conductor on the Underground Railroad, she returned to the South so many times to liberate others, she came to be known as Moses. She's quite famous for that, but it's less commonly known that she later got involved with the Union army and actually led a military raid that freed hundreds of slaves at once (far more than the seventy-some she led to freedom in her prior efforts), then served both as a nurse taking care of Union soldiers and a scout doing recon in and guiding soldiers through

Confederate territory. Beyond the Civil War and freeing of slaves, she turned her attentions to fighting for women's suffrage. Harriet lived to be ninety-one years old, a remarkably old age for the era she inhabited.

People with far less trauma in their upbringing have declared the rotten things they suffered to be good reason to hate and shut down and focus on all the ways life has failed to support them. Harriet Tubman persisted in believing she was divinely inspired and guided and kept showing up for the next way to offer herself for the good of all concerned. Amazing, inspiring woman.

Did we get too grand again? The thing is, all of those people were just people—people who refused to interpret events in a depressing, self-defeating way or in a way that somehow undid all the beauty and strength still accessible to them within the poignantly real limitations of their realities.

So let me tell you about Piper—perhaps more relatable—who felt deeply defeated after being asked to leave her job. She felt exhausted and powerless as she reviewed the sequence of events and difficult relations with her supervisor that led up to this ending. Her mind, on the other hand, seemed tireless in offering up interpretations about what was wrong with her and how she was ultimately ill-equipped to get along with people on the job. Projecting a future in which she would never work in her field again, she proceeded to find an entry-level position in retail grocery, with a significant pay cut. Though she saw this initially as another sign of failure, she also started scooching toward better interpretations.

For starters, the job she found was in a whole-foods store, a place she liked, an environment that felt good for her to be in, with people who felt like her peeps. Because of these things, she was able to frame her current work less in terms of punishment and demotion and more as a good and safe place where she could regroup and make a viable living with less stress. A great beginning for reframing her story of defeat.

From there, she was able to go back and question her thoughts about the so-called failure. Culturally speaking, I find Americans tend to go very quickly to the concept of failure, and we're horrified of losing jobs, starting businesses that don't make it, or being moved out of a department we're not thriving in. (For some, this applies to breakups and divorce as well—instant assessment of failure, even when it's clear that the relationship was no longer serving anyone concerned or even when it contained a toxic component.) People typically don't think to find the benefits of such events, even though these endings so obviously open the door for new beginnings, though they deliver lessons that won't be forgotten, though they point the way toward work that constitutes a much better fit. What if we didn't see such endings as failures, ever? What if we always took them as good news? What if Byron Katie's "I've been spared" were the first thing we thought of to say to ourselves? It would be so much more empowering. It would also require harnessing the power of interpretation.

Piper did the work of finding the benefits of being released from the ill-fitting environment she was in. She also looked for all she'd done that constituted good work—evidence that the failure (if it was that at all) wasn't all-encompassing. This allowed her to then review where she'd want to address some weaknesses in herself if she were to return to her field. She identified in clear terms what she'd like to do differently.

In the meantime, she had some bolstering and strengthening experiences in the world of whole foods. When she received occasional negative feedback, for instance, she saw she was quick to take it to mean she was no good at all, or at the very least more problematic than most. She was able to recognize these reactions as interpretations—not reality, not truth—and got interested in learning how to receive feedback in a way that felt open. She worked on seeing it as a gift, allowing it to inform things she wanted to improve without entirely erasing or somehow annulling all she was truly doing well. She placed her focus on what she knew she was contributing to her team and made it a point to notice the praise and positive feedback she got, along with any evidence of good relations with co-workers and supervisors that came her way. In general, she got interested in viewing events through the lens of a friendly Universe. (She's also one of my clients who fell in love with Tosha Silver's *Outrageous Openness* and used the writings there to bolster her in believing nothing in her life could be going wrong.) She started to relax into the possibility that she hadn't somehow gone hopelessly, shamefully off-track, but was in fact experiencing exactly what was needed for her to move forward in life valuing herself and more boldly choosing the directions she wanted to go in.

It took a year and a half for her to feel stirrings related to returning to her field. She was finding that she didn't want to make a lifelong career of the whole-foods work, and synchronicity supported her by bringing to her awareness some job openings in her field in new, appealing places. No longer perceiving herself as a failure, she pursued a few options with an open heart and mind, watching for where it felt she most belonged (and the friendly Universe had given her a palpable taste of belonging in her interim job in whole foods). She's right where she wants to be now, doing the work she feels she was always meant to do. The story may have gone differently if she'd held to the interpretation of failure. She didn't, though: she harnessed her power of interpretation.

The most alarming aspect of this power-of-interpretation stuff is that it could stop you from being the loser once and for all. Are you ready for such a thing? Will you claim winner status and be bold enough to interpret anything that happens as evidence you're still on the way to a win? If you refuse to see anything as proof you're not okay or you're being barred from doing what you most want to do, you can interpret every *no* and every shut door as guidance, as good information to have: how the light bulb doesn't work, who isn't your mentor or helper, who's not the right partner, where you're not going to work, what program isn't for you, what entrepreneurial project isn't your ultimate calling, what isn't the right color or material or spice, what it's not yet time for. You can keep moving toward your vision any way you see how (just the one next step to take right now), detached from any particular way it must look, eyes wide open and curiosity engaged to find out just how it'll all turn out.

It's an inspired and fun way to live. Sometimes it takes courage; sometimes it takes blind trust—otherwise stated, the willingness to experiment with the possibility it's a friendly universe. In my work as a coach, I sit with people trying to get pregnant, start or change relationships, change careers, break patterns of self-sabotage, take on and carry through major projects related to art, home, healing, and spirituality, and I listen to their interpretations all the time. They sometimes have major perception shifts just from coming to see that what they're treating as fact is just interpretation, and other ways to frame events are not only possible but truly desirable—even crucial to their healing and evolution.

I'll throw in another Edison quote for good measure: "Many of life's failures are people who did not realize how close they were to success when they gave up." That would be because they interpreted their results as failure.

You can always ask yourself, Is there another interpretation here? There is, and you can even make a game of finding it. This is your power of interpretation, and it never runs out. You may have no power over any number of things happening in your life; but you can always (by which I mean, every single *now* moment) harness your power of interpretation.

chapter 14

Two Liars: Guilt and Shame

Guilt and Shame are liars. Never trust them. Never believe what they tell you about yourself. You can rely on them to be unreliable, and that's about it.

Still, don't be too quick to send them packing. Think of Guilt or Shame as the unwelcome guest who shows up uninvited. You can try to slam the door in its face but it will persist. It will stalk you, hide in the bushes, slip in through the crack next time you even try to peek out. You may as well invite it in. Sit down with it awhile. Look it in the face. What could be scary in meeting your accuser? The discomfort you'll feel is the same discomfort that's there when you try to ignore it. (I've heard Byron Katie say a number of times that the hell we fear is the hell we're already in. I love this.) A harsh emotion may appear in a more concentrated dose when you give it your full attention, but that also means you can process the worst of it and move on.

Honestly, what's scary about meeting your accuser is that it might be speaking the truth. You cringe from Shame and Guilt because they keep showing up with new evidence to confirm your worst fear: you really are bad, weird, unlovable, too special, too forceful, too flighty, too demanding, too defiant, or some degree of *not enough* that's simply unbearable. But each moment Shame or Guilt returns, you have the chance to look again, scooch in closer, follow the spiral down closer to its roots. You may even get to truth this time—and the truth of your essential nature is all about abiding love and limitless potential, not transitory fluctuations into contracted states with *What's wrong with me?* written all over them. The contractions will come: but be clear that they're not telling you the truth about who you are.

Let me bring you back again to both minding the pain body and tending the mind. It's most effective to meet shame and guilt at both levels. Both are equally important, and together they add up to a clear case of bigger-than-the-sum-of-the-parts. This two-part process is the stuff of true healing.

115

The work of minding the pain body asks that you locate emotions in your body. Where do you feel shame or guilt? At the first hint of its presence—pause to feel it. Do you notice a discomfort? Pause. Take the time to locate it, just like you'd go searching if something in your house started beeping unrelentingly; you'd go through every room and closet and open every drawer till you could find the thing and dismantle (possibly throttle) it. So go on a bit of a hunt for where that alarming emotion is hiding. Zero in. Does it have you by the throat? Is it lodged in your gut like the residue of the bully's punch? Is it squeezing your chest with its talons?

Remember, you can depersonalize emotions a bit and move away from taking them so seriously—so personally—by stating it just this way to yourself: *The pain body is active.* Notice how different this is from *I feel horrible* or *I'm ashamed.* (You may as well say, *I am Shame.*)

Beyond acknowledging it, bring kindness to bear. Remember that child running in with the skinned knee? Take the time to attend, even for a few moments, by giving your pain body awareness and breath, as you'd willingly pause to give that kid some attention and healing balm, maybe even a cool Phineas and Ferb Band-Aid (my favorite).

At the level of tending the mind, let's begin with Guilt. It's useful to ask yourself, *Am I actually guilty of something here?* Answer these questions (whichever seem useful to you, perhaps even just one of them):

- Am I actually guilty of something here? Is there anything I've actually done wrong or would like to have handled differently?
- Is there anything to learn here about how I want to handle similar things going forward?
- Are there any amends I need to make?
- Is there anything I want to change now to make it right or to feel better about it?
- Can I get completely okay with this [event, behavior, decision], however imperfect it may be?

Getting okay always begins with opening to being okay—giving yourself permission, if you will. Nonresistance!

I say Guilt is a liar, but you can extract whatever crumbs of truth it brings by answering questions like the ones above. These enable you to

116

look at yourself clearly as a human being doing human things and to get okay with all of it. You can't get through a human life without tasting this piece of the pie. You must learn how to forgive yourself if you're going to forgive others. And you must learn forgiveness if you want to live love. (There's a whole chapter on "Ongoing Self-forgiveness," coming up next.)

Let me add, too, that quite often, perhaps more often than not for most people, the answer to *Am I actually guilty of something here?* is no. You may walk around feeling guilty because someone felt hurt by something you did (but it was nonetheless the right thing to do—like saying no to helping out with their project because you're full up with your own); or breaking family tradition (like not joining the clan for the holidays); or telling the truth ("I need someone with a calmer presence to take me to chemo"). Any number of things may not feel good to you or to others, but that doesn't make them wrong. The resulting guilt is simply not legitimate.

Guilt takes off from something you've done and declares not only that the action is wrong, but that you're wrong for doing it: "You're guilty"— as if what you've done somehow morphs into who you are, tainting your identity. The truth is, you can acknowledge anything you've done, you can make it right with someone else however you see to do that, and beyond that you must learn to let it go as surely as you benefit from letting go of what anyone else has done to you.

Guilt asks you to remember, to hold on with a death grip. Its unspoken promise is that you won't do it (or do it wrong) again if you keep feeling guilty. But have you noticed you're at your worst when you think ill of yourself? Guilt actually doesn't bring out the best in you.

We're not meant to accrue things and stack them up in precarious psycho-towers. In fact, all the painful things that come our way are meant to be moved through and out of; they're meant to be handled and released. We can extract a gift from anything we do or anything that happens to us, but we don't need to hang onto the guilt to get the gift. Don't hold on to the bathwater to keep the baby!

I know someone who experienced such abuse in childhood that only fragments of those memories remain (or flash in at random). Cal lives with guilt over long-ago things he can barely conjure a whiff of. Yet he sometimes fears—is tormented by the fear—that he did very bad things (possibly harmed animals) out of seeking approval. If a child does something bad, even very bad, for whatever motive, does it follow that the child is a bad person? Does that child grow into being a bad adult, forever stuck with that fixed identity of *bad*? Creativity coach Jude Spacks likes to point to what she calls the innocent motive: surely the innocent motive here was survival?

(Hey, I always love the part in books where they tell you to run get professional help if you're dealing with something atrocious and off the charts. So, okay, off you go, then, if you must read it here.)

Should guilt hang on till the grave and keep someone from thriving and creating—thus also keeping them from giving their highest gifts to the world? Do you live in a punitive or loving Universe? Is forgiveness ever available and applied, or is it withheld? (You get to choose.) The thing is, at whatever level you're dealing with guilt, you're burdened with a sense of your own wrongness, carried over from past deeds, that will get in the way of what you want to do now. It's worth the work and time and all manner of resources to clear your guilt.

Shame is a worse liar than Guilt. Its crumbs of truth are even crumbier, sometimes microscopic. While Guilt may imply that what you did is who you are, Shame goes straight for the jugular of identity and throws into question your essential nature and value. The bold-faced lie of Shame is its assertion that there's something wrong with you—not that you did something wrong, but *you're wrong, you're bad*.

Sometimes people worry they'd stop sensing the right thing to do without shame. Ay. Your guidance system speaks to you through joy, through sensations of expansion and relief and pure, simple knowing— never by making you feel bad about yourself. Sure, shame could serve you by pointing to something you'd like to do differently or never do again, but you could actually get to that (and more quickly) through neutral or compassionate evaluation. Shame's blaring message that you're worthless—you don't even belong on the planet—isn't part of your guidance system, and needlessly complicates any other message it's trying to deliver about course-correcting.

There's no good in Shame. It tells you there's no good in you, then you get stuck in some negative version of yourself. You're no longer free to be who you really are—never mind who you're ready to become next.

Try questions like these when Shame appears (I like the last one, which cuts right to the core of it):

- Is shame actually warranted here? Can I find one good, peaceful reason to hold on to shame?
- Is there really something wrong with me?
- Am I wrong? Am I bad?

Reviewing the shaming scenes in your mind, watch yourself as you would someone else. Imagine any other person, several other people, in the same situation—doing or experiencing whatever it was that brought on the feeling of shame. Imagine a child in that place. Would you steer anyone into shame here? No one else is any different from you. If others shouldn't be ashamed, neither should you. (Whatever you'd vote for for the human race, you'd better be willing to claim for yourself as well.) If you genuinely believe you belong in the realm of shame, you need to stay with the questioning, perhaps with a reliable helper. You can also ask yourself, facing shame, the same questions I offered for guilt in order to consider what you might want to do differently or how you might make something right (if that applies).

Ultimately, the question you're asking is, *Who am I? Who am I really?* You are not whatever you've done that you don't approve of; you're not whatever has happened to you that was awful and exposing. Give some time to finding love for yourself, to approving of yourself. Give it ample time, more time than you've ever given to reviewing shaming evidence. Take time to envision and honor your highest intentions for yourself. (As I reread this, it strikes me how radical it is. People are more comfortable shaming themselves than holding themselves in high esteem. It somehow seems more reasonable, or at least less suspect, to give precious time to shame than to self-honoring. Wow. Would you like to flip that for yourself?)

Both Guilt and Shame get in the way of your personal evolution. They'll tell you that you can't pursue your fondest dreams—not you. They'll say you can't be who you want to be, you can't get too big. Shame and Guilt are liars. Don't believe them, especially when they're telling you who you are, what you're capable of, what you deserve. Even when they're not huge for you, when you allow either shame or guilt to sort of buzz along with you at a low-grade level (those fruit flies again), it's like a constant irritant that you're barely aware of—one that saps your energy and affects how well you function. (Classify any degree of embarrassment as shame.)

I invite you to clear out Shame and Guilt, at whatever level they exist for you. After you've sat with them a bit, show them the door. They'll be willing to leave when you stop being such a good host for them. They may try to come back—and then you know what to do: Welcome them for a moment, but don't pour tea for them, don't plump the cushions. Take the time to look them in the face, check out their allegations, speak back to them with truth; then, one more time, firmly usher them out.

chapter 15

Ongoing Self-forgiveness: Live Free and Clear

Have you noticed how you bind up your energies by getting stuck in all the ways, small and large, you can't forgive yourself? Plainly put, in not forgiving yourself, you're not free. It doesn't much matter whether it's some seemingly huge, shaming event—the affair, the ugly breakup, the fiasco at work; or something minor that's been blown up in your mind—the rampant PMS the other day, the rude moment with a customer-service person on the phone: either way, you get all tied up with some past vision of yourself that you allow to define you. You give it the power to limit how you can show up here and now and who you can become next.

It's an issue of presence: you can't be present when you've got feelers out to some old story you think you have to keep referring to, keep checking in with. If that past story involves something unforgiven toward yourself, you walk around feeling like a bad person, like there's some *wrong* that colors everything else, like you're not worthy of better than *this*. You can't dance with your potential. You can't even be at ease.

At the School for The Work, I heard Byron Katie talk about moving without a trace from one moment to the next. Her words struck a sort of stunned chord inside me. I felt like I'd never done any such thing—like it wasn't in my repertoire! It was as if some Velcro or another always kept me stuck to a few boulder-sized transgressions and countless minute missteps that should be bygone. I saw for the first time how this kept me from being fully present, ever—or fully free, fully me, fully anything!

Just try to get through a human life without having done some (sizable) thing, that could bring on shame when put under a microscope. Just try to get through a week—sometimes a day or an hour—without some little moments that just aren't the most sterling examples of the levels of loving-kindness and serenity you're capable of. What if you gave yourself full permission to be human? Can you let yourself witness your bad moments without judging or attacking or shaming yourself?

You might learn from your observations if you just allow those moments and get curious about them.

Let me tell you about an ugly evening with my children, still in memory because I wrote about it in 2012. I growled at my son (literally, I felt so frustrated that I just let out this warped, oversized-feline growl), and I railed to my daughter, overriding the look on her face and the knowing in my gut that I'd completely departed from the realm of clean communication. I'm sure I said what I needed to say three times over, instead of the once that would have done or, better, instead of waiting for a calm moment another day—like most space-sharing issues, it was nothing that wouldn't keep. And I'm sure I didn't speak sweetly. Okay, you know that harsh-Mama off-key strident tone that you just don't want to hear coming out of you, ever? When I went to bed, I felt all disturbed. I felt mean. Mean and rotten.

Lying in bed, I said my forgiveness prayer, which I created from the teachings of Marianne Williamson, remembered from a good while ago. Let me be clear: the memory is dim, and I have no idea what her words actually were or where I heard or read them. I only know my own certainty that it was Marianne who originally pointed me to this idea of connecting through prayer to the forgiving force that's able to hold for you what you can't hold for yourself, so it's important to me to credit her. Because she elucidates *A Course in Miracles*, her language is full of Jesus and the Holy Spirit. My prayer doesn't go near all that. I have people send it out to whatever Higher Power they connect to, the Universe, the Force—whatever: God or Current Resident.

Here's the prayer applied to the self: "I forgive myself. And where I can't or don't know how, Universe, you forgive me for me, and hold that while I catch up to it. I acknowledge that it is done. Somewhere beyond time and space, the forgiveness is complete."

The obvious beauty of this prayer is that it doesn't require you to be ready to forgive, only ready to let the Universe bring in its endless supply of forgiveness, freely given to anyone anytime, under any circumstances. There's no issue of merit in the Universe's capacity to forgive. This prayer helps you scooch toward forgiveness when you intend to forgive but you're not there yet; however ready you are, it helps make forgiveness feel more tangible and complete.

After I said the forgiveness prayer multiple times that night, I witnessed my behavior in my head retroactively. I saw very clearly that I had simply exhausted myself that day by walking far more than my body was ready to walk in the wake of hip surgery. That failure in self-care cost me my patience with my children. (It's very good to notice what your lapses in self-care cost you and those around you—a good way to keep collecting evidence that practicing self-care is a very good idea, and not a bit selfish.) I looked at the good reasons I had walked so much— identified the innocent motive for the lapse: my son and I were on a joyful mission to find him some boots. I told myself I would be more careful henceforth to figure in my limitations, because that works better and is kinder for all involved.

What follows is important: in the name of not telling myself lies, I put specific application to this broad concept. I decided to check in with myself on school nights (this could mean lying down!) at least half an hour before time to cook dinner. Thus, I could gauge my energies, hold them up to the needs of the day, and plan accordingly. After that, I felt as caught up to the forgiveness as I was going to get that night, and I slept well. The next morning, when I woke my beautiful son, he was just my son: he wasn't the boy I'd been mean to the night before. When I next saw my daughter, I was just happy to see her.

Thanks to The Work of Byron Katie and the School for The Work, I no longer tolerate holding on to grievances against myself. It's too painful, and I don't make room for pain when it's optional. It disrupts the joy that I love to cultivate on an ongoing basis. I'm stunned at the self-loathing that people allow to take hold in them, to take up the air waves in their heads, to fill them, body and soul. Actually, I recognize it quite well, and for years never imagined it was possible to be without it.

It's possible. It's even imperative. Do whatever you need to do to question your thoughts about any punishment you deserve, anything that's proof you're not worthy, anything that you must hold on to— perhaps from the good but misguided motive to make sure you never do it again. Find (or at least notice that it's possible to find) a way to manage what you do or don't do again without the fabricated handicap of never forgiving yourself. Practice lavish self-forgiveness daily for anything and everything, minute or momentous, that you or anyone else would hold against you. Because when you can move without a trace from one moment to the next, you can live free and clear; you can spend a whole lot more time in peace, joy, love; and you can do a whole lot more good both for yourself and for others on the planet.

chapter 16

Application in the Moment: Impermanence, Stone Statues, Green Smoothies

Let's talk about impermanence and blowing up stone statues. My intention here is to turn "if only it were that easy" on its sharp, pointy little head so you can just do what's needed right now and be kinder to yourself. Honestly, if this chapter doesn't hold something for everyone, I give up. Add whipped cream, if you must, or drink a green smoothie while you read it, then you will surely be fulfilled, at least for a moment.

I have an inspired, inspiring twenty-something client who took to my concept of stone statues and together we coined the term *statuefication*—which it turns out exists as a word in French (just drop the *e*, bring not just your lips but your whole face forward as you speak it, and land in your sinuses at the end). The idea is that living life well puts us face-to-face with all kinds of concepts, ethics, and aspirations that are flexible, open to interpretation, abstract, not literal, not made of matter, and, perhaps above all else, impermanent, and we sit around like a bunch of frustrated sculptors seeking to make stone statues of it all. Does that sound like a good idea?

Here's an example. Let's say that, like my client Manuela, you have the truly sensible idea that you don't want to react to your partner when he (substitute your preferred pronoun) has hair-raising reactions to your driving. It's a common ideal among spiritual types: I don't want to react. I want to walk around like a thin, fit Buddha who drinks green smoothies or bone broth, and just smile beatifically when people around me react. I just want to love them in their humanity and stay solid in my equanimity. So that's nice, right?

It's nice as long as you stay out of statuefication. Stone statues violate impermanence, which is a law of the Universe. Not reacting to others, contrary to popular belief, is not a law of the Universe. It's just a really good idea a lot of the time. It's just an ideal, which means that you, as a mere mortal, won't always achieve it, though you can aspire to it if you wish. And there may even be times, since it's not a stone statue, when reacting is a truly inspired idea and your best bet, as when you scream STOP before someone hits someone else with a moving vehicle. (You might even scream it in a hair-raising way.)

Make a concept a stone statue and you're saying it's a THING, it's solid, it's real, it will sit there for a very long time because it'll still be cute when its arms fall off. If you statuefy not reacting, as with any concept, you're bound to get in trouble. People react. That means you need permission to react. You need to keep away from guilt when you react—because you're in fact guilty only of being human, of doing what human beings do. You haven't violated a universal law, or even a federal or local law; you haven't done anything wrong.

So what if you want to be nonreactive (that's your intention) and you find yourself reacting? I'll cover this in detail in "The Power to Change" in part 3. For now, let's simply say this: catch yourself reacting, celebrate catching yourself, and then, in that moment (*now* is the only time for change), step toward your intention: course-correct. In this case that could mean apologizing for your reaction, offering another response, getting quiet so you don't react some more, noticing that you're also reacting to your own reaction, and beginning to direct kindness, forgiveness, spaciousness, at the very least, toward yourself.

Remember the two things you can always return to: mind the pain body and tend the mind. Pull in, and tune in to the pain body—find the place in your body that feels the ache or raw pain of whatever just got churned up by the thing you reacted to, compounded by your belief that you shouldn't have reacted. Your pain body wants awareness and breath, so give it those two not-so-much-to-ask-for things. (At the risk of repeating myself, this actually does something.) As soon as you're ready, you can address your thinking and start to identify and dismantle the belief that caused you to react (children shouldn't shriek at the top of their lungs, teens shouldn't make unhealthy choices, your partner shouldn't have hair-raising reactions to your driving).

In my usual way of exhorting my clients to be in a two-part process of minding the pain body and tending the mind, I asked Manuela how she did with these. She said she was *trying* to do those things in the moment but kept getting sucked back in to her own judgments of herself, which got her irritated at him again, which got her judging herself some more— one of those seemingly (seemingly) no-exit existential-nightmare loops.

So I told her about me, something my clients seem to love and which I get to do because I'm not only a mere mortal but also a mere coach, not a therapist. I get to tell on myself. I told Manuela about something that happened for me recently that brought up full-blown shame—so weirdly, blessedly unfamiliar now—the kind that makes you feel sick through and through. It actually made me feel weak: I had to go lie down. I swear the last time I felt this way I was wearing that hoopskirt dress and they were still marketing smelling salts, but there was just no such thing to reach for this time—just all I know to practice for being with pain.

I accessed the compassionate, dispassionate witness and gave myself to the pain body. I breathed into the place that hurt, and let myself really, really feel it, the full extent of it, the breadth and depth and exact quality and pitch of this particular pain-body event. I wrote down my thoughts, and then I went back over them and found how they weren't true.

Then something beautiful happened: I landed in humility instead of shame. I'd never thought of humility as the light side of shadowy shame, but there it was. I found it helpful to name this thing I was feeling, because something was still there but with palpable shifts—what was it? Humility! Much better.

Ah, but humility is no stone statue, and damned if it didn't flip right back to shame. I witnessed the pain body. I sat in the question, *Do I really have something to be ashamed of?* I sat till shame flipped to humility, again. And it flipped back to shame. Humility, shame, humility, shame … There's no stone statue. I just kept meeting what came up and consciously steering toward humility, because it's so much kinder and truer. (Shame is a liar, right?) Some of this flipping back and forth happened not sitting or lying down, but simply going about my business. I held the pain body, I held the question, I steered toward humility and, perhaps miraculously, kept locating kindness.

I invited Manuela to that kind of process. Blow up the stone statue that represents "I shouldn't react." Then blow up the stone statue that says, "I should bring myself back from my ugly reaction and stay put in the prettier place." Now you're in a much more realistic and even more Buddha-friendly (certainly more you-friendly) process that doesn't violate the law of impermanence. Now you can simply witness yourself going back and forth from clarity to murkiness, from light to dark and back again, and get okay with all of that. This is how you blow up your stone statues, and maybe it's not a truly glamorous or gloriously gritty process (no actual explosive exploits), but it sure does a lot to realign you with reality, which is as full of impermanence and kindness as you'll let it be.

Does this make sense to you? Manuela's first response was, "If only it were that easy." Wait a minute—that's stone-statue thinking right there! Forget easy. Forget hard, too. The greatest effort required here is to be present and allow what's really happening. (Nonresistance!) You might want to exert some effort to access the compassionate, dispassionate witness—but you don't have to *do* anything; just watch what you *are* doing and how you *are* feeling. Then if you want to live intentionally (and here we have the intention not to be reactive), point yourself kindly toward what better fits your intention than what you just caught yourself doing.

Hard? It's hard to be someone who never reacts; it's hard to shift out of a reaction into some super-serene state then stay put at that new setting: stone statues are hard, hard, hard. If you're willing to be in flux, if you're willing to get real, if you're willing to get present—that means, now and now and now, to simply witness yourself without judgment; if you're willing to move toward where you want to be because you've found yourself where you don't like it so much—then where's the problem? You're great … but only right now. You're not a stone statue's worth of great. I personally choose to follow such a process until it spends itself—that is, carrying on with the above example, until the shame stops reasserting itself and even humility becomes a moot point.

chapter 17

Healing Meditation for Meeting Your Past Selves

I'm continually amazed at the healing power of simple rituals. I've been playing for some time with rituals that involve meeting a former self to clear out things I feel stuck with. I want to insist on the *simple* aspect—nothing needed beyond intention, imagination, and words. Some of my rituals happen spontaneously when I'm lying in bed at night (or in the wee hours) and notice something that needs to be addressed. In other words, no props, no prep, no nonsense.

Let me give you an example. It came to my attention at some point that I was divorcing myself from certain past versions of myself. I would have memories come up that made me cringe and shudder and I'd go into some kind of internal muttering that I was glad not to be that person today. Actually, I am that person. I noticed this, and noticed that this unconscious disowning of self I was engaged in constituted a shame response. You know I'm not an advocate of letting shame have its way. Because shame is the most potent of self-destructive emotions, best to face and clear it as soon as it comes to awareness.

So one night, I lay in bed with the idea that I needed to embrace each version of myself that I've traveled through in this fascinating lifetime. I've moved through so many phases, experimenting with some version of spiritual seeker in every one: sad child burdened with her emotions and everyone else's; the one who lived in France, the one who came from France, the one with nothing interesting about her whatsoever (*What? How'd you learn to speak French like that?*); born-again fundamentalist Christian, raging feminist and card-carrying lesbian, Waldorf mom and wife in traditional nuclear family, divorced single (lesbian again) mom working as a life coach. ...

I decided to progress year by year, beginning at the first age when I could find any crumb of belief there was something wrong with me. This set the start line at age three. There was this scene of showing a grown-up that weird vein in my inner thigh and she was horrified by the frog-leg spread of my little legs. Too much revealed: oh, the shame. I then went progressively through the years, watching whatever visions of myself I could call forth from each one. With each character I took in (the three-year-old, the four-year-old, the five-year-old, and onward through teens, twenties, thirties, forties), I repeated the same words, which went something like this: *You have been part of my journey. I thank you and embrace you. I love who I have become, and I extend that love to you. You are part of me.* Note that this repetition of the same declaration infused the process with a ritual quality and also facilitated the integration I was after.

It was a powerful exercise. By the time I got up to my age at the time (forty-nine), I felt cleansed. I felt relieved, and calm, and whole— integrated. Something really happened. In the wake of this ritual, my mind cut way down on playing that mean-spirited teasing game of randomly visiting a shaming memory on me. I don't want to say never, but it's pretty much gone. Before clearing it, I hadn't been fully conscious of this habitual mind pattern of reaching back in time for something to shame myself with in the midst of a happy, connected present time. (In the absence of current shame, let's see what we can dredge up from way back when!) Sometimes those random mind-bombs can still happen with more recent things, coming to show me what's not fully cleared. I go in as quickly as I can and clear it as best I can and continue to vote for standing fresh in each moment. Sometimes the smudge on the glass needs just one more wipe. I believe in profound and lasting transformation.

I guided a client to go back to herself at various ages when she was engaged too early in sexual activity with peers who, typically enough, weren't looking out for her well-being. She talked to her younger selves to help them see what was protecting them even though they weren't being protected from the bad kind of sex. She also gave them hope by telling them about herself now and letting them know about the wonderful partner she would end up with.

I find it's very powerful to go back to a former self if you believe it's still in there holding trauma. Just today, someone told me about the sad and scared five-year-old inside her who still believes ... I hear this all the time. It's both crazy-easy and truly potent to step in as your older, more evolved self and give these young aspects of you what they didn't get in the past. In your imagination, you can hold the child you used to be and tell her it wasn't her fault that someone was awful to her; it didn't mean she was awful or deserved it; it didn't mean her whole life would hold nothing but the same. Give the child that thing Byron Katie calls the turnaround: if she felt unsupported, let her know all the ways life will support her over the years (from her age to yours in the present moment). Give her a lot of concrete, specific evidence. Tell her some good and true stories from your life, her later life.

I also think it's especially useful to let your younger selves know who they get to become—tell them things you love about yourself as you are now, or some of the marvelous, unexpected things you've gotten to do, or the stunning ways grace found you at various times and landed you in just the right place, with the right people, doing the right thing. Let them know how much you like who you've become; invite them into the wonderful-me club.

These rituals don't have to be bare-bones simple: I just want to insist that they can be, and their power is in no way diluted for that. If you want, however, you can add candles and incense or sage, music, creative actions that symbolize clearings and completions—whatever you dream up that's doable. Invite allies and witnesses. If you have access to some healing modality—if you can do Reiki on yourself, or know EFT techniques, or use ecstatic dance to express shifting rhythms—it can be a great integrator to end a ritual in such ways. Just don't stop yourself or even stall by concocting something too complex to realize. If something's up for you, follow the energy that brought it to light and go for the clearing.

Finally, I urge you to hold a consciousness of transformation. This sort of ritual has the potential to fully release something you've held on to and (falsely) identified with. In no way are you stuck with your past identities unless you continue to claim them. Allow your intention plus the power of simple ritual to bring you fully, and fully grounded, into the present.

PART 3

Scooch into Your Personal Power

In 2013 at the Michigan Womyn's Music Festival, I taught for the first time my workshop called Personal Power Surge. Its purpose was (and is) to invite those present to get out of any victim mentality and step into the most powerful available version of themselves. As I write this, the 2014 festival is just underway without me. I'm taken back to the beautiful workshop areas carved out of the woods, circular(ish) openings edged in ferns and contained by trees, some of these stunningly beautiful—the kind of trees even diehard no-nonsense scientific types might see as spirit, with branches as the arms of love holding space for whatever sorrow, joy, humor, love, sex, sickness, healing, and song the womyn bring to the woods. (Please indulge me: I must spell *women* with a *y* where the festival is concerned.)

The workshop begins with my disclaimer that I'm not after power over others, ever. I'm not interested in the kind of power that makes others smaller, lords anything over anyone, or discounts or plows through the well-being of others. What I advocate is the kind of power that represents you standing in your strength, being as big and as beautiful as you can be, living up to your full potential, channeling all the light you're here to soak in for yourself and radiate to the world. (Hey, take a moment to google Marianne Williamson's gorgeous quote about our deepest fear, which she posits as related to our power, not our inadequacy. Reread it if you already know it!)

You'll be most powerful when you mind first the relationship between you and you, knowing that anything that passes between you and others can only reflect that essential primary relationship. When people think of personal power, they tend to begin outside themselves. They give primacy to how others perceive them, or the impact they have on others, or their ability to influence or to make things happen out in the world—which often enough has to do with rallying, impressing, or convincing others, or any number of tactics that fall, for better or worse, into the realm of manipulation. That's the wrong point of departure: your personal power begins with your relationship with yourself.

Remember, this is not about power-over. This is about you, about your experiencing and expressing the highest version of yourself that you currently have access to. When you take in fully that this power is nurtured within yourself, and then expresses outward, you may quickly notice that this awareness in itself is power. That is, you're stronger just knowing you hold the reins for this power-growing process: it doesn't rely on what others think of you or how they respond to you or what they give you or withhold, or anything else that comes from the outside. Your power is yours, for you to grow or not, to remember and forget, to keep coming back to and experiment with (please, make it a grand experiment!)—no matter what anyone else is doing out there, no matter what they think of you.

Let's look to the beginnings of French feminism to see what light it sheds on the topic (oh, why not?). In my first explorations of feminist thought in the early eighties, I read Simone de Beauvoir's *The Second Sex* and was struck by her discussion of *seeming* versus *being*. It's a simple, brilliant concept. She wrote (in 1949—ay, how far have we come, sisters?) that men are taught to *be*, while women are taught to *seem*. Thus, she posited an essential inauthenticity or pretending that women are directed into by societal systems, a falseness that certainly contributes to the lesser power they enjoy as compared to the power men have. In essence, Simone says, women are being taught to appear in certain ways and cultivate appearances (and not just physical appearance), while men are taught to actually be what they want to be, become what they want to become, do what they want to do. So, with all due respect for the (significant) gains women still need to make as a population and across cultures, let me appropriate this idea for all human beings in this way: in order to have

134

true personal power, you must really truly actually be what you want to be, not seek to appear that way to others. Don't seem: be.

Your relationship with yourself is the best place where you can truly and consistently cultivate such a thing. Between you and you, you need to be solid. You need to like yourself. You need to like who you are, how you choose, what you're up to, what you think about, what you're interested in, what you're grappling with, and so on. You need to attend to what hurts, what feels good, what feels off, what feels right—for you personally. If you think you're awkward, for example, you'll gain nothing by seeking to convince others that you're at ease. Your power doesn't lie in appearing to be at ease. Your power lies in actually being at ease—and being okay with where you are as you scooch that way.

So if you're awkward now and wish to move toward being truly at ease, you might begin with noticing the presence or the reality of awkwardness from a place of no judgment and no cringing. Aren't you a human being, and don't human beings sometimes feel awkward? (Again and again and again, do welcome yourself to the human race.) Then, how you face the fact of your awkwardness—how you hold it, work with it, talk to yourself about it, set intentions around it, protect yourself or push yourself out of your comfort zone, self-evaluate, and so on—sets the tone for your process and determines how fruitful it will be. Are you in a kind and intentional process—that is, a process aimed toward the true development of power in this realm? Or are you in a mean-spirited, self-abusive, self-defeating process that keeps you forever awkward, because you become self-identified as awkward and keep reinforcing *awkward* as you behave awkwardly and judge yourself for having awkward experiences?

Note that all the material in parts 1 and 2 preceding this section provides a good basis toward cultivating a solid relationship with yourself. Once you've got a good beginning in (and keep course-correcting toward) basic self-love, kind self-talk, and a gentle growth-and-healing process, you're already attending well to what's between you and you. From there, you can build a level of personal power that you haven't gotten to yet and that will only support you to keep living well with yourself, and ever better with others.

Let me also add the very important point that there is no stable, measurable number we could assign to you that rates how powerful you are (*Take this internet test now and find your personal power quotient!*). Your power fluctuates from one moment to the next, one era to the next, one set of circumstances to the next. You can recognize sometimes alarmingly differing levels in your sense of feeling solid and equipped to handle all that life brings you or any encounter with another human being, whether unexpected or scheduled, whether they adore you or barely tolerate you. The following chapters will offer you ways to come back to your power when you feel you're out of it and to cultivate mental and behavioral patterns that will support you to live more often in clarity, authenticity, integrity, honesty, and whatever qualities you aspire to or define as the stuff of a powerful character.

If you don't habitually stand in your light, it may feel like a long shot to get there. Perhaps more than anywhere else, most people cannot, in the realm of personal power, whisk themselves instantly from where they are to where they want to be. How do you move through life at ease when you're used to constantly straining and striving to feel you're good or okay? How do you know and radiate your full worth when it's hard to believe others could consistently take you seriously or think well of you? How to stay solid when the rug is always in danger of being yanked out from under you by a capricious Universe (or the unreliable people who populate it)?

The chapters that comprise this section are full of the stuff of scooching. There are so many ways to step gradually (now and now) into fuller experience and expression of your power. I invite you to begin by being in a kind, gentle process with yourself and to prioritize what happens between you and you. I invite you to *now*, because you in your power are no stone statue, but may fluctuate notably along your own personal-power spectrum from one moment to the next. I invite you, predictably enough, to scooch.

chapter 18

The Power to Change

You have the power to create change in your life: you can change your circumstances, you can change your character, you can change how you operate. None of this is fixed. Your personal power increases when you hold the conviction that you can change the things you want to change. Otherwise, you're stuck being whatever you've come to define as you, and that supposed identity may include any number of negative limitations (and they're still false, no matter how much identification you've invested there).

Sometimes people who take to The Work of Byron Katie get confused about whether it's okay to change things. Aren't you just supposed to *accept* everything? Love what is, right?—don't change it. Well, now you've made a fixed religion of Katie's work. By *Katie*, I mean the one who teaches questioning everything and making a religion of nothing.

Here, step with me into the kitchen for a moment. That's you cooking an African peanut stew (or whatever sounds fragrantly mesmerizing to you in the savory realms) and, tasting from the pot, you find that the spicing is off. So now what's your task? Do you accept that the spicing is off? Or do you correct the spicing?

People sometimes make confusing what isn't when they bring spirituality—or their concepts of spirituality—into the mix. It's not inherently more spiritual to accept than to change. Sometimes it's your spiritual task to get okay with what is. Sometimes it's your spiritual task to correct the spicing.

I do find again and again that it's easiest to correct the spicing when you're in a place of acceptance, or nonresistance. If you taste the soup and are appalled that it tastes off; if you're riddled with shame that the spicing is *so not* what you thought it should be; if you think something terrible is happening and anyone who tasted your stew would be damaged or offended (their taste buds would wilt and shrivel); if you project a future in which you'll never get the spicing right again—all these forms of resistance will certainly make it more difficult to simply take the right next action to get that spicing just as you want it to be. You're likely to get flustered and dump in a boatload of cayenne when a touch of turmeric would do.

When you're in a place of nonresistance, change happens more easily than most of us tend to believe or expect. Here's a simple, scooch-friendly, three-part formula for any kind of correction you wish to make in your world:

1. Set the intention for the new way in contrast to the old way.
2. Catch yourself in the old way.
3. Course-correct toward the new way.

In order to change, you have to notice what you want to change and clearly establish a new intention. For example, noticing you're often the one swooping in on a breathless flurry while the one you're meeting is solidly settled (if not starting to sag) and gazing at the clock, you might set the intention to be punctual. Setting your intention, or defining the new way in contrast to the old way, is step one. It's also your declaration that you want to do it the new way, you're ready, you're willing to do what it takes to get there.

Popular thought would have it that step two is to start doing it the new way. This misconception takes people off-track (usually into self-flagellation) and slows down their progress. After setting the intention for change, don't expect to do it differently: expect to next catch yourself in the old way—because that's how it works. *Oops—I'm leaving the house when I should be walking into the coffee shop.* What's lovely about calling this step two is that you can't possibly mess up: step two invites you to do it wrong. So you can dispense with beating yourself up when you find yourself in the old way. What's to be dismayed or distressed about? You're right where you belong. You can therefore celebrate catching yourself: you're onto yourself; the old way no longer feels right to you, and the discord between old and new gets your attention. Yes!

Now waste no time moving to step three: course-correct toward the new way. Do anything you see to do: text to say you'll be late and declare that you're buying in order to express that you do value your friend and her time; interrupt yourself mid-sentence, change your words, shift your tone or volume, choose a different action, cancel the event, apologize, make a plan for next time, tell the truth—do whatever makes sense to you that constitutes movement in the moment toward the new way. This is no different from what you'll see in the visioning section (part 4): the intention for the new way is your vision. Just keep aiming toward that vision, taking any step small or large that you see to take, in roughly the right direction.

My client Molly reinforced for me the power of this three-part formula by declaring it the best advice she's ever gotten in all her life. (No, shut up. Of course she wasn't exaggerating.) She started playing with it consciously by applying it to a long-standing habit of locking her knees when she stands. She sent me an e-mail about her progress:

> I used to berate myself whenever I noticed I was doing it, thinking I should have moved beyond it already (I decided to stop this over a year ago). But now, whenever I catch myself locking my knees, I just stop doing it; and I have a 2-second celebration in my head that I'm onto myself. I'm having a devil of a time breaking this habit, but I don't fret about it so much anymore. I just keep noticing and correcting, trusting that I'm making progress.

Do I need to point out that if nothing else, this process is kinder?

Molly's knee-locking example is in the easy-breezy category because it's about a physical phenomenon that occurs and gets regulated just between her and her. What about more complicated things that involve others? You may be attending some event with a whole cast of characters (and maybe you dressed up for it, so it's loaded) or even interacting with one other human being (and maybe you're naked, so it's loaded), and you actually get confused, finding yourself torn between the old way and the new, and uncertain about how to proceed? That is, you've just caught yourself in the old way but, in the heat of the moment or with witnesses present, you don't see how to aim toward the new. In that case, consider making your process transparent.

Here's a low-stakes example of what I mean by that: Let's say you're seeking to stop reviewing how incapable you are of making money (old way) and to speak instead about the money-making power you exercise well and freely—or at least to express and emphasize any scooching you're doing in that direction! You're in a party-conversation with an acquaintance and tell her that you've started selling those black-and-white sweaters you knit that she so admires (*"Aw,"* she says, *"that's awesome!"*) but of course (sip of wine, unconscious party chatter) since you don't know how to assign proper value to anything you do, you're charging way too little for them. Hearing your own words, you've just caught yourself in the old way.

Now, even if you know that you're in the right next step (caught yourself), and even if you haven't gotten out the inner whips (could be as close to celebrating as you're going to get right now), you may simply feel muddled and confused by what just came out of you—what now hovers in the air between you and this other shiny-eyed being in black—in contrast to the new way toward which you want to course-correct. If you keep making small talk, you may find yourself feeling increasingly distracted and pressing your cheeks into a false smile that has no bearing on your inner reality, trying to keep up with the outer conversation while, mentally, you're groping blindly for what on earth that idea of course-correction could look like right about now. *How?*

Make your process transparent: simply speak out loud the mismatch between your inner reality and your outer. You thus course-correct by saying clearly and explicitly what's happening inside you, dissolving the dissonance troubling you as you speak. For example, "Can I go back to that thing I said about being incapable of valuing my work? I threw myself off when I heard that come out of my mouth because I'm in this major project of changing that: I want to see myself as entirely capable of making money, because I am. And seriously, the fact I'm selling the sweaters instead of giving them away along with a pot of jam and a secret recipe is a huge victory for me. My plan is to get better and better at this thing until I forget it was ever an issue. So could I try again? What I meant to say was, I'm so proud of myself to be selling these. I'm pretty sure it would make sense to raise the prices—still working that one out. I'm on it. I do really want what I'm paid to match the time and skill I put into these." Course-correction complete.

When this concept of making my process transparent first dawned on me, I was in the last stages of learning how to stop yelling at my children. I was a scary yeller in the beginning. When things got stressful in Nuclear-Family Land, I was appalled, truly, to find myself acting out

140

some award-winning renditions of some amalgam of the Terrible Mother and Wicked Stepmother archetypes. This caused me more suffering than anything I've dealt with in my life, hands-down. It also got me serious about healing what needed to be healed and finding another way. That's the short version of what launched the journey that got me to The Work of Byron Katie.

So once I'd learned how to question my thoughts about what was wrong with my kids, and once I'd begun to accept that the yelling was here until it was gone (it didn't stop just because I really, really wanted it to), I surrendered, and started simply witnessing myself when the yelling took me over. And I noticed something fascinating: it looked like there was way more going on inside than outside, and the inner process was actually in opposition to the outer. As the yelling carried on or even escalated outwardly, inside I was horrified to hear myself, hating the behavior, dropping ever deeper into self-loathing, not even believing a word I was saying, and then seeking to counteract all of that verbally with a self-righteous insistence on my good and valid reasons for yelling, which I then reiterated, loudly, in my mean-mama monologue that got meaner and meaner as I went. So much friction! (So painful, for all concerned.)

It somehow occurred to me, in order to interrupt this, to simply speak out loud what was happening internally. Yell, not speak, because if I could have just stopped myself from yelling I'd have done so years before and skipped the whole AFGO of it. So I kept yelling, but now instead of making the content about what was wrong with them, I switched to a narration of my inner process that went something like this: *I hear myself yelling at you and I can't stand the sound of my own voice, I hate it when I do this. It's not even about you, it's about me and how frustrated I feel right now, and you don't deserve to be talked to like this, but I swear to Goddess I have no idea how to get you to* [fill in the control issue of the moment], *but that's not the point, the point is I've gotten myself all upset, and that's not your fault, and I'm going to go calm myself now, excuse me.* And then I walked away while my wide-eyed kids used both hands to press their jaws shut.

Catching yourself in the old way once you've set the new intention, you may have no clue how to proceed toward course-correction in the confusion of all that's happening in the moment. When you make your process transparent, you not only catch yourself but also speak it aloud so you don't implode from the dissonance between the inner world and the outer. This also interrupts the external behavior that results from that tug-of-war, whether it's being the fake-smiley, distracted version of yourself in a conversation or screaming and yelling at kids who will not benefit even one iota from your words delivered that way—or whatever you've got going.

What you might love about making your process transparent is that it's entirely reality-based and perfectly compatible with scooching. So are these three steps toward change:

1. Set the intention for the new way in contrast to the old way.
2. Catch yourself in the old way.
3. Course-correct toward the new way.

In case it's not perfectly clear how personal power increases when you know your power to change: There is no fixed identity. If you tell yourself, I'm someone who can't have that, who can't do that, who never follows up (whatever it is), you can only be telling of past events. You're not telling the truth of who you are or what you're capable of. However many times you've played out a pattern, still, no true fixed identity follows. You can't change it in a fixed way, either. No decision or declaration to be something else will make it so forevermore. Change happens only now—each time you course-correct toward the new way.

You teach yourself what else is possible by stepping into something else now and now and now. What doesn't ensue: you don't get a (new) fixed identity. You get a new experience. You get to expand. Still, string enough new *now* moments together doing it the new way, and you can change your default and have that new, preferred experience the majority of the time. Don't teach yourself that you are your negative patterns and limitations. You're a powerful being. You have the power to change.

chapter 19

The Power of Being in Good Standing with Yourself

I have a client I'll call Cleo because I've come to think of her as the Egyptian Queen. She landed on that moniker in our work to declare how she moves through the world—and it fits. She's truly regal in her appearance and demeanor: self-contained, gorgeous, tall, sometimes adding a good three inches to her height by piling up her hair in an elegant, crowning way. This is all a natural expression of who she is. Few would guess that she feels very thrown off anytime it comes to her attention that someone has a less than perfectly approving response to how she's handled something, or when even minor negative feedback comes her way. She struggles with worry about maintaining the respect of her colleagues (or anyone).

In the fall of 2014, when people across the nation were disturbed by the rioting in Ferguson, Missouri, and by the fatal violence directed toward Black men by police that caused the insurgence, Cleo organized a program at her university to invite people of all races into a facilitated conversation. The idea was to provide a forum where people could engage together in a respectful exchange looking at American racial issues to date and expressing the impact of these distressing current events on them personally, on various populations, on the nation as a whole. She invited a history professor to set a historical context and assigned herself the role of framing the evening with opening and closing remarks, and she facilitated the discussion. Because she's both African-American and in a position related to supporting minority groups on campus (she jokingly calls her sphere the Brown-Black-Lesbian Office), Cleo was an obviously politically correct choice for this role—she wasn't treading into dangerous waters here as a random white staff person or administrator might have done.

As soon as e-mails and fliers went out to publicize the event, there was backlash. Obviously, this was already a heated topic. Cleo spent a morning unpacking her inbox, fielding e-accusations of stirring up negativity and of creating a situation that would surely escalate into something ugly, even violent. Tricky start: she certainly didn't garner instant approval and admiration—or anything resembling unilateral support. Any number of people threw in their interpretations and judgments that had nothing to do with her clear intentions of respectful discussion that admitted all viewpoints. Still, there were some shows of support and plenty of folks opting in, so the event was on.

Sitting down together two days before, Cleo and I determined that this event brought up full-scale the issues of personal power we'd already been working on. I invited her to be in good standing with herself. It had never been more obvious to her that life didn't allow for her, however careful and well-intentioned she was, to be in good standing with everybody else. (Life seldom does.) Was she in good standing with herself? What was her own self-assessment in this story?

Cleo realized that all her life, raised by intelligent, liberal parents, she'd been involved in activism in some form or another. Currently, there was little available expression for that part of her. She saw that this forum was an opportunity for activism in the relatively sedate academic setting where she lived and worked. It was something she could do and it made sense to do it. Further, she could see for herself (never mind who agreed or didn't) that the gathering was worthwhile, perhaps sorely needed. The entire nation felt emotion around these current events, and she had her own strong feeling: it stood to reason other live, local beings did too, and could use a safe container within which to process their thoughts and feelings.

Well, thoughts, certainly, but the realm of feelings isn't readily welcomed into academia. Next, Cleo determined that her worst fear for the event wasn't some gross escalation of frenzied emotion in the crowd but the danger of her busting into tears. It was interesting (and important) to look at this. Could she be okay with crying while speaking about a charged, personally meaningful issue? Could she hold to not abandoning herself in the spotlight should that happen—stay close to her pain body, make space for her tears just as she intended to make space for any idea or emotion that anyone brought to the fore? In the end, Cleo stated a strong preference for holding her equanimity and still found the clarity that this event was worth hosting even if she found her professional self crying with a roomful of witnesses.

What if someone thought ill of her for that? Actually, several someones might. Could it also be true that others (perhaps most) would view her with compassion and even feel grateful that she was expressing a level of emotionality they themselves were feeling—and possibly not feeling master of?

The next day I wrote her these words:

> Cleo, it's so obvious you're *more* in your power doing something that carries the risk you'll cry in front of a group than avoiding doing that thing because you could cry. Throw yourself into this, as this is you in your power standing up for what you believe in, and doing so in a way that's inclusive and respectful, while holding firm to what's important to you. It doesn't get any better than this. Put your focus on that. Give your attention today not to crying or what else could go wrong, but to the courage, importance, and beauty of this event.

What did ultimately come of the gathering was a thought-provoking discussion among intelligent people. She reported back to me:

> One person cried [not Cleo], one person cursed, the room was somber and tense. People expressed a need to have more forums like this. I was encouraged by everyone's honesty and pleased with how it went. I'm still getting e-mails about it, but now the e-mails are from attendees and they are positive.

It's been fascinating and humbling to me to be allowed to come close, as a life coach, to the insecurities accomplished and impressive people have that most observers wouldn't dream they carry around. If you feel insecure and agonize over what others think (even if it's not habitual but episodic, attached to certain specific conditions or events), welcome yourself to the human race. And remind yourself that you can't get through a human life without people thinking ill of you at some point or another, or being unnecessarily harsh and critical about something that could be evaluated in a neutral way.

Let the good opinion of others come and go, and stay in good standing with yourself. This is so much more important (and more possible) than staying in good standing with others. In fact, the second usually follows the first, but don't get attached to that one!

Remember, whatever people do to anyone, someone will do to you (and in turn you'll do, or you've already done, to someone else). People make up stories about other people all the time. If you live impeccably, this is still bound to happen—someone will create something out of nothing, or interpret something you do in the most skewed way. Let it be, because it is. Make it your intention to stay in good standing with yourself—whether others are looking or not, whether they're seeing you clearly or not.

Have you noticed how inauthentic you get when you want them to like you? How you say yes when you mean no? How you smile when you don't mean it? Forget about whether they like you: that's their business. Step into your business (and your authenticity, and your power) by getting clear about what you want to say and do and then following through. In other words, stay in good standing with yourself. Whoever then likes you will like you for you.

When you find yourself wanting validation from others, or actively seeking it, or frustrated because you're not getting it—it's time to come home to yourself. Give yourself what you want from others. The one who needs to think you're okay is you. The one who needs to approve of your choices is you. The one who needs to confirm you're on the right path is you. Sometimes validation comes in from the outside as a gift, a mirror held up by another so we can see ourselves in that light. Certainly, love those moments, feel the gratitude. And walk yourself onward.

chapter 20

The Power of Self-referral

Personal power requires self-referral. This isn't a term that gets much press, I've noticed. People tend to perk up and lean in when I say it; they want to know more. The concept of self-referral, or being self-referential, has an instant appeal for many—as well it should. It's your key to letting yourself be you, and being done with what anyone out there thinks about it, or what they are in contrast. But how to define it? How to live it?

Begin with referring inward, not outward, to determine what you want to do and how you want to do it, what you want to believe and value. This can be tricky for people, as most of us are raised to organize ourselves around external concepts of right and wrong. Whether we're pointed to religion or logic or a certain wing of politics or what-the-clan-has-always-done, it's Out There somewhere, and we're directed to line up our insides with that instead of finding what's out there that lines up with what's inside. Abraham-Hicks puts it roughly in these terms: parents teach their children to do what will make them (the parents) comfortable, systematically training said children to follow outer guidelines they lay out for that purpose. What parents should do instead, Abraham gently preaches, is to point kids inward—teach them to connect to and follow the guidance that comes from within. Ah, I wish I'd learned about this much earlier in my own parenting journey. (I'm on it now.)

I first heard about self-referral from Deepak Chopra (in his *Magical Mind, Magical Body* audiobook), and worked out for myself the details of what this might mean in practical terms. I got a lot farther with applying it once I had The Work of Byron Katie to help me question my mental constructs; then, more conscious about how I perceived and approached things, I started noticing when my point of departure was what other people thought or valued. We're not in self-referral when we size up other people then make decisions about our worth in reference to them. All of that needs to go out the window—which means noticing the external measuring, or catching ourselves in it, and coming back to an inner gauge.

In "That Crazy Comparison Thing" in part 2, I began to treat the importance of a personal-best model that leaves others out of your self-evaluations entirely. It's not what people tend to do, so it requires a certain discipline (catch yourself).

I've been thinking about spectrums lately, and how just about any human quality could be set up on a spectrum model. Think of the Kinsey scale for sexuality (that spectrum actually got named), in which "exclusively heterosexual" is on one end and "exclusively homosexual" on the other, with charming labels in between like "predominantly homosexual but only incidentally heterosexual" or "predominantly heterosexual but more than incidentally homosexual." The idea is that not everyone would head for the polarities if they claimed their rightful place on the scale. All of humanity would cover every speck of the spectrum. What if we all agreed this was just fine? What if we valued every position on any scale just because it exists? That would be truer to the actual value of each spot (as opposed to assigned value, whether assigned by culture at large or by various groups therein).

Or think extrovert to introvert. A client of mine recently argued that Western culture values extroversion more, and while that may be true, some people or certain circles consider those with high extrovert quotients to be flighty, or somehow lacking in substance. In academia, introverts are certainly more highly regarded. If both traits were seen as neutral, or even as equally desirable and simply representing different ways of being, we could simply—just out of fascination and admiration for the wonder of diversity—invite everyone to go find their place on the spectrum and stand there. Wouldn't it be fun to claim your place and see who else is about? There'd be some adorably geeky IT type or librarian, maybe a horse whisperer, on the pure-introvert polarity, and there'd be a rapper or an actor, a wedding planner or a carnival barker, over on the pure-extrovert end. In the vast, glorious spread in between, people of every imaginable kind would stand proud where they belong and love being the one to inhabit that very spot. Isn't this fun—or is it just me?

In real life, we tend to assign value. You know how people with curly hair wish they had straight hair, and people with straight hair crimp and curl it. Playing with this thought, I found on Wikipedia, under "Afro-textured hair," a twelve-point scale (1-4 with a, b, c gradients in each). It begins at 1a with straight (fine/thin) hair and goes to kinky (wiry) at 4c. In between are coarse straight hair ("bone-straight," apparently hard to curl) and corkscrew curls and eight more kinds you too could go read about. You could also determine your number. Mine's 1b, and damned if identifying that didn't immediately produce the thought *Ugh, boring*.

Even if we posit a spectrum that obviously has a pretty universally agreed-upon better or worse side to be on—let's say brilliant to stupid—and maybe put Einstein on one end (2c hair, I'm guessing) and someone too stupid for words on the other end (well, since we're on hair parenthetically, *blonde* could be the word—I know, not funny): what would people do if they found their actual true scientifically determined or Goddess-given place on the spectrum? Well, they would probably look one direction to make themselves feel inferior, and one to feel superior. The thing is, both of these feel just awful. And neither has much value for inspiring people to be their best selves.

When people place higher values on their end or particular spot on the spectrum, hideous cultural phenomena result: white supremacy, male dominance, gender binary, religious wars and crusades—in short, horrors. In more individual manifestations, it can look like arrogance or narcissistic carelessness toward others. When people place higher values on what they're not, it can only stop them from being all they can be. Instead of connecting to all that's possible for them, they focus on what they haven't gotten to, what they can't do, how they're not enough. So they don't move into, never mind fulfill, their potential. It's crazy-absurd, even tragic.

The powerful antidote is self-referral.

I created a simple workshop exercise to give people an active experience in self-referral, complete with that contrived this-would-never-happen-in-real-life thing specific to workshop exercises. I have people in pairs stand face-to-face, usually after some wordless eye-gazing (more on this later in a whole chapter on eye-gazing), and they take turns consciously saying four sentences to their partner: "I am not less than you. I am not greater than you. [Name], I honor you. And whether you honor me or not, I honor myself." Everyone speaks these words to a variety of people—who have various impacts on them, who create different kinds of connections with them—to fully absorb that this is a stance they can take toward any human being. It's a stance toward others to foster as a way of life.

I invite you to it. Practice saying those words in your mind as you notice your better-than or less-than reactions to people, or when you catch yourself even reaching for the measuring stick to start the reckoning.

There's no self-referral without checking in with yourself. This bit is brought to you by the fact that I paused for a check-in. Before I sat down to write this, I was in that whirlwind of whooshing through the to-do list. I caught a whiff of my own frenetic energy (in my mind I was reaching for the phone to take care of a quick call while in physical reality my fingers and toes were already committed to carrying a box up the stairs)—so I came to a full halt. I reached for a question (no hands needed!) and found this: How much time do I have till my next client? And this: What do I actually want to do with that time? That's how I landed here, joyfully writing.

How many little explosions, harsh words, confused moments, weird encounters, rotten decisions, states of prolonged irritation or vague dissatisfaction (etc., etc.) could be staved off by simply tuning in to what you need or to what feels right for you right now? The act of checking in with yourself allows you to locate simple truths like "No," "I'm not up for this right now," "I need food," "I'm still mad at him and it's leaking through indirectly," "This feels very important to me on a soul level and I keep not giving it my time and attention," and so on. ... It's so easy and so powerful: check in.

What is it you need to check in with yourself about? The more you're onto yourself, the more you know typical areas where or times when you need to have check-ins in place. If you tend to say yes to everything, you might want to mandate a check-in before taking on even the smallest new commitment. If you forget to eat, you need to check in for hunger— and be clear about the alarms that alert you to low blood-sugar. Do you stay up beyond what's good for you? You might pause before choosing the evening's activities and see if you're going for what makes sense to get you to bed on time and in a sleep-ready state. You know the tendencies you need to watch for and counter.

What alerts you to check in? Like everyone, you've got your own little buzzy alarms that go off to call for a check-in: feeling woozy, getting irate, hearing a certain tone in your own voice; having any emotion descend, distract, or seem to take over—feeling confused, sad, angry, jealous, scared, threatened, unsettled; getting tense in every muscle, going unfocused, finding yourself to be all over the place. (Checking e-mails again? Opening another document and a chart while dialing the phone? Heading for the laundry room as the kitchen sink fills with sudsy water?)

The bottom line is that any physical sense that something feels off indicates the need to check in. I remember being stunned when I first heard Deepak Chopra's simple observation that the Universe guides us through sensations in the body—which I've come to think of in terms of on/off signals. (In part 4, I'll cover this from another angle in "Accessing Guidance in the Moment.")

What could keep you from checking in with yourself? It's so easy: it's free, and there you are, no matter where you are, ever available. But while a check-in may be obviously or desperately needed—still, you too, like so many others, may forget to check in at small daily junctures or even huge turning points in life. Why is that? A few typical reasons follow. Notice how they keep you from being self-referential.

Being too focused on others

How much effort do you expend sending out tentacles to probe for what others think, want, expect, feel—then seeking to manipulate their feeling states (*I don't want to hurt her feelings*) or their thoughts, especially about you (*He'll think I can't manage the class*). The coming chapter, "Tell the Truth," deals with all the ways you might turn into a liar when you organize around not hurting feelings or offending, making sure no one thinks ill of you, and avoiding certain reactions. When this is what determines how you proceed, there's no self-referral in sight—and no need to check in: you can just look outward to what they tell you they want from you, or go for what you imagine based on your best guess or your worst projection.

Attaching to a particular process or outcome

When you're fixed on some particular outcome or some way you want things to go along the way (or both), you'll forget to notice what's actually happening. For example, having high hopes for getting a job, you don't quite register during the interview that the boss is already

151

micromanaging with nit-picky questions and speaks disrespectfully of the past two people in the position. Or noticing it, you keep bringing back to the forefront the concept you came in with (you want this job!); thus, you lose track of reality.

The antidote is simply to show up for what's actually happening ... not what you thought should happen, not what you wanted to have happen. (Remember chapter 2?) When you're in self-referral, you're noticing your current inner gauge for whatever process or situation you're in, not some past assessment or expectation you must hold on to and navigate by. It may have made sense to knock on the door when you did; once it's opened, notice here and now whether it makes sense to go through it.

Riding the momentum of what you started

Many (many) people tend to have a belief in place that, once in the midst of something, they have some obligation to see it through to the end. They feel the momentum of it (or sometimes even the drag!) and push through to the endpoint despite the many possible station stops for cutting the journey short along the way. Have you seen yourself do this? Have you figured out yet that it's not necessary? More important, have you given yourself permission to stop anything you've started?

Pause right now to check in about the particular thing you suspect you may benefit from stopping. Are you sure it's too late or too much trouble? You actually do have the right and may be wise to cancel the subscription, end the first date before the first beer is down, take the kid out before the end of the school year, process the data differently in the middle of the project. ... Do you have to finish everything you begin? It's a great thought to question. (There's actually no universal law that you must.)

Not having check-ins as part of your worldview

Most of us, growing up, aren't taught to check in with ourselves. We're taught to follow certain concepts and codes of conduct. We're taught to obey certain authority figures—or may along the way construct a default identity of categorically defying authority. (Neither model represents freedom!) We're even taught to follow clocks and schedules over our inner dictates.

Will you teach yourself another way? It's such a simple thing, to learn to check in—to go inside for your next operating instructions, thus being self-referential. But until it comes fully into your consciousness, you simply won't think of doing this.

Not knowing how to check in

Checking in is about connecting to yourself and tuning in to the inner voice that actually knows what's right for you. Be still and quiet. Feel your body. What feels off? Where is there tension? Simply bring awareness and breath to those places. Then, reach for the right question to ask yourself.

- What do I really want?
- How can I best get that?
- Is this my priority right now?
- Is this the best use of my time?
- What's missing?
- Is some form of self-care more important than anything else right now? If not, can I carry on with what I'm doing in a way that's better for me, that incorporates self-care?
- Is there something I need to attend to first, then come back to this?
- Is it time to step back and look at the overview, then come back in to the task at hand?

If you're trying to decide whether to do something, look for the next layer. What is it you want to get or think you'll be getting from this? By exploring the motivating factors, you may find a better way to get what you're after. For example, you may be thinking about going to a party because you want to have a social life; you want to have fun. Ask yourself questions like these:

- Is a party the best way for me to do this? Would this be fun for me?
- How could I connect to people socially in a way that works better for me?
- Could I actually have more fun doing something alone right now, while holding the intention to create a vibrant social life?

Reach for other useful questions particularly suited for decision-making:

- Am I getting an *on* or *off* signal here?
- Does this move me toward or away from my intention?
- Is this the right time?
- Am I getting tripped up on some *should* or something someone else wants from me that keeps me from my own clarity?

The simple act of checking in with yourself could be the difference between:

- revving up into full-blown everything-irks-you irate versus soothing your irritation
- yelling at loved ones versus noticing and tending the upset someone ignited or bumped up against
- letting a default *yes* determine how you spend your time versus giving time and energy to what most matters to you and moves you closer to your vision
- doing what people do versus making an authentic choice that feels true for and ethical to you, and that expresses who you are now or who you're stepping into becoming
- making yourself sick versus practicing excellent self-care
- having your life slip away from you versus choosing it consciously

It's not a big deal in the moment but it makes a huge difference in both process and outcome: check in with yourself. Be self-referential: refer inward instead of outward.

chapter 21

Tell the Truth: The Perils of Caretaking and Manipulation

What could be more important than telling the truth? Why would you ever want to speak something that doesn't match your understanding of reality—or keep silent when a truth needs to be told? What could cause you to stop seeing truth as an overriding ethic, or even an option?

When your primary concern is to take care of others, you'll go directly to what others need and want. You may not even be able to locate your needs and wants—or your opinion, for that matter, or what is or isn't okay. Your imperative becomes to determine what they want from you (go ahead, just make it up) and then do that. If you do happen to be aware of what you have to say or want to do, first figure out if it will cause them any disappointment, hurt feelings, or discomfort of any kind, then shut down what you had in mind if they'll be less than thrilled. In this model, what's true for you doesn't matter in the least, no matter what the issue or how high the stakes: what restaurant to go to, what color to paint the room, what does or doesn't get spoken, how the job gets done, how the money gets spent, how someone treats you, how often you visit them, whether to pull the plug, whether you stay or go.

Maybe you're the one who worries about what others think of you and prioritizes that over telling the truth. Here, you might get tripped up on taking care not to offend, be rude, sound stupid, look uncool, or appear to be anything that bothers you (bossy, mean, selfish—name your emotional bugaboo). Isn't it fascinating that people can have such a religion of being nice and polite, they're willing to become liars? This could apply to something innocuous like, "I do, I love your new bangs"— but people take it as far as staying in a love relationship they don't want to be in because they can't stand to hurt someone with the words "I'm leaving." It can strike in any realm of life: someone told me a story of engaging an attorney she didn't trust (a visceral *no* hit her in the gut) for something important enough to take to court—all because it felt rude to walk out with her money still in her wallet when she'd come to this person for professional help. Wow.

In his book *Protecting the Gift*, geared toward parents wanting to keep their kids safe, Gavin de Becker warns against raising them to be polite. I was most struck by his example of waiting for an elevator. The door opens and exposes someone who instantly registers in your system as unsafe—you can't miss the alert to danger. But this is your elevator (going up), and you were obviously poised to enter, so what do you do? Most people go ahead and walk in. Humans are the only species who'd get into a steel box with a predator because they wouldn't want that predator to think ill of them.

Then there's the concern about reactions, to keep truth telling at bay. Anger seems to be the most common dreaded reaction people factor in to their willingness to tell it like it is—but other predicted reactions can equally inspire silence or lies, including sadness, disappointment, disapproval, despair, emotional coldness or shutdown, sexual withholding, criticism, blaming, disdain, and then some.

Anger may top the list because sometimes the angry party gets violent or threatening, and keeping silent to stay out of harm's way is understandable enough. (Here's one of those please-go-get-help places: if you're in a relationship of any kind in which someone controls you with violence or threats of violence, or you monitor yourself based on their volatile nature, you need to get help getting out.) I've noticed, however, that plenty of people just don't like anyone to be mad at them, ever, so it doesn't matter that the other party in question has no history of actually putting physical violence to an angry response. They just won't tell the truth if it could piss someone off.

Want to tell the truth? It'll be easier with these three things in place:

1. Don't make it your job to take care of other people's feelings
2. Don't manipulate what they think of you
3. Let them have their reactions

Mavis was overcommitted. A medical doctor, she doled out her time and energy among three professional ventures, not to mention a husband and two children, and couldn't get to the work of making her dream career a reality. Not that there wasn't a bit of kinda-sorta heading that way.

156

When she started coaching with me, she was already in a gradual process of setting up an office space for holistic nutritional healing: the place existed, the stage was set, and she was slowly but surely filling it in with the right props.

Perhaps it was more slow than sure. She couldn't seem to get to the part of calling in the clientele—no marketing plan or activities so far. It's not just that she couldn't find time for all that. There wasn't even space in her schedule to place herself in the new office space—which she loved more and more with each addition or adjustment she made, one little tweak at a time. So what held her back?

Not a lack of passion. She had a long-standing concern about the nutritional-healing blind spot in the allopathic world, and she wanted to be part of the remedy: her aim was to support people to get more of what they needed to counter disease and to maintain health through diet. She'd managed to acquire hours of training in the margins of her life with a particular teacher whose approach she was entirely enamored of. That program wasn't 100 percent complete, but she also knew she could keep training till the grave; knowing her, she probably would.

She noticed she had some fear about not being quite ready to provide a legitimate service, but it didn't take long for us to work with her thinking to counter that: it was truer that, as a physician with many years of family practice under her belt, she was hardly insecure about her knowledge and experience; she knew how to research what she didn't know; she was comfortable with the fact that addressing some problems required a certain amount of trial-and-error.

Was she in the right place? Surely Atlanta was progressive enough for this kind of work, or city enough that the cross-section of folks drawn to explore this shouldn't be too puny. She also knew that plenty would be willing to go down this path with her precisely because of her MD status.

There seemed to be no good reason not to go for it, except for these pesky prior commitments to three other jobs.

It took one question and two seconds of reflection for Mavis to put her finger on which job it made the most sense to let go. (When people feel they have an impossible puzzle before them, with pieces that don't fit together, I ask them a simple question: What is it you need to let go?) The obvious tweak to her schedule—dropping her post at the not-for-profit clinic—would free up a single day per week. Just one day, but that was a sufficient opening to get her into the new office, get some structures in place, and start inviting clients in. Okay. So, ready to resign?

Well, no. If she were to quit right away, she'd be putting another human being in a terrible position. Nora, the heart-of-gold operations manager, would have to find a qualified person to replace Mavis, and Mavis couldn't forget how relieved Nora was when she first stepped in—what, only a year and a half ago? Had Mavis even worked there long enough to have made it worth anyone's while? Now poor Nora would have to start over with another search, and it just wasn't that easy to find local physicians who could carve out a day a week to support the clinic's nurse practitioners.

Poor Nora? To my mind, Nora had chosen her job and probably loved it (or at least valued what she was doing). She was probably pretty clear about her job description, too, and either already accepted or needed to learn to accept that it was her responsibility to maintain a good staff, whatever that took. In other words, Mavis wasn't putting Nora in any position at all. Nora had put herself in this position and likely wanted to be there. If not, she could certainly get out. If Mavis's resignation turned out to be the straw that broke the camel's back, so be it.

In short, Mavis wasn't telling Nora the truth ("It's in my best interest to resign now") because she was prioritizing—or making more important than truth—taking responsibility for someone else's feelings. People do this to be considerate of and careful with others—they want to be nice—but it's inappropriate nonetheless. Plain and simple, it's never your job to take care of other people's feelings (unless the other party is under five years old). You can certainly tell the truth kindly, to someone of any age. (Don't say, "I'm quitting, so go to hell, you pork-faced puke bag.") You can be aware of your impact on others, and where it's appropriate, mitigate that impact. But do you see the insanity of withholding truth until you've determined that no one's gonna have hard feelings about it?

Ah, if I had a dime for every time I've told someone, *Leave them to their journey!* Mavis, like so many good-hearted folks, was more than willing to accept the concept of a human journey for herself, and willing to allow for some suffering and discomfort as a normal part of that trek. But for others? For Nora? Who was such a good egg and gave so much to the clinic? Mavis wasn't so sure. And if Mavis was to be the agent of the discomfort or suffering—if someone should experience such things because of her—she could hardly stand that. (We'll come back to this form of insanity.)

Then there was image control. Beyond considering the impact on Nora and wanting to take care of her, Mavis was concerned about what Nora would think of her for bailing (can't call it *resigning* from a place of stressful thinking). Nora would think Mavis irresponsible, selfish, unreliable. She'd think Mavis wasn't living up to her commitment. She'd think Mavis didn't have much of an ethic for community service. All of these thoughts were intolerable, the result being that Mavis then needed to manipulate what Nora thought of her by staying in her job so she could be seen as responsible, selfless, reliable, and committed to public service.

(Think of when you smile so people will know you're nice, or you're safe, or you think well of them. We manipulate in small and large ways all the time. Note that I'm not saying this is all bad. It's fine to choose to smile to set someone at ease. It's equally fine not to. It's good to be in choice with the matter and know that the whole world doesn't need you to take care of it all the time. You know the subtle version of racism white people exhibit when they smile at Black folks to set them at ease, make sure they know we know they have the right to be here? Ay, I used to do that. Black people don't need me to let them know they're okay. No one needs me to let them know they're okay. In certain contexts, I can certainly choose to extend that to some human being because it makes sense and feels right in the moment—but it's no longer my default or my mission; it's not what I walk around doing.)

Notice that Mavis stirred up all those negative descriptors—irresponsible, selfish, unreliable—in her own thoughts and projected them onto Nora. And sure, it was entirely possible that Nora or any number of people could choose to buy in to this line of thinking. Here's where some of those tactics for tending the mind might come in: Mavis needed to be still with and meet these accusations coming up from inside her. She needed to determine for herself her true levels of irresponsibility, selfishness, unreliability. And if she was welcoming herself to the human race and found with equanimity where she did embody those flaws on any level, she wouldn't be in honesty, clarity, or truth until she went to the other polarity to check out how she also was and had been responsible, selfless, reliable. Could Mavis still validly embody those positive qualities if she quit the job at this point in time—or did all of that somehow go null and void with her resignation? (Remember Byron Katie's Gift of Criticism tactic that I describe at the end of part 1 in "Oh, the Messy Process of Applying It All"? Once you find the negative trait on one end of the spectrum, look for evidence of the positive trait on the other polarity as well. This might get you closer to a balanced view of things.)

More important, did any assessment of Mavis's character change the fact that it was time for her to step out of her position at the clinic? The truth was, it was time to go, no matter what anyone decided that meant about Mavis's goodness. Integrity, here, lay in going, not in managing the stay-or-go decision based on what others would feel or think.

Finally, Mavis could have warded off telling the truth out of fear that Nora might get awful—perhaps mean, or back-stabbing, or otherwise vengeful—in response. Since Mavis had no such fear, predicting and averting a reaction didn't play into her decision to speak or to withhold. (Though remember it's possible, too, to fear someone's alarm, or sadness, or defeat—not just aggressive responses.)

I invite you to notice the mind-reading game you sign up for when you don't simply tell the truth. It's a game of skill and chance with a warped crystal ball thrown in. The object is to foresee how someone will feel, what they'll think, or how they'll react to what you have to say: if you don't like what you see, avoid saying it at all costs.

What you'll project, of course, will come from your worst fears and bleakest thinking and the ugliest of what you've decided the other party is capable of—in other words, you sure won't be seeing them in the highest light or giving them the benefit of any doubt, never mind actually checking out with them what their thoughts might be. Big-hearted Nora has no capacity for seeing that Mavis has her own life, path, career track beyond the clinic? She can't trust that the right people to keep the place going will come in at the right time? She doesn't get that individuals come and go and the larger workings remain intact? The best she's got is to crumble when things don't stay today the way she set them up yesterday?

Hey, your guesses could even be right—you may be quite skilled at this game, or you may have a super-predictable Other Party on your hands— but it's still not fair or appropriate to go into someone else's head. Nor do you actually have access to what will happen in the future (the Universe's business every time). Even when you know someone pretty well, you don't ever know the ins and outs of who they are and what they're capable of. You don't know who they are right now.

More to the point, it's in fact not possible for you to be in someone else's head, and you never belong there. You're out of your business every time you try to read minds, or anytime you use your excellent intuition to decide you know what someone else is up to, what they're thinking, what their motivation is, what they want from you, how they'll think of you, how they'll react, what they'll say or do next.

If there's reason to, check it out: run your hunches, projections, worries, and fears right by them. More often, though, what's needed is for you to reorient, recenter to think in terms of *you*, tune in to what's right for you, and make your best choice here and now. I invite you back to the power of self-referral. If it feels appropriate to figure in to your decision how someone else is impacted, ask questions. Engage them in the conversation. This requires that you talk (not imagine), and tell the truth. Mavis's first thought, instead of being to protect Nora (or herself from Nora's opinion), might have been to ask Nora directly how Mavis's resignation might impact the clinic and Nora herself.

Consider the cost to Mavis of shutting down the truth. It's high—prohibitive, I'd say. The implication is no less than being stuck in the life she doesn't want to live, doesn't feel good in, and doesn't experience as offering her greatest gifts in the highest way. I consider that too high a price to pay.

Mavis can't stand being the agent of suffering for others? She has to. You have to. You must be willing to inconvenience people, to get in the way, to be a burden, to cost others time, money, energy—any number of resources. You must allow them to think ill of you, because sometimes they will. You must be willing to witness their negative reactions of all kinds. You don't have to take those reactions personally, because they truly have nothing to do with you. (Do move away from those reactions when that's what's best for you. You're not required to stick around while they run their course.)

I'm not saying you can't minimize the people-impacting equivalent of your carbon footprint, but you cannot set life up so you maintain a steady zero: not possible. Just for being human, you will inconvenience and upset people. You might hurt their feelings. You might even hurt them physically through no fault of your own (accidents will happen). You may cost them money you can't pay back. (Hang in there—life just might give you the chance to pay it forward, especially if you invite that.)

It comes down to this: if you organize around not having any impact on others, it won't work. It's impossible. The effort to do so will require any number of crazy contortions, fitting square pegs into round holes, shoving down what you want or need or what feels right and good to you right now. You will tell lies. You will step out of integrity. You will betray yourself.

Betrayal is a great sidebar to the topic of the craziness that comes of caretaking and manipulation. When clients bring me stories of betrayal, I tell them everyone must play the roles of both betrayed and betrayer. There's no way around it. If you still hold guilt or sorrow about being a betrayer, notice you've also been betrayed. Welcome yourself to the human race. I urge you to clear the guilt. (Go back to "Two Liars: Guilt and Shame.") If you still have amends to make (in a way that won't cause further trouble) or see any way to make something right—ever, in any scenario—by all means, make amends, do that thing. And then move on.

If you still feel wounded or incensed for having been betrayed, find where you've also been the betrayer. You would never betray anyone? Even if you do nothing that constitutes actual betrayal, someone will interpret something you do in that way: there, welcome to the role of betrayer. People can feel betrayed, for example, when their love-and-life partner wants to leave the relationship and does so in a clean and honest way without starting something else before they go. (Everyone has the right to leave a relationship, and they get to have their own reasons for doing so. I'm stunned by how often I encounter people who think the only good reason to go is outright abuse. Out of that belief, they sometimes create some harrowing scenes to play out that will eventually, then, allow the leaving. Or they stay stuck in a dead-end relationship.) Still, with the departing one going well and honestly, the one who doesn't want it to end sees the very desire to leave as a cruel violation of what they were doing together, all they've ever said to each other, all their history together holds, how deeply connected they were: betrayal.

This brings me to the most fascinating and possibly most absurd instance of caretaking and manipulation that I encounter. People actually stay with a spouse or primary partner they don't want to be with because that one still wants to be with them. "He would just be devastated," they tell me, or "I couldn't possibly hurt her that badly." Ay, good people, we're never doing anyone a favor by treating them like a victim. How do you think you're serving someone by sticking them forevermore with someone who doesn't want to be with them? So your partner is such a loser that you have to stay with them because no one else will have them? People follow this line of thinking even when they can give me ample evidence that the other could very well, would most definitely, be attractive to someone else. So why not set them free so they can be with someone who actually wants to get in bed with them and who might even be excited about sharing a life with them?

People will organize themselves around other people's feelings, thoughts of them, or potential reactions at any existing level of human interaction. Here's a range of examples. Is this you?

- You buy something you're not sure you want (or are pretty sure you don't want) because you feel sorry for the salesperson.
- You stop to talk to someone (friend, acquaintance, client, stranger, ax murderer) on the street when you have a commitment elsewhere or just plain aren't in the right space for stopping at the moment. (Don't you love giving your time and attention in a way that's divided, strained, begrudging, resentful?)
- You stay on a committee or board or in a group when it's not feeding you and doesn't fit into your life (never mind align with your vision)—but wouldn't it leave them in a bind or upset them if you went?
- You have coffee with someone just because they really want to have coffee with you, and they seem to really need it.
- You give money to someone just because they really want to get money from you, and they seem to really need it.
- You open your home to someone just because they really want to come into your home, and they seem to really need it.
- You have sex with someone just because they really want to have sex with you, and they seem to really need it.

It's harrowing what people will do to take care not to hurt feelings or cause disappointment, disruptions, or discomfort of any kind, making sure no one ever feels bad on their account; what they'll do in the name of being nice or polite or to be seen in any way at all; what they'll do to keep someone from reacting in a way they don't want them to react or from saying in response what they don't want to hear.

Would you like to know how things worked out for Mavis? Nora accepted her resignation graciously. Together, they came up with a schedule to taper Mavis's appearances there during a time of transition. This made Mavis feel responsible—she wasn't just bailing—and Nora only wished her well in moving on to where she felt called. But for the record: let's be clear it would have been equally fine if Nora had lost it and gone off on Mavis about what a loser narcissistic slacker she was to leave them high and dry. It would have then been Mavis's task to question all that brought up for her, to mind the pain body and tend the mind, and to come back into good standing with herself. That's what anyone needs to do when leaving the partner, dismantling the business, redirecting the project—whatever unpopular decision, thought, or point of view you've got to declare.

Want to tell the truth? You'll find that easier to do with these three things in place:

1. Don't make it your job to take care of other people's feelings
2. Don't manipulate what they think of you
3. Let them have their reactions

chapter 22

Never a Victim: Cultivate a Consciousness of Choice

I once heard Byron Katie give a definition of *victim* that changed my life, truly. It continues to inform my persistence in living in power and in guiding my clients to live there—no matter what life is dishing out or who's doing what.

Katie said that anytime you're believing something or someone outside of you can keep you from your good (joy, success, health, love, well-being of any kind), you're a victim. You're a victim because you're placing responsibility for your well-being outside of yourself, beyond your grasp—so you're screwed, you have no power, you're really not okay. I was struck by the fact that we all do this to some degree or another: the economy! health care! how my mother treated me! how he won't take *no* for an answer! this body! how late I entered the game! my insufficient talent or lack of connections or puny resources! their crazy driving habits! hetero-normative mentality! the way she talks about me to others!

So who isn't a victim? This stuff is universal. Accepting that it's universal could very well take the sting out of simply noticing where you're a victim. It's very useful to notice.

At the time of this epiphany, I decided I was the Queen of the Victims. Sometimes I say this in a workshop and someone vies with me for the title, so I let her have it. I'm done with it, having made a firm and clear decision to be a victim no more. (And need I remind you that there's no such thing as instant, blanket change? So what followed that decision was catching myself in victim mode, again and again, and finding my way back out.) When I heard Katie offer her definition—you're a victim when you believe something or someone outside of you can keep you from your well-being—I was pacing around my house in rural Maine listening in on a teleconference she was giving shortly after I'd returned from her School for The Work. There, we participants were encouraged to look at ourselves so deeply and unflinchingly, that I was wide open to a self-scrutiny that looks for the truth without applying judgment or self-flagellation. (Katie insists that people use The Work in a way that's kind.)

I took in how deeply unhappy I'd been (agonize, despair, suffer, suffer, suffer) all my life, almost forty-three years at that point. (I'm a Four on the Enneagram, pure and simple.) At the time I was in a miserable marriage with a man, my lesbian identity sealed away. I was dealing intermittently with wretched insomnia (which I now understand as part of my guidance system, seeking to wake me up to something); struggling with pain and limitations in my body from a car accident I'd had at thirty-one; still seeking to right a systemic yeast imbalance (candida) that had been with me for more than a decade; working hard to clean up some yelling patterns in my parenting that created plenty of suffering for others in my household (absolutely the hardest thing for me to forgive myself for); and still bumping up against the self-loathing that had long since become my habitual way of perceiving myself (well, if I wasn't in hubris). Ay. All of this, I saw, I'd made into someone else's fault. Having just spent those days at the School taking responsibility for anything and everything that I looked at in myself, I was ready—so, so ready—to go deeper with this process by getting very conscious of victim mentality. I took this on with missionary zeal.

Since I'm so verbal in my orientation to life, I started identifying victim language and watching for that. Anytime your words put the responsibility for your well-being outside of or beyond you; anytime your language points to some idea of your being without choice—you're talking (thinking, living) like a victim.

Have to: "I have to pick up the kids." No, you don't. You actually want to be there when school closes to bring them home. Sometimes when clients tell me harrowing tales of what they have to do (or do without) because of their kids, I remind them that the orphanage is an option. It makes them laugh and brings them back to all they're willing (choosing!) to do because they actually want to parent these particular beings, and parent them well.

Can't: "I can't go because he'll get mad at me." Nope, you could go, but choose not to because you'd rather organize around his wrath than around what you want for yourself. "I can't get a word in edgewise." So be silent, or leave, or forget the edges and stand up to loudly plunk into the middle of things what it is you've got to say. Note there are any number of permutations of *can't*. Here are two popular examples:

Can't afford: "We can't afford to go on vacation this year." Actually, you made certain spending choices (possibly very good ones) that make going on vacation a bad idea, and you'd rather stay home than go into debt. (So you could still choose to take a break and do some fun things, eat yummy food, and go where the tourists go in your own region during that time. I love to go hang out in Ithaca's gorges and take in the force and spray of the waterfalls.)

Can't stand: "I can't stand how my boss talks to me anymore." Really? Because you're still standing as you tell about it, and you keep going in to work every day. (I don't remember when or how she said it, but Byron Katie made me see that if I'm not in a coma or dead, I can still stand it.) If you've started looking for new work, now quit talking about what you're trying to get away from (that boss you can't stand) and talk instead about what you're moving toward (the vision!—what you want to create in your work life).

Expressions of overwhelm or being burdened by a greater measure of responsibility than others have: "It's all too much"; "It all falls on me"; "If I don't do it, it won't be done right."

Any declaration that someone or something makes it impossible or whatever the adjective of the moment might be (hard, tricky, miserable): "They make it impossible for me to lead the meeting." Sounds like something isn't working that needs to be addressed. Where do you have agency to address it and invite others to look at it with you? "She makes it so awkward to have those conversations." So mind your awkwardness and leave anyone else's alone—not your business—and make sure you take responsibility to have whatever conversation you think needs having.

Anything that implies some external permission being withheld, especially when permission isn't literally someone else's to give: "I'm

167

not allowed to state my opinion." You're not stating it because you don't like how it's received. You're not establishing your own right to speak; you're staying put with people or in conversations that don't honor it. "She won't ever let me pick what we do." So why are you still going wherever she wants to go? Let her call it, if that's what works between you, and if it's not working for you, get help, get a plan, or get out.

Anything else (besides permission) that someone withholds from you: "My boss won't give me any good leads." It sounds like time to invite your boss to another way, learn all you can about getting good leads yourself, find other allies, make the best of what you've got, or get another job. "She's not very affectionate." You can be the change you want to see and slather her with affection, ask for more (and keep asking), get it elsewhere (in a way that doesn't break an agreement), or get out of a relationship that doesn't meet your needs.

Declarations of lack (stated not as fact or interesting challenge but as what prevents you from living the life you love): "I don't have wheels," "I'm just not built that way," "I never had that advantage," and the ever-popular "I don't have time." In fact, we all have 24 hours a day, 7 days a week. We also all have handicaps and limitations. What if all that you do have going for you is enough?

Metaphorical words and expressions that posit you as the victim of forces of all kinds. This is treated in detail in the next chapter, "Watch Your Language." Short version: "I'm drowning in this," "He's got a noose around my neck," "They're watching my every move," "She's got me wrapped around her finger," "I'm between a rock and a hard place," and on it goes, till the cows come home (if they ever do).

Any description of someone that makes you smaller, put upon, overpowered, or in any way squashed or crushed: "He's toxic for me," "She's a force to be reckoned with," "They take over the room," "There's no getting around him."

Any overt expression of the absence of choice: "I've got no choice"; "I don't have much choice, do I?" "I really have no say in the matter." Are you sure? Find what choice you've got. There's probably plenty before the ultimate and perfectly valid choice to get out.

The more I explored the idea of victim mentality (as expressed and uncovered through language), the more it seemed to boil down to choice. At some point I came up with a way to articulate the antidote to victim mentality, and the phrase has stuck as a powerful admonition: Cultivate a consciousness of choice. I posted it on Facebook once and one of my beautiful Michfest workshop attendees translated it to Spanish on her wall: Cultivar una conciencia de elección. (Thank you, Fabiola! That just sings to me.)

It's hard to be a victim if you're standing firm in choice. It's hard to focus on what someone else or life itself is visiting upon you or withholding from you, if you're standing firm in choice. My pep talks about choice over time have come to be distilled to five basic points:

1. In any situation you're in, find where you do have choice.
2. If you have little to no choice, you've always got the choice to harness your power of interpretation. (This concept is so important that I gave it an entire chapter in part 2.)
3. Choose consciously—make the best choice you see to make.
4. Get 100 percent behind your choice.
5. If you find over time that you can't get or aren't getting behind a choice, do one of two things:
   • choose again (do something else);
   • get into place the supports you need that will allow you to get behind your choice.

Let's look at the December holidays as an example of how people lose track of choice and cause themselves all kinds of stress in so doing. "I have to go to the office party," "I'll be expected to host my in-laws again," "We need to make this super special," "I have to buy more princess outfits for Muffy." You don't have to do any of those things; you may certainly choose to do them—or not.

If attendance at the party isn't or doesn't seem to be optional, then by all means, choose to go. Choose it because you value this job: it's worth it to you to attend the occasional required gathering. (You could just as well choose to quit your job, or to simply let your boss know you won't be attending and stay tuned for what happens next.) Choose to visit or host family members because you want to foster connection with these specific human beings, and this season looks like the best time to put that into action. (Do I need to say it's a valid option *not* to visit or host them?)

Remember you have choice, and choose consciously. So many people automatically go by duty and tradition to plan their holidays. If this is you, consider this: You get to define *duty*. You get to follow, toss out, or recreate tradition. If you want to continue to visit certain people during this time of year, that's a fine choice. But it is a choice: embrace it as such. You're someone who wants to do your duty, who wants to follow tradition. Maybe other things motivate you: you don't want to be disowned, or you don't want to deal with disappointing your family or having them be mad at you. Any number of factors may inform your choice. (These factors can be questioned and challenged; they can also simply be noted.)

All things considered, you're still in choice. Don't lose sight of this! It's an option to disappoint, or to anger, or even to be disowned. Do realistically note that you may equally disappoint or anger family members in your presence and participation! And if being disowned (or some less extreme family threat) is a land mine in your reality, then it probably represents a whole cluster of land mines that a whole lot more than the holidays could set off. You get to choose how and whether to let tricky or toxic issues inform your holiday choices.

If you choose to host or visit family—whatever your reasons—get 100 percent behind your choice and stop talking about everything that's a pain about it. Remind yourself that you actually want to be with family for the holidays. Become a master of extracting from the experience all there is to enjoy.

It may help to consider more deeply why you choose what you choose. How does it serve you to maintain good relations with those you work with? Can you best do that through sugar, alcohol, and tiresome conversation? What do you value or even love about being with family? What is it doing for you and yours to take a trip during vacation time in December? What's behind the choice? A very simple question to ask yourself is, *What do I hope to get from this?* A nice follow-up question would be, *Is this the best way to get it?*

If you're out of touch with the underlying aim or value, you may sabotage the very thing you're after. For example, let's say you want your kids to have grandparent time. If you focus on everything your parents or in-laws do that makes you crazy, the kids may get grandparent time, but they may also get a confusing experience of divided loyalties; they may wonder if it's really okay for them to cozy up to these people you seem to despise. ... Choose clearly and consciously, and get behind your choice by connecting to, speaking about, and interacting with what you love and appreciate about these grandparent figures.

When it's hard to get behind your choice, choose again. You can leave in the middle of a visit, or make a judicious note to self to do something else next year. But if you want to hold to your choice, in this instance or as a way of life, learn to pause to consider what supports you need in place to do that—to make the choice sustainable. It may even be a matter of making ongoing choices to support an important choice you've made. You might support a holiday choice by choosing to take excellent care of yourself while in someone else's home or while others are in yours: carve out alone time; eat in a way that doesn't throw you off or make you feel bad about yourself; tune in to your true yes/no on/off responses so you're not perpetually doing what you don't really want to do. Emotional support may be important too. Since you could get thrown off despite your best clear choice-making, have someone in place you can call or pull aside so you can vent to a kind listener who will love and support you. When I need an ear, I go to someone who can compassionately hear whatever I'm feeling but won't treat me like a victim or support me in vilifying someone else. (This is very important to me.)

Taking such measures makes it possible for you to get 100 percent behind your choice by making sure your choice is humanly possible or sustainable. It also makes it possible for you to take full responsibility for your well-being during the holidays—victim no more. And why be a victim of the holidays? It's pretty absurd that as a culture we treat a time of vacation, sacred celebration, gift-giving, and downtime with loved ones as if it were a time of war.

Ellie: Get behind every little choice

I ran into my former client Ellie outside the food co-op and she wanted to tell me about the Friday night that had just passed. It had felt like it was passing without her: she was grading papers while a group of her friends were going out to hear live music. She said that because of our work together, she gave herself a talking to: "You're *choosing* to stay home and work," she told herself, "so there's no need to sit around being upset about it and hating it."

"And it was a good choice?" I asked.

"It was a great choice," Ellie said.

There might be an obnoxious edge to running into your life coach (who has no off-switch) when you're shopping. She might want to offer a little refresher course on the spot, whether you need refreshment or not. "If you embrace those choices," (I just had to add) "and you're not sitting around feeling bad about your life or hating yourself, then you can just catch the next wave and make a choice toward fun when that's what's best."

"Yep," she said. (She was already on it.) "Something came up just today and we all got together and had a blast. I had the perfect weekend."

Why be a victim of anyone or anything? If you live in a friendly universe, no one can keep you from your good, and every force that seems to be outside of you can be seen as moving you forward in your evolution, supporting you to thrive. Can't see it now? Keep watching, keep scooching, and act as if you trust. Life is good. You and your life are rife with potential—drop your focus on anything that would keep you from realizing it and locate (now and now and now) all that supports you to evolve, thrive, be fulfilled, and offer your highest service to the world.

Evelyn: Self-care in service (or, don't be the victim of those you serve)

My client Evelyn was preparing to fly to her sister's city to help her get through a harsh, invasive surgery. She was clear about wanting to do this—choice—but she also dreaded feeling stuck in a horrible hospital atmosphere with her sister in the room, especially in the role of patient. At some point, she told me, no way around it, the woman would get thrown off, she'd get hyper-distressed, she'd get loud and shrill, and, for some time, there would be no calming her. "I just want to jump out of my skin when she gets that way," Evelyn told me.

She and I talked about her getting comfortable with her discomfort and worked on how she might mind the pain body and tend the mind in the moment. We also gave a lot of focus to this choice thing. In choosing

172

to act as her sister's main support person for this surgery (and checking in with herself, Evelyn continued to feel good about this choice), she saw that part of getting 100 percent behind the choice was to accept that she'd inevitably find herself in a closed space with her sister at her worst, and this could in turn (quite likely) bring out the worst in Evelyn. She decided she wanted to work on accepting both parts of that equation.

Sometimes when people have a truly difficult person to deal with (a narcissistic boss or parent, an intense, high-needs child, an ex who's pretty reliably difficult during necessary transactions about shared kids), I suggest that they witness the person with fascination for how very well they play their role. You can even enjoy this. You can sit there laughing or barely containing laughter about how gloriously well they do what they do—an Oscar-worthy performance!—and how just when you thought you'd seen all their tricks, here they come with something crazy-fresh, truly outdoing themselves. You've gotta admire that! Evelyn decided to play with this. She ended up writing me later to say, "I loved watching how quintessential my sister was at being the difficult person she is." Note that this is an example of putting a structure or support in place (in this case, a mental trick or mindset) to ensure being able to get behind a choice.

Further, Evelyn wanted not to beat herself up if she found herself being at her worst. In speaking of accessing the witness to mind the pain body, we expanded this to accessing the witness, period—and remember, once you're in touch with witnessing at all, scooch toward the compassionate, dispassionate witness. Thus, when she found herself in close quarters with her sister suffering harsh circumstances, Evelyn remembered to access the witness. She created distance (and thus, the possibility of less identification and less judgment) by watching herself interact with her sister. She found she was better able to control how much she reacted and better able to get okay with whatever reactions she had.

We spoke once during her time away, when Evelyn was having a moment of not being completely thrilled with herself. I challenged her to accept her reactive moments—there's room for reactiveness in the universe, maybe especially post-surgery in the hospital. What if there's no problem here at all? How many people wouldn't be at least a little bit reactive in such a situation? Evelyn started using any level of reactiveness to her sister as a reminder to check in with herself, locate the self-care she needed, and respond to that need as quickly as possible.

Self-care was an important piece (perhaps the crucial piece) for her getting fully behind her choice to assist in her sister's surgery adventure. It was another structure to get in place to support the choice. Evelyn knew her sister to be very self-absorbed, especially going through what anyone would agree to be hardship. From her sister's perspective, it would rightly and truly be all about her. Therefore, Evelyn could count on the fact she wouldn't get praise or appreciation for all she did for her sister—and, in fact, was likely to get reprimanded for anything she didn't think to do. Further, her sister wouldn't be looking out for how tired Evelyn was or what needs she may have—which brought home the reality that this was Evelyn's job to do for herself. Accordingly (lining up with reality, getting behind her choice), she determined in advance some things she knew she'd need, and made a point to secure those things for herself while she was there. Note that it truly began with giving herself permission to make self-care part of her mission, and to consider it equally as important as anything she was doing for her sister.

This included permission to set limits for how much she was willing to do (boundaries!). She was willing to give a lot: that didn't have to mean 24/7 with no breaks; it didn't mean she had to listen to anything her sister wanted to say, in any way she wanted to say it, and for however long. Having considered that there would be moments when the hospital room would feel like a pressure cooker over high flame, she was ready for those moments and even proactively staved them off. She went out for daily walks, stepped out for a cup of tea or breath of fresh air, took time to talk with her wife by phone, left the room abruptly if the pressure felt potentially explosive, and more—whatever she saw to do in the moment as she minded her pain body and tuned in to stress or reactivity registering in her system. As she later wrote me in an e-mail, just as she knew it would, the situation did often feel like "endless chatter and endless caregiving and total stress zone."

Because she was so solid in her sense of choice, Evelyn knew there was nowhere outside herself to place blame if she didn't like how things went. Her sister was her sister, behaving in the predictable ways she behaved, and Evelyn was entering the whole scene fully cognizant of the risks and fully willing to take them. The result of this clarity in terms of choice was that Evelyn went through this experience more swimmingly than she imagined she could. By no means was it a picnic at the beach. It was something Evelyn did because it felt right and good to do it, and she took care of herself the whole time. In the end, she felt good about standing by her sister, and great about staying close to herself.

Rebecca: Don't miss choosing your life

When Rebecca first came to talk to me, she felt conflicted—even somewhat tormented—about what wasn't in place in her life. She worried that she had somehow entirely sold out because she wasn't living according to certain values she'd always held dear. She suspected she'd abandoned some key parts of herself and felt trapped by the choices she'd made that now seemed to make other choices impossible—and weren't those things she wasn't getting to at least as important as what she *was* doing? She loved her husband and felt well matched with him in many ways, but he had a business that predated her and wasn't willing to join her in the homesteading life she wanted that would have required both their energies combined. Nor did he have any interest in communal living, while Rebecca had been enamored of intentional community since she'd first heard of such a thing. What was she doing in this insular world of nuclear family? That she and her husband had had two kids together—little people she loved and loved mothering!—somehow only made her feel more trapped in old choices. Had she chosen all wrong?

One of the reasons I love offering Rebecca's story here is that she didn't have the funds to enter into what I typically do with coaching clients—which is to work with them for six months at a time to do deep work. Nor could she buy a block of four sessions, which I make available so people can experience a shorter run with me (whether to warm up to longer-term work or to simply do a piece of focused work). Together, we keep meeting what life brings to them during their time with me, and I walk them through how to do it differently. I support them in creating clear intentions and in holding to these as they move through life day by day and week by week. Thus, lasting change can take hold. Rebecca saw me once.

When she wrote me some months later, I was so excited by all she'd done with that single meeting that I invited her to a second free session to see how I might serve her in pointing herself ever more clearly in the direction she wanted to go. Rebecca is living proof that a little can go a very long way. She's also proof that you get from coaching, or any growth process, as much or as little as you put into it—it's largely a matter of applying what you get. With minimal input from me, she transformed her life in remarkable and beautiful ways. (Note that I never imagine I'm the only influence or resource, and seek to honor my clients' own widom and to point them inward—but here I'm specifically addressing what Rebecca took from my offerings.)

The thing that most affected her was this idea of getting 100 percent behind her choices. Yes, she had made certain choices, and for very good reasons. For now, true enough, these choices did preclude some other options. She could wake up every morning dismayed at her choices (that *what have I done?* line of thinking), or she could embrace her life anew each day, declaring, *Today, this is what I choose. This is where I want to be. These are the people I want to be with.* If she couldn't do that, there really was the option to choose again.

Here are two mindsets Rebecca adopted in order to get behind this new way of looking at things. First, she decided to think of her choices as being for now. At another time, there might still be the possibility of homesteading or, in an attenuated version of that dream, taking on some form of farm work that could be satisfying. She might end up living in community down the road: where she was now was good for now.

Second, she consciously dropped a standard of perfection that required her to live all of her values and preferences at once and to the hilt, with nothing left out. Perfectionism and all-or-nothing thinking are toxic (or at the very least exhausting and depleting) in most circumstances. Recognizing both the toxicity and how she'd been perpetuating it with her thinking, she refused to keep exposing herself to it. She was willing to work with her thoughts and change her focus.

When I first met Rebecca, she presented a number of things she wanted to be doing that she couldn't possibly get to. When she laid it all out on the table, it was like she'd crowded the space with total chaos—a puzzle with so many pieces and such a level of complexity that there was nothing for us to do but declare it hopeless. But it's never hopeless. Sometimes (I've said this before), when it feels like the pieces just don't fit together, there's something to let go. After our talk, Rebecca found some things to let go.

Soon after we met, she followed through on one of her dreams to get certified as a celebrant: this would allow her to officiate at weddings and funerals. The certification wasn't hard to get, but required initial research, then a bit of time and money, and she got behind all of that to bring it to completion. This was satisfying to her, and fit into her life without tipping any balance in terms of abusing available resources (her energy levels included). Having launched that, and before it was all done, she researched divinity school. As she followed open and shut doors, she began a program that would likely take her a good decade to get through, one or two classes at a time, with payment also to be determined one step at a time. The first few classes were covered through funds she found to apply for and which she was awarded.

Let me add—this is important—that she also failed to get the funds she wanted for the program she originally thought she most wanted to attend. Remember, the open and shut doors are equally good news, both guidance. Forcing nothing, grasping at nothing, we can simply allow ourselves to land in the right place at the right time. "Honestly, I'm in the perfect program," Rebecca told me—only two hours' drive from her house, one day a week, and in the same city where her sister lives.

When we spoke the third time, precisely because I wanted to use her story in this book, she had her celebrant's license and four weddings under her belt. (Her website beautifully expresses the rhythms-of-life vision she brings to this work, as well as how she works closely with clients to tailor ceremonies to their values and visions. You can check it out at fullcircleceremony-dot-com.) Further, she was six classes into her long-term divinity program (one quarter complete!) and loving it. And— gorgeous development—having previously spoken a few times at her Friends' meeting (which, atypical of Quaker meetings, engages speakers for each gathering), she'd been asked to speak monthly for a modest stipend, and was reveling in getting to practice in her current reality what she was seeking to do in a greater version once the divinity program was complete. Friendly Universe, anyone?

"I was all over the place when I first talked to you. Now I feel like my life is streamlined, and it makes sense as a whole." ("All the parts fit together," I threw in, because I love to remind clients of this: all the parts of your life are *supposed* to fit together.) Essentially, she was talking about being in alignment. Getting there in the imperfectly perfect present required letting go of some things and truly getting behind her choices.

When she did that, the next best steps for her to take to allow her life as it currently looked to bump up to the next level made themselves apparent. The way opened, the resources came in, and she kept teaching herself to daily love her life and embrace her choices even as it all kept looking and feeling better and better. What she realized from our first talk was that when she kept thinking about all she wasn't getting to, she completely lost touch with all she had. Rebecca put it in simple and crystal-clear terms: "I feel like I narrowly averted the tragedy of missing my life."

chapter 23

Watch Your Language

"It seems like a flying cow shat on my head," my client Nigel wrote when he got some unexpected news. I dashed him a quick reply encouraging another interpretation with maybe way less-evocative imagery! Janine once sent me an SOS, "I actually feel like I'm falling apart at the seams." I wrote back calling attention to her metaphor by looking at it literally: "You're absolutely not falling apart at the seams. You have no seams. You can look right now and notice that you're intact. Your body is intact. Your hair is intact. Your face is intact. Your history is intact. Your personality type is intact. Your coaching process is intact. Your soul is intact. Your home is intact." She found such solace in this recasting that she reviewed it enough times to be able to quote it back to me. (I learned this when she thanked me for my words next time we Skyped and I looked at her blankly.)

As you move through hard times, harsh circumstances, or tricky situations, it helps to be very clear about what is and isn't actually happening. How you speak (think, write) about it matters. I often point out people's metaphors, which may seem harmless and even fun—who doesn't love colorful speech? Sometimes people feel like it's okay to talk about harsh things going on for them if they put some interesting linguistic spin on it: somehow they sound less like complainers; or they can at least provide a bit of entertainment for the poor souls listening to their travails. (And here's where they might throw in a fake-laugh for good measure—a power zapper to be sure.)

Once I've made clients aware of their language, they sometimes get self-conscious and start sentences with disclaimers—"I know I should never talk like this but ..." Actually, you should talk however you talk. Speak your uncensored mind, and it will serve you well if you also hear yourself and catch the distorted, overblown words you speak. Do they exaggerate your difficulties? Declare that what you want is impossible or that there's something wrong with you? Posit you as the victim of anyone or anything?

The phrase *Watch your language* is apt, but not if it means to refrain from talking a certain way: let it mean, instead, Notice how you do talk and come closer. See what you can learn from the things that come out of your mouth. Recently, I didn't realize I felt isolated in dealing with a family situation until I heard myself start a sentence to a friend with the words "I'm all alone here. ..."

Question the thoughts revealed by your speech. Consider whether you actually believe what you're saying. In fact, in the above example, I wasn't all alone by a long shot; in that very moment, I had my friend's rapt and entirely compassionate attention. What was truer was that I felt temporarily disconnected from source and guidance and needed to spend some time reconnecting, then questioning my thoughts. I proceeded to do just that.

Someone told me of a song and dance she had to do for someone. Nope. No song, no dance, and no *have to*. Last chapter, "Never a Victim," stressed the importance of catching victim speech (it's so disempowering!). You're a victim if you *have* to do something for someone else—even more so if this thing involves contortions and manipulations. I don't seem to tire of repeating that you can't be a victim when you're in choice. So if you choose to sing and dance, by all means, do just that, and do it with gusto or grace or whatever pleases you. You could also choose to stand firm and speak clearly and simply say whatever you need to say to someone with no embellishments thrown in to make them feel okay about you or what you're saying. Don't wanna be a victim? Let me repeat myself: you can't be a victim when you're in choice. Your language can support you in the effort to cultivate a consciousness of choice.

While looking at the possibility of working on a project with someone reputed to be difficult, my client Sandra once metaphorically used the words "I may not want to get in bed with him." I told her that I personally would be very quick to drop that particular turn of phrase. Maybe it's just me, but don't you think it feels very different to get in bed with someone than to collaborate with them professionally and creatively? Using that language, I can't imagine being on my surest footing as an equal with someone who's a challenging match in a professional situation. Notice that you can actually make yourself smaller and weaker or somehow put yourself at a disadvantage by the way you describe your position in a game. Or you can do just the opposite with different language.

Again, don't try to control your language; just notice it, and scooch toward what works better. Allow your word choices to show you more about your perceptions. If what you hear sounds sketchy to you, make like a smart phone and auto-correct. My client Cyndi once told me that she felt the world was passing her by. As soon as that came out of her mouth, she beat me to saying, "That sounds like victim language."

Let me be clear: I encourage gentleness with this awareness. It's not about catching yourself being wrong. It's about witnessing what doesn't serve you and course-correcting toward what does and what better matches the intentions you hold.

When Cyndi said that, she was engaged in some bold explorations to rethink her career path, and the world could only be passing her by if she interpreted her colleagues' promotions and new jobs as meaning they were achieving what she couldn't get to. Actually, she didn't even want the kind of changes they were making, as they were moving around within a system that she was seeking to exit altogether. If she interpreted their gains as a sign that success was very close by—*Success all around me!*—and also honored all that she'd been up to get to the right job in due time (or divine right time, if you will), then the world was her oyster, containing and supporting her, with some beautiful new pearl in progress. (A month after I wrote these words, Cyndi effortlessly landed in a job that couldn't have fit her more perfectly. The position was actually within the same system, but with so much in place to improve her lot—including a pay raise and a shift to the autonomy she craved and work content that she's passionate about—that it represented significant change.)

Let me flag once again the importance of harnessing your power of interpretation. Nigel, with his metaphorical flying cow, saw with little prodding (he's quick) how his words to me showed that he felt—well, shat upon. He considered that he might interpret everything happening as guidance and direction in certain realms where he was actively seeking to make changes. How could this not be good? He recast what looked like bad news initially as a sign that life was supporting him to shift gears sooner than later. Nigel also looked for and found the safety nets actively built into a situation that challenged his sense of security. Life is long on safety nets, we decided together, and actually pretty short on flying shitting cows.

chapter 24

Make No One the Villain:
Meet Every Face as the Face of God

You know you're making someone the villain (or making what's happening to you about them) when you go over the details. In no way did this observation come to me from personal experience, as I hope I made abundantly clear at the end of part 1 in "Oh, the Messy Process of Applying It All." We fixate on the details, we tell them again and again; privately, mentally, we keep going over that particularly odious detail—the can-you-be-LIEVE-it bit that sends our loyal friends rounding up the posse. And then we firmly clamp down on a huge, ugly, certainly well-substantiated story about the other.

It's never about the other. What I mean is, it's never about the other even if he or she really did do and say these odious things that everyone would agree with you are just awful and grossly unacceptable. (They really truly might be those things.) If it's happening to you—if the other is bringing up anything in you that feels dreadful or miserable or makes you launch a defense (even that wee-hours impassioned speechless speech before the nonexistent jury in your head)—then it's surely all about you, and it's all for you. It's here to support your healing and evolution, not to squash you. So drop the other person out of the story and see the whole thing as happening between you and God—another way of saying, between you and you.

The antidote to making someone the villain is to meet every face as the face of God. A client of mine widened her eyes at this and breathed, "Easier said than done." Another said, "You haven't met my boss." Actually, that boss is exactly the face I mean. And even with that boss, with anyone, it's just not that complicated. It may not be fun and it's probably not your current default, but it's still not that hard. You can simply ask yourself, *Why would the face of God show up for me this way?* Even if this really is a particularly odious face of God (they're out there), you can consider with this simple question what useful purpose it serves here—only for your good, your healing, your evolution.

On that note let me throw in that people sometimes misunderstand me on this topic and take my words to mean you need to go along with anything anyone comes to you with, give them your time, do what they ask—all because they're the face of God. Nope, I don't mean that. Some faces of God are the ones you must learn to say no to—or to keep out with a slammed door, or to stand up to, or to call out on what they're actually doing while they're pretending to be appropriate, and so on. There's nothing about being a doormat in what I'm speaking of here. The one who shows up trying to make a doormat of you would be the face of God to walk away from or send packing. This would be the face of God to keep from crossing the threshold and to hold some very firm boundaries with forevermore.

Abby: Face yourself before you face your accuser

I'd like to tell you about Abby, a client of mine whose work involves serving a particular group of people. Someone from that population— we'll call her Cruella—decided Abby was failing miserably in her work and angrily scheduled an appointment to tell her all about it. Got dread? Abby's mind climbed onto the trepidation treadmill and, for several days running, would not get off.

There are so many things Abby and I talked about as this meeting approached, and so much courageous work she did around all of it. In particular, it provided us a sort of living laboratory for working with this concept: make no one the villain; instead, meet every face as the face of God. Another way to say this is that nothing that happened had anything to do with Cruella. It was all about Abby—and all for her.

It was astonishing to me how Abby took Cruella's bad opinion of her and, for a window of time, seemed able to look only through that lens to frame a vision of herself. Through this woman's eyes, Abby saw her professional self only in terms of what she was doing wrong, what she was failing to do, what she hadn't done enough of, what strengths she lacked, what she hadn't yet developed in her program—and onward down the spiral from there.

As you know by now, The Work of Byron Katie is my (non)drug of choice for questioning limiting thoughts. Question 3 in this process serves to explore cause and effect; it allows you to look at the life you get when you believe the thought you're bringing to the inquiry process. The actual question is "How do you react, what happens, when you believe that thought?" and many subquestions can be used to tease this out from several angles. One subquestion for #3 is "What do you lose track of, what do you fail to notice when you believe this thought?" It's a good one.

When Abby took on Cruella's version of her performance—in a nutshell, "I'm doing a terrible job"—Abby couldn't see anything she was doing well. She couldn't see all she'd done all year that had had a powerful impact on the people she served. She couldn't see her good influence, her dedicated presence, her effective, creative development of a successful program. She lost track of all the appreciation she received on an ongoing basis.

Not yet realizing the extent to which her mind had run with this, I innocently asked, "Well, you've had a big success recently, right?" She looked at me blankly. She said, "You mean ..." and named a recent moment when she'd responded to something mundane in her personal world in a nonhabitual way. I said, "Uh ... the grant?" She'd just gotten funding for the new program she was launching. Her face gave a funny little twist, then laughter broke out. "Oh," she said lamely. "Um ... forgot about that."

We were both fascinated. As I probed deeper, I learned that Abby hadn't been talking to people about the grant she'd been awarded. No announcements, no celebration, no relishing the success. In fact, she'd adopted the warnings people above her had delivered about what the grant meant (an interpretation): all eyes were on her, everything had better go just so—all kinds of ways to frame it to make it a burden instead of a joy.

In other words, Cruella wasn't the only one failing to take note of what Abby did well.

When Abby and I first sat down to prepare for her meeting with Cruella, looking together at how she could actually receive what her accuser might say and what she might say back, Abby was completely focused on defending and trying to get Cruella to see things differently. She was making it all about Cruella. She was making it about the other.

In this book's introduction, I talked about one of my favorite questions from Byron Katie: If it's a friendly Universe, how is this perfect? I gave a few rephrasings to look at it from other angles. Let me offer them again here: How is it all perfect? How is it growing the muscles you lack?

185

What's the invitation here? What healing is possible right in the midst of it—not despite it, but because of it? What is this situation teaching you that you need to learn? And my favorite, if you think in terms of meeting everything as consciousness, every face as the face of God: why would the face of God show up for you this way?

Why would All That Supports Her show up in Cruella form and accuse Abby of doing a bad job? Because Abby doesn't know how to focus on what a good job she does. Abby is her own worst accuser—but she couldn't see this till it came before her with someone else's face on it. If it hurt when Cruella came around prodding Abby about what's not good enough, it's only because she was jabbing the sore spot from Abby's self-inflicted harm.

Abby was so ready to face Cruella by the day of their meeting. I coached her in literal listening (Byron Katie's trick for deleting the tone and dropping subtext or interpretations—just taking someone's words at face value and giving the simplest, most direct answer); seeing Cruella with compassion; getting curious and inviting Cruella to say more about anything she put forth; agreeing with any part of what Cruella said that could be true and remembering later to look for how the opposite could be true as well—sure, I can find the program's weaknesses, and now, for my own clarity, I'm going to find all its strengths (again, Byron Katie's Gift of Criticism); remembering that Cruella has a right to her story, but that doesn't make it the gospel truth. ... We covered all this and then some, and Abby felt equipped to meet her accuser.

But more important, Abby had sat, by her Day of Reckoning, with the things she needed to face in herself. She took in the level at which she neglected to savor her own successes, to appreciate her own hard work, to value what she did herself. This neglect kept her perpetually low on fuel; that is, it kept her from cultivating the creative energy to do more, and to do it with joy and increasing effectiveness. She committed to tooting her own horn, to spreading the word about the grant she'd been awarded, and to enjoying the work as she stepped into the new program. She made the event between her and God—or her and her: a new way and new level of valuing her work was being required of her, and she was stepping up to the plate. Cruella was just a player in the scene to help her look at herself.

Want to know how the meeting went? I can't tell you that. Cruella never showed up.

chapter 25

Be the See-er, Not the Seen

There was a moment in one of my workshops in the woods at the Michigan Womyn's Music Festival in August of 2013 when I stopped being the see-er and became the seen, and in that shift I became weirdly self-conscious. It was a moment—and it passed quickly—but such a fascinating, completely unexpected moment that here I am writing about it. I believe it holds something for my readers, because it exemplifies becoming the seen (and it's a fun example).

It happened on the one day at Michfest when I didn't like my hair. You may wonder, Who thinks about hair while camping? To which I can only answer, You've obviously never been to the Michigan Womyn's Music Festival—which happened for the fortieth and final year in 2015. In brief, there was a whole fashion show happening there on so many levels, the topic could fill its own book. Let's call it a range between outrageous, campy costumes and clothes that simply best expressed an individual's sense of attractiveness, style, and/or personal freedom, with ratios of skin to cloth that followed no rules, and with zero sometimes figuring on the cloth side of those ratios.

As for my hair, I set it up to be something I don't give much thought to; so I rarely give it much thought. Further, I set up my presenting so I don't give much thought to anything about me. This, in fact, is why I'm able to present in the first place and why I present with such ease and have so much fun while I'm at it.

When I started coaching, I got a great gift from a master coach and teacher out of Arizona named Steve Chandler before I ever gave my first presentation. In his *MindShift* audio series, he says that you can't freely speak in front of a group if you're concerned about how the people see you, what they're thinking of you, how you're being evaluated. (There, in my language, you're being the seen.) He recommends bringing what you're passionate about to the fore and keeping your focus on that. (This makes you the see-er.) He also places the priority on relating to the people present, harping on a single, beautiful point: "Only connect." Equipped with this simple philosophy, and feeling quite passionate about what I wanted to bring to groups, I was pretty fearless about entering the realm of public speaking. Ah, friendly Universe.

Back to hair. I got experimental that year and grew my hair out from a short, spiky look to a cropped cut with longer meshes in front. It was fun to change and fun to get a little frillier, and I mostly loved it. Sometimes I would pull the front meshes outward (which just felt weirdly and deliciously capricious) and more often I directed them down and in—much more no-nonsense, but still femmy. And, according to this scheme, the meshes did need directing, as one side wanted to head one way and the other flipped the other. On the day of that particular workshop, the sides refused to come into sync. I made a valiant thirty-second effort to tame them then reached the end of my willingness to bother with hair. I stepped into the world and into my workshop with hair I wasn't thrilled with, but I had no plan to give it a second (hmmm—by then surely third or fourth) thought. I was willing. I'm willing to be one more human being on the planet having a bad-hair day. I'm willing not to be a victim of my hair by wrongly believing it could make the difference between connecting or not connecting or giving a good or bad program.

I was certainly passionate about my topic and able to put my focus there. This would be my third time at Michfest presenting my Personal Power Surge workshop. A key point in the curriculum is this: Be the see-er, not the seen. When you're the seen, you become an object; you're no longer the subject of your life—never mind the hero of your own journey. You become self-conscious, looking at yourself from the outside through the eyes of others (and all the thoughts you invent that *must* be going through their heads). You're no longer able to be curious, engaged, present. Rather than living through your sensory perceptions and experiences, you're mentally at the mercy of how (you think) others perceive you. The see-er watches, takes things in, is free to hold back or step in according to choice. The seen, at worst, gets paralyzed; the seen, at best, dances and contorts to win approval. It's no fun to be the seen, and it's a power zapper, to be sure.

Power zappers (stay tuned for their chapter, coming up soon) figured in the workshop in an exercise that most people loved. It did alarm an introvert or two, but they had the option to simply watch. Willing participants acted out in mini-skits the various ways people lose their power, sometimes on a daily basis, while those watching tried to guess what was being depicted. Two womyn (remember, no women at Michfest, and no ladies, either) were enacting *making comparisons*, and the skit opened with one of them pointing across the way and saying something about someone's hair. I was the apparent someone she was pointing to, but my brain somehow translated this gesture as being directed to some fictitious, invisible person standing somewhere between the actors and me. Still, given the wiring between brain and hand, a finger pointing in my direction with the word *hair* attached caused the bizarre, instinctual flight of my own fingers to the unruly side of my hair.

As I stood there caught in an uncomfortable hair-holding stance instantly followed by an uncomfortable vision of myself that I disapproved of, the next words in the skit made it clear that, *oh fun*, they were actually talking about me. I'd been incorporated into their skit. This second comment was about my glasses. In quick succession, they then went to my torn-jeans look and by then I'd let go of my hair, literally and mentally, and gave a little spin so that my jeans (the ones my tidier sister had recently counseled me to throw away) could get a 360-degree viewing. At this point I was genuinely laughing, and I felt only a twinge embarrassed, not even close to the mortification my former self would have felt. (In my younger, unhealed days, I could easily raise a burning, crimson blush if even positive attention came my way.)

I stepped out of that moment by bringing my focus back to what needed to happen next in the workshop and giving my full attention to that. All told, the whole episode lasted two minutes tops and I was none the worse for the wear. I had a brief experience of being the seen, not the see-er, and I moved back into being the see-er so I could do what I was there to do. I could have hugely sidetracked myself, and done some damage to my beautiful workshop, if I'd gotten caught up in evaluating the moment, internally apologizing or atoning for my lapse, wondering what others had seen and what they now thought of me, being dismayed by my own self-judgment, and so on. All of that did suggest itself (typical thoughts will typically run through the mind), but for nanoseconds. The point is—and this is the way to live in power—I stepped out of being the seen and moved back into being the see-er.

I'd like to take a tiny side-trip to talk about *now*. What I also did was to simply step out of one moment and into the next. I had no belief that the content of the prior moment would contaminate the next. It's possible, and very desirable, to make this a way of life. To achieve this, it helps a lot to practice ongoing self-forgiveness, to believe and trust that all of life loves and supports you, to rid yourself of any belief that you should be perfect or practice anything in some constant, sustained way (more on that below), and, finally, to be the see-er, and not the seen.

Through that brief episode in that sweetly contained workshop grove surrounded by embracing trees, I inadvertently demonstrated another important principle to the group—though (hindsight!) I wish I'd spoken it out loud. It's a principle I love to include in this power topic: living in your power doesn't mean setting it up so you're always there. (Good luck.) As with everything, you will step or fall out of it, maybe fall right on your face, but you can simply step (or grope your way) back in. (Scooch!) At that point in Michigan, the concept of the power to change hadn't yet expressly made it into my personal-power material, but I've always included some version of catching yourself kindly—no self-flagellation allowed, as this will keep you in a negative vision of yourself and likely deplete and defeat you. Applied to being the see-er versus the seen, catch yourself in the position of the seen, and simply course-correct toward the perspective of the see-er. Turn away from how you appear to others and refocus on what you want to pay attention to and what you wish to take in with your senses and sense of curiosity.

Now apply being the see-er to any moment public or private, to scenes involving multitudes or one other, to everything in your life. I was recently reminded by a question from a client that you can apply it to sex, because when you become the seen instead of the see-er, you'll get caught up in ideas of performing and forgo all spontaneity and joy, forget to have your own sensory experience, lose track of connecting, and possibly literally stop performing. Finally, you can even apply it in solitary moments, because (crazy humans) we mentally bring in others and their supposed thoughts of us even when no one's around.

Get present, get curious; step into *now* and into your power; experience your amazing senses: be the see-er, not the seen.

chapter 26

Keep Your Word: Increasing Self-trust

If you show up consciously for your inner work, personal evolution, or spiritual growth; if you value things like integrity, reliability, and responsibility; if you've got a stake in having others count on you in various roles (as businessperson, parent, teacher or mentor, partner or spouse, friend, collaborator)—you probably agree that keeping your word is important. Perhaps especially if it's tied to your livelihood, you see how keeping your word affects your relationships: people can rely on you when you keep your word; they see you as trustworthy, and they'll keep coming back.

What you may seldom think of—and this may well be even more important—is that keeping your word affects your relationship with yourself. Whenever you tell others you're going to do something, you're telling yourself too. And when you tell yourself you're going to do something, you're obviously telling no one but yourself. Ultimately, every transaction is between you and you. If you don't come through on what you say you'll do—or you come through partially, later, differently—you teach yourself that you can't trust yourself. You erode your self-trust.

Why does that matter? You need self-trust in order to change, to grow yourself, to create. You need substantial measures of self-trust if you want to change radically, to grow yourself in a new direction or configuration, to get bigger than you thought you could be; or if you want to create something big, something uncomfortably dear to you, perhaps the thing you feel you came here to do. In order to make such changes, you must believe that you have the power to make happen what you say you want to make happen.

This comes up sometimes in coaching when clients break their commitments to the process—don't do homework, show up late, don't send the check on time. Our work together is about profound and radical change. How can they believe in their capacity to change if they don't keep their word and therefore don't experience themselves as trustworthy? The problem, anytime they fail to do what they said they would do, isn't that they're disappointing me. The problem is that they keep reinforcing for themselves their own image of themselves as unreliable.

Conversely, the more you keep your word, the more you build self-trust. Creating is deeply linked to language. In his slim, potent, easy-read, gem of a book, *The Four Agreements*, Don Miguel Ruiz posits impeccability in using your word as the first and most important agreement. He links the spoken word to power, to creation, to manifestation. He even goes so far as to speak in terms of magic—tracing whatever you've got in that department back to how you use your word.

Whether the concept of magic irritates or delights you, consider how words truly are the building blocks of creation. There's nothing you create in the physical realm that you don't first envision (or hold as a vision) and put words to. And to bring it into being, you must imagine it some more and put more words to it. When you bring in other people, you use words to draw them in, share the vision, exchange ideas. With words, you make agreements about meeting these people, getting help from them, perhaps giving them something back for what they give you. Words figure significantly, in any number of contexts, in your process to bring vision to fruition. In short, you rely on your word to create, so your word must be reliable.

Children know the value of words. They take everything you say you'll do as a promise. Have you noticed? Whatever you casually say can happen *someday* means to them it will definitely happen, and this in a time frame that makes sense to them—soon—or at the specific time or in the situation you named if you veered into anything remotely resembling specificity. ("We'll stop at the ice cream stand next time we come this way.") If you're a grown-up who has any dealings with children, you've surely had a child say, "You promised!" when you never used the word *promise* at all. You were just talking. But children know the value of words.

Or at first they do. Over time, children learn to devalue language, because grown-ups show them the way. Kids eventually stop trusting, and they learn not to be trustworthy.

This very likely happened to you at some point, perhaps long ago. Would you like to renew your reverence for your power to create through your word? Would you like to increase your self-trust and thereby harness your power to create? Warning: this could seriously impact how much you accomplish moving forward.

You can begin by making fewer agreements. Does that sound simplistic or even absurd? It actually works! If you haven't been 100 percent clear about doing what you say you'll do, start with saying very little—that is, agreeing to very little—then be sure to do that little bit you do agree to. You'll have a golden track record in no time.

Differentiate, *explicitly*, between an agreement or promise and a statement of likelihood or speculation. If you're not committing, use clear language like "Maybe I will, maybe I won't" or "Sounds good now, but I'll go with what feels right when the time comes." Especially if you know you've got work to do on this keep-your-word thing: start by speaking words that clearly promise nothing. When you say yes to something— "I'll help you move," "I'll come to the party," "I'll mind the no-fracking table and field questions for an hour"—do it consciously: make sure it actually fits into your life and schedule; record it in your calendar; take care early on of any preliminaries, such as sign-ups, registration, advance ticket purchases, coordinating rides, preparation of clothing or food you'll need—anything that could make a liar of you if you leave it till the last minute.

When you don't mean a firm *yes*, be clear that you're not giving one. Let me take the three examples above in reverse order and elaborate. Tabling for anti-fracking work: "That's the kind of thing I feel good about doing but I'm not sure I'll be up for it that day. When's the latest you need a firm answer?" Going to the party: "I like the sound of it now but I'm not always in the mood for socializing when the moment actually comes. I may show up and I may not—do you want advance notice?" Helping someone move: "My impulse tends to be *yes* when people want help moving—good karma, right? But life's been overfull lately and I'd like to play it by ear. Why don't you text me on moving day if you still need another body and I'll come over if that works for me then."

Some people are horrified to give such honest and open-ended answers. If that's you, ask yourself, *How could it be horrifying to speak the truth?* Consider that it might be much worse for all involved (including you!), to say you'll be there then flake out. It could be worse (much worse) to make a day of suffering out of it, first finding yourself dreading to go and later hating being there. Who benefits from false commitments, unnecessary pressure, or resentful, half-assed participation?

One thing I've learned from Byron Katie and take care to apply in my personal life is that when you do something you don't want to do out of some impulse to be kind to others, you end up being most unkind to yourself and, somewhere down the line, probably not that kind to them. Some break-the-straw moment may even trigger you to totally unload all your frustration and resentment on someone who simply asked you for something you could have said no to. (Ay, have you seen yourself do this? Doesn't it feel rotten?)

Don't agree to anything vague, ever (another power zapper). There's little I find more tiresome than "Let's get together sometime" or "We should have coffee." Either make a date or don't, but if someone throws you a vague line for a rendez-vous you don't want to make, I recommend you firmly refuse to bite. I like to say things like, "I'm not making many coffee dates these days" or "It doesn't work for me to make vague dates, and right now is not a good time to set something up." Try anything that's true and doesn't put it on something external or beyond your control. For example, I'd opt for "I'm giving most of my time to work and my kids right now" (here, you're making choices) over "I don't have time" (here, you're a victim of that great bugaboo, Time). You can even just watch them do the let's-have-coffee dance and say nothing instead of pretending to agree. The power and art of looking at someone in plain face is covered in the chapter on eye-gazing in this section.

So what about when you've made a commitment it turns out you can't keep—or, if you don't have this whole thing down yet, what if you said you'd be there without absolute clarity about your commitment level? There has to be room for renegotiation in life. The unexpected happens, and there really are things beyond your control. There are also times when self-care or some occurrence in another realm of life truly makes it a better idea to renegotiate than to push a mountain upstream to keep your word. What you thought would work when you made the plan honestly doesn't work when the moment comes. I've seen people put their health in jeopardy by following through when canceling just plain made sense. Don't make a religion of keeping commitments. Do renegotiate clearly.

The rule (if you will) for clean negotiation is simple: Let them know as soon as you know. That is, once you know you need to change a plan, let all involved know as soon as you can possibly communicate with them. I've noticed people especially fail to do this when they feel bad about renegotiating—thus making things worse. If you're concerned others won't be happy about the change, please do notice that the impact on them tends to intensify as the time draws nearer and nearer. Letting them know as soon as you know allows for best-case scenario on their end even as they manage inconvenience or disappointment: they're more likely to find replacements, come up with plan B, or regroup however they need to. Obviously, if you can help with any of those things, go for it! But this is by no means a requirement. Again, there has to be room for renegotiation on the planet, and people (you're people, too) have a right to change their minds.

Note that if you're renegotiating too often, you've just stepped into another version of not keeping your word: you're back to being unreliable. If it comes to your notice that this is happening, pause to consider what's up. Are you saying yes when you don't really mean it? Are you trying to do too much—that is, are you being unrealistic about how much energy you've got, or how much you can cram into the hours of a day? Are you answering in the moment of being asked from a place of pleasing others rather than giving the right answer for you? Have you lost track of what you're up to and what your priorities are? (In the chapter "Line It Up" in part 4, we'll look at the importance of choosing into your vision, which asks you to let go of even wonderful opportunities that take you in the wrong direction and squander resources you could put to that vision.) See if you can locate what's going on and set an intention to correct it.

Let me repeat that a great way to work on keeping your word is to simply agree to less.

The last thing I want to say about renegotiation is that it's good to renegotiate consciously with yourself too. We're so casual about breaking our dates with ourselves and dropping our promises with no more than a bad feeling we shove down. (Quit swatting the fruit flies!) Instead, bring it close, and look at what you're not doing that you said you'd do. Make it a conscious choice to do something else (*I'd honestly benefit more from a bubble bath tonight than a trip to the gym*). Then make a new plan, write a new date on the calendar, hold on to the original intention in whatever way makes sense—or clearly decide and declare you won't be doing this and firmly shut the door.

Nobody's watching these transactions, so you won't get gold stars or satisfied customers or anything else from the outside. (Actually, my client

Molly gets gold stars because she gives them to herself on a chart she made to track these agreements with herself!) You will, however, come to know yourself as trustworthy, and this will increase your power to create and possibly cause you to hold your head high and whistle while you work. Watch the impact on your self-trust and your sense of personal power: as you get increasingly good at keeping your word, even to yourself, I predict the change just won't be that subtle.

Do I need to admonish you not to slow down your progress by beating yourself up when you catch yourself either failing to keep your word or renegotiating too often? I hope not. Just keep course-correcting toward honoring the power of your word; course-correct toward telling the truth. If you don't do what you say you're going to do, you make a liar of yourself, and you erode self-trust. It feels better and it's more powerful: do what you say you're going to do.

chapter 27

Yes or No: Be Someone Who Gives the Right Answer

One thing people sometimes need spelled out for them—especially if they grew up in a household with bad boundaries (that's most people in my generation, with fewer but plenty in the next)—is that *yes* and *no* are ways to create boundaries. It's a boundary issue not to be able to say no; it's a boundary issue to give the wrong answer. When you say yes when you mean no—when, for you, the right answer is no (and boundaries are entirely subjective and personal)—then you let people in where you don't want them, you let them cross lines that you need drawn. You abandon yourself. Self-honoring means declaring and holding your own boundaries. Self-honoring means saying yes when you mean yes, and no when you mean no.

If a professor were to give a yes/no test, as opposed to true/false or multiple choice, would it be a valid test if the right answer were always yes? That test wouldn't measure a thing. It would be a waste of time and a drag. See the students dashing through filling in *yes* answers before getting the hell out to smoke something fragrant or down a few beers, even if they don't normally smoke or drink. A valid yes/no test would need to alternate *yes* and *no* answers in random patterns.

Think of life as such a test, because it is: sometimes the right answer is yes, and sometimes it's no. Weirdly, though—in American culture, at least—people have come to believe that *yes* is the right answer. *Yes* is nice. *Yes* feels good. *Yes* doesn't hurt anyone's feelings. *Yes* means you're cooperative, you're a team player. *Yes* is desirable. None of this is true, but it's how people tend to conceive it, often quite unconsciously.

Conversely, *no* is mean, uncooperative, selfish. *No* is a rejection. *No* is negative (duh). It's rude, sometimes cruel. *No* isn't nice to say and just plain makes people feel bad. It's a bad idea to say no, or to say it too often. None of that is true either, but these concepts are deeply ingrained.

Could we please start over? Let's give equal weight to *yes* and *no*, because, in truth, they weigh the same. (An Indian swami named Baba

Muktananda spoke of praise and blame as weighing the same. I want to shamelessly appropriate this here for *yes* and *no*.) The fact is, sometimes the right answer is yes, and sometimes it's no. Do you want to be someone who says yes, or someone who gives the right answer? Another way to say this is, Do you want to tell the truth? (Reminder: you have more personal power when you do.)

It's fascinating all that could keep a *yes* default in place, and while the motivators may vary, they really don't get that unique. Some people say yes automatically if they're asked for help, especially if asked in a pitiful way or in a way that implies they're the only solution (not likely to be true) or even the best solution (also suspect). Others give an instant *yes* if they're asked to do something with prestige all over it or if they're made to feel special for being asked. Some cough up a reflexive *yes* for a community effort or a cause that they love. *Yes*, for others, might be attached to specific people; sometimes it's specific to those someone loves or wants love from, so that *yes* ultimately serves to get or keep love. Another popular *yes* producer is the impulse not to hurt feelings, not to make others feel bad. A *yes* default may be unconsciously linked to security—thus applied to any requests at work, reasonable or not; applied where physical or emotional safety seem at stake; applied when the good opinion of the tribe appears to be threatened. You may want to identify your motivators for *yes yes yes yes yes*.

It's useful (supremely useful) to begin with understanding what *no* means to you. I learned from Byron Katie to tease that out by making a list. If they say no to me, what are they thinking about me? What are they really saying? An example follows.

- She doesn't like me.
- I asked for too much.
- I'm a burden.
- She doesn't value my contribution.
- She thinks I'm a pain.
- I can't find the support I need.
- She doesn't see me.
- No one sees me.
- She's rejecting me.
- I'm a loser.

If *no* feels this loaded on the receiving end, how could speaking it to others come easy? Given that list, I'm now doling out the following messages anytime I tell someone no:

- I don't like you.
- You asked for too much.
- You're a burden.
- I don't value your contribution.
- I think you're a pain.
- You can't find the support you need.
- I don't see you.
- No one sees you.
- I'm rejecting you.
- You're a loser.

Wow, who wants to deliver all that? An instant (dishonest) *yes* looks lovely by comparison.

I use this idea in my power workshop by having one participant (A) ask another (B) for a favor. The question isn't random, because first B comes up with something that someone might actually ask her (or recently asked her) that she would find (or found) it hard to say no to. Let's say the person is asking if she can join a committee that B's in charge of. A asks the same question repeatedly, while B keeps saying no, using her own list to embellish each *no*. "Could I join this committee?" "No, I don't like you." "Could I join this committee?" "No, I think you're a pain." "Could I join this committee?" "No, no one sees you." The exercise makes people laugh, while also making glaringly apparent why *no* isn't easy to say with all the attached subtext—usually hidden and here called out.

Let's get clearer than clear: in actuality, *no* delivers none of that. None of it! You simply unconsciously feel like that's what it means to give a *no* if that's what it means to you when you receive one. Clear enough, then, why you can't say no? Why you feel terrible when you say no? Why you go back on your *no* when you've said it? Why you have to agonize to get to *no* and offer a bunch of rationales for that answer? Why you can strive to say it once or twice then short-circuit on the third asking so the yes/no switch snaps back to *yes*? I like to help clients notice what I call their false quotas. It's okay for you to say no how many times until a *yes* is required

199

next? (Let me emphasize the *false* part of *false quota*.)

If *no* meant only *no* (that's all it actually does mean), you wouldn't even have to deliberate most of the time. You'd really just need to check in for the truth: what's the right answer here? You have inner signals that are capable of giving you an instant *yes* or *no* for most of what comes up in day-to-day life, and for those larger-ticket items too—certainly in emergencies. Honestly, people who decide to divorce after months or years of going over the facts and swirling around in eddies of pointless guilt almost always knew for some time that the answer to *Do I still want to be with this person?* was no.

Mona: Give your children a powerful no *(they'll need it later)*

My client Mona came to me because of a messy family problem I won't describe here. As we looked at her parenting style, we found that she had a very hard time saying no to her two sons. She just didn't like telling them no. She liked being a nondictatorial parent; she liked listening to her boys and hearing what they wanted and cared about; she liked giving them choices and letting them help make decisions that affected them— all beautiful values. Somehow it felt to her that saying no violated—even somehow negated—those great parenting values.

The result was that her children, smart little creatures, didn't believe her *no*. They didn't accept it when they heard it. They ignored it, whined about it, went into wheeling and dealing, threw tantrums, dug in their heels, and even, in the extreme, got violent. Mona responded in a classic way most parents respond: she relented and gave them what they wanted.

Thus, Mona kept effectively teaching her sons not to believe her. She taught them that they couldn't trust her *no*. And what wasn't necessarily apparent yet—but this inevitably manifests down the line—is that she taught them not to respect anyone's *no*. She even taught them that their own *no* had no meaning or value. Seriously: parents seldom realize that with their own flimsy hold on the word *no*, they take away access to *no* from their children, keeping them from ease in either giving or receiving it. Just to get through adolescence, never mind life, kids must have access to *no*. They need to hear it and accept it; they need to say it and hold it.

This pattern created a lot of unhappiness for Mona's whole family. As soon as I talked to her about the importance of being friends with *no* and holding her *no*, she began to be very careful about when she said no to her boys. And when she did, she held the *no*. She also learned, through her self-observations and our explorations, that she felt compelled to explain and justify any *no* she gave them. This is an important point, and a common thing people do in all kinds of relationships.

Mona realized that this explaining thing was instantly taken as hedging by her children. It sure didn't make the *no* more solid. Instead, it led them to talk her reasons down. Sometimes she found she over-explained or got confused, especially when she didn't know why she was saying no—but felt a strong *no* nonetheless—it was the right answer! We looked at the idea that she didn't owe her kids explanations for *no*.

Mona began to interrupt herself when she started explaining a *no*. She opted to just hold it instead. (Repetition of just-plain-no is no problem—notice how many times kids will freely repeat themselves in their efforts to get what they want!) Not only did dropping explanations very quickly translate to greater peace with her children, but she felt so much more serene within herself knowing that she didn't have to explain it to herself. She could figure out the whys and wherefores later, if she felt like it. (This was a huge revelation for me personally at the School for The Work: I saw that I didn't owe myself explanations for any *no* that came up without good reasons attached—and knowing I didn't have to fabricate reasons for myself liberated me from a false obligation to provide them for others.)

As her experiments progressed, those boys listened to Mona more and more. She was laughing with amazement the day she recounted a shopping moment when one son said to the other (as she walked away from them), "Didn't you hear what she said? She said, *Stay right here.*"

It's crazy how often being nice is the motivator for not saying no. It's somehow not nice to say no, to disappoint people, to refuse them what they want. (Being seen as nice was a high motivator for Mona.) What happens then is that things don't go so well because you said yes when the right answer was no. You end up frustrated, resentful, or experiencing events in the outer world that were the very things you were trying to avoid when the *no* came up from inside. For example, let's say you want to say no to one more round of a game because it's important to you to get to an appointment on time. But it's the culminating round of a game your kids love and you talk yourself out of your *no*—it would just feel so mean to say it. Then, down the line, you end up scrambling to get out the door, and when someone notices he's barefoot and has to run back in for shoes, you lose it and end up screaming, lecturing, blaming—upsetting everybody and entirely corroding your own inner peace. Wouldn't it have been kinder (and even nicer) to just interrupt the game? In the long run, you're often much meaner with a false *yes* than with a kind and solid *no*. It's even worse when you don't take responsibility for the mess by acknowledging you failed to say no. (You make it about what they did that caused the problem.) That's definitely not nice.

I suggest dropping *nice* altogether. Don't aspire to *nice*—you may end up being most unkind, perhaps especially to yourself. If you'd like to be kind—a lovely thing to aspire to—then be someone who gives the right answer. Say yes when it's yes, and no when it's no.

Finally, in the interest of scooching, you may catch yourself giving or having given the wrong answer after you've set the intention to give the right ones. In that case, you've basically got two options: correct it, or follow through with what you said.

Correcting it involves speaking again, telling the truth this time. Renegotiate, or simply assert what's right for you. Speak it directly and simply, as in, "I changed my mind" or "I misspoke" or "I answered too quickly and now I see that I gave the wrong answer." Feel free to apologize if you think that's warranted, but that means apologize once—and then it's over. Feel free to offer compensation if (and only if) that's appropriate, and then hold the right answer unapologetically and without worrying that you need to keep offering more to make up for your temporary loss of clarity.

Following through means you're getting 100 percent behind your choice (the answer you already gave). Resolve to carry it out in this situation, here and now, noting what you'll do differently next time and, if it's appropriate, communicate clearly about this with the other parties involved.

Please be kind to yourself and be clear that if your wrong answer violates a boundary that you really need to hold for yourself, you'll do best to pick door number 1 and correct the wrong answer. It's okay if that bothers someone else; you'll be bothered if you don't properly take care of and honor yourself.

Be conscious and strong in both how you use *yes* and *no* and how you respond to them. Like it or not, intend it or not, *yes* and *no* are constantly being used to draw, uphold, and violate boundaries: use them wisely, truthfully.

chapter 28

Eye-gazing, Personality, Possibility

While eye-gazing can be a formal practice with a meditative quality and powerful results, it can also be a way to connect with others during normal, brief, everyday encounters with personality and manipulations set aside. Using it the second way constitutes both an ongoing spiritual practice and an effective way to live in personal power.

Eye-gazing, as the name implies, involves simply looking into the eyes of another human being (cats are really good at this too—hey, try it with anybeast willing to gaze back). When I have people practice eye-gazing in workshops (and I do this a lot, because I love it, and they often come to love it) (I've done it with the womyn in the woods of Michigan), the single most important instruction I offer is to gaze with plain face. There's no need to suppress anything that comes up—sometimes a smile just takes you or you burst out laughing or crying—but the idea is to let any facial expressions melt back into plain face as quickly as they arise.

Plain face, in part, allows you to drop personality and just connect at the soul level, that place where we're all one and no detail of similarity or difference matters in the least. I'm not against personality. In fact, it's one of my great fascinations. I was musing about what the different types on the Enneagram might be up to (habitually, unconsciously) when they make eye contact, and this led to me to create a word caricature of each of the nine types in action. Check them out:

Type #1 (The Reformer): I've just shoved down how much I disapprove of myself today, so I can't help but notice that something's off about you.

Type #2 (The Helper): In one glance I'm going to make sure you feel special and know how important you are to me. (That makes me important to you, right?)

Type #3 (The Achiever): This is the face of success—you noticed right off, didn't you?

205

Type #4 (The Individualist): I'm really not in the mood for this right now, but let me look at you soulfully so you know how much I mean it when I meet your eyes. (I've already started agonizing over the lapse in authenticity.)

Type #5 (The Investigator): I'm watching you closely without seeming to and, we'll see, I might use it to make myself feel out of it or I might breathe thanks that I'm not part of your club.

Type #6 (The Loyalist): There's a small herd of butter-elephant-flies rampaging through my gut right now and it reassures me to remember that you and I have the same politics.

Type #7 (The Enthusiast): I have this disarming way of looking at people that conveys I'm amused and amusing and I'm using it now because I need a cup of java in the worst way and there's nothing funny about how substandard this so-called French Roast is.

Type #8 (The Challenger): Whether I flash a smile, give a wink, or withhold all but a tiny lift of an eyebrow, I've already alpha-ed you before even glancing your way.

Type #9 (The Peacemaker): Oh, absolutely, let's connect—but I only have so much energy for that and I'm going to get worried and start to disconnect internally if it looks like you're not sending energy my way too.

Aw, aren't they all adorable? But what happens if we drop personality altogether? Because one marvelous possibility in the whole rich and complex arena of personality is to put it all down and simply connect. Don't know how? Keep reading.

Another thing plain face allows is the absence of manipulation—what else is personality up to? (Please note that I'm not saying all manipulation is inherently bad. We're all just trying to get our needs met, whether we need to or not.) It's so useful to notice how putting anything on the face constitutes manipulation. It can actually be frightening to us human beings, or discomfiting at the very least, to just look at others without organizing ourselves around some facial structure to either communicate or hide something—often both at once:

- *I'm doing this thing with my cheeks and mouth and eyes because I want you to like me, or I want you to think I like you.*
- *I'm reassuring you, me, both of us, neither—because something here doesn't feel right.*
- *I live in the U.S. so I think I'm supposed to smile all the time, I think smiling is good and not smiling is bad, and maybe you'll think I'm not nice if I don't.*
- *I'm uncomfortable because we had that awkward moment at the picnic table—remember? I do, obsessively.*
- *I'm actually not here because I've jumped ahead to what my boss will say about that slapdash report—this smile is my stand-in.*
- *I'm super attracted to you and can't figure out if you're attracted to me, which throws me off but I don't want you to know I'm thrown off, so I'm now willing my face, body, and clothing to strike that sweet spot between sexy-and-aloof and welcoming-girl-next-door.*
- *I'm out of sorts and don't wish to be seen right now—my face is a mask and my enthusiasm about you is a decoy.*
- *I've got this little bruise under one rib from yelling at my kid earlier and somehow stopping to really look at you is like pressing hard right where it's tender—my defense is to act way more rushed than I actually am because I cannot get away from you fast enough.*

All of that is just human. If you're happy to be caught up in any such feelings and thoughts, defenses and manipulations, there's really no problem and nothing to correct. If, however, you'd like to (even sometimes) make your movement through the world a sort of walking meditation; if you'd like to connect with the people you meet beyond personality (or simply meet consciousness in other sentient beings—same thing), then you might want to try eye-gazing.

As a formal practice, you sit or stand across from another willing eye-gazer, and gaze for a set amount of time (could be 2 minutes, half an hour—whatever you're up for) or for an open period to be ended by either party at any time. To bring it into your daily world, simply go about your business sometimes conscious of meeting eyes in this way, if only for a few seconds or even a fraction of one. Please (please) note that I'm not proposing inappropriate staring or boring a hole in someone's face. (If someone gets uncomfortable, you've gone too far!) I mean that during select moments, you connect with eyes conscious of connecting with eyes. In those moments, be only consciousness meeting consciousness, seeking to force, convey, or manipulate nothing. For those moments, drop personality.

The best way to drop personality, externally, is with plain face. Internally, you can witness what comes up for you without judgment and just leave it alone—since nonjudgmental witnessing also means there's no need to shove anything down, adjust it, or feel bad about it. Then, just as you keep coming back to the breath or a mantra in sitting meditation, you can seek to keep bringing your focus back to simply meeting another set of eyes to connect to the mirror-soul gazing back.

I learned from Byron Katie the crazy-brilliant concept of not taking your own thoughts personally. You just don't have to identify with the stuff that streams through the mind as predictably as oxygen streams through air. Just let it go by, along with your impulses to make any impressions on (to manipulate) other people with your smiles and other facial expressions. Look into eyes with plain face while witnessing the mind, and move on. Without all the pretending and posturing, you'll feel closer to others and to yourself.

When the morning routine with my son feels like a crisscrossing through the house navigating bathroom/kitchen stairs/refrigerator doors/ toaster oven/reminders/and where-did-that-thing-get-to?—I stop him in the moment of parting with a single word: "Eyes." He's such a good sport. He pauses and turns my way with his beautiful, clear, miraculous blue eyes. Something palpable (visible?) happens in this dropping in, a moment of finding each other. Sometimes his face relaxes, or a little smile plays across his whole demeanor, or some small anxiety prevails and I tune in to that and give back whatever connection and calm I can convey.

Should I even bother spelling out the application to couple life? Okay, let me put it in terms of choice. It's a choice to allow ourselves to play the ships-passing-in-the-night game day in and day out, or to stop and remember who the other is, who we are together, all that's still possible that we haven't even gotten to. It's a choice to think in terms of "I know all about you" (or worse, "Oh, you again") versus "I'm still discovering you right here, right now, and I must pause to savor this moment of discovery." But even beyond all that, there's the fact I'm a soul and you're a soul and we can provide each other the marvelous service of holding up a plain mirror to reflect that—to remember that—a spacious mirror that holds acceptance, unconditional love, forgiveness for everything, openness to anything.

If you play with eye-gazing out in the world, you might find that things feel a lot easier, because you're just connecting—not striving in any way, not manipulating, not putting anything on. You also maintain a better connection with yourself because your energies aren't all dispersed and externalized. What could come up for you that's potentially unpleasant (initially) is being stripped of your masks. You may feel discomfort in bypassing your default settings for how to behave out in the world, how to meet and greet people—and these things are in place to give you the safety and familiarity of a set identity. (That doesn't mean you actually need them there.)

Why bother to step out of this known territory? Well, it's like any movement out of the comfort zone. It will grow you in marvelous, unexpected ways. It will open to you a realm of experience you haven't tasted yet. It will show you what else is possible, and this will affect you in every part of your life.

If you play with eye-gazing as a formal practice, you may witness any amount of awkwardness moving through your mind and body, and you may (initially) hate watching the workings of your own mind as it worries about what the other thinks of you, or catches things you think of them that you don't want to think, or wanders off to make grocery lists because there's such solace in the mundane. You may find that you feel like you're staring weirdly or hyper-intensely. I once had a nature-guide type (Susan Rausch of Camp Earth Connection) come to one of my retreats to teach the participants new ways to move through the physical world, and she directed us to beware of tunnel vision and seek to include awareness of our periphery as we visually took in our surroundings. This felt revolutionary to me! As a group, we later included tuning in to peripheral vision during eye-gazing. We found that doing this relaxed the whole thing, as it allowed for a softer meeting of the eyes instead of a locking together.

As in any meditative practice, it helps to give some attention to your breath in order to anchor yourself in your own body. During a workshop last summer, I spoke aloud while participants were eye-gazing: "If you're not aware of your own breath right now, you're way too involved with the other person." These words came back to me on the feedback form because people were struck by the truth of this, and by the effectiveness— the support—of moving back to the breath. Honestly, if you have no interest in touching this eye-gazing stuff, you could take that one piece and benefit hugely from this reading: go about your business with some of your focus constantly coming back to the breath.

I don't seem to tire of the topic of *now*—I'm pretty sure it's the last word in spiritual growth, in cultivating a sense of wonder, even in living the good life. Eye-gazing brings you squarely into *now*. It's a pause. You can enter it fully, land in it, know that for that moment all of the Universe lands with you. In that moment, it really doesn't matter who you are, who carries the other set of eyes, what's in the past, what's in the future: right now, pure consciousness.

Could eye-gazing change your life or your experience of who you are? Could spending even 30 seconds a day in this practice with your significant other make a difference? I'd bet my bottom dollar on it. If you're curious, check it out for yourself. Play with it. Experiment (make it a grand one). I find that eye-gazing often yields some gorgeously surprising results, but here are the standards you can pretty much count on:

- It opens the way for moments of authentic connection with any sentient being.
- It trains you to drop manipulations in interactions with others.
- It allows you to create deeper intimacy with loved ones.
- It deepens your connection with yourself.
- It promotes a pure experience of *now*.

So much is possible. So what's not to love?

chapter 29

Power Zappers

I came up with the power zappers when I first put together my Personal Power Surge workshop for the womyn in the Michigan woods. It was a way to lay out the typical things that take or keep us out of our personal power, sometimes on a daily basis. You'll recognize yourself somewhere in here. I invite you to read through them with open curiosity—rather than, say, fear and loathing, or any propensity toward judgment. Notice the ones that aren't issues for you—or not much—and those that still apply more than you'd like or even that exist for you as primary defaults. If you're struck by how many of the power zappers you fall prey to, do not be alarmed, and don't despair.

Awareness is the first step in your readiness to clear them: as soon as they're in view, you're on it. So if you're ready to scooch into your power, please don't slow down your process by being horrified by what you do or by believing it's not okay. Of course it's okay: these are things people do. Once again, welcome yourself to the human race.

For each power-zapping tendency, there's a new intention or affirmation given. This provides language to help you connect to the new way, or to a clear intention to counter any power zapper you find in yourself (or, more accurate, in your habitual behavior). You know the drill: catch yourself in the unwanted behavior (celebrate!), then simply course-correct. Do that in the moment if you can, or go back later and, in a neutral way (no judgment), consider how you might have done it differently. This will support you in doing it differently next time and in catching yourself earlier in the process. Please tweak the wording of the affirmations as needed or come up with your own: the language should feel relevant and good to you. I invite you to actually make use of these, especially in the moment you catch yourself in the old way.

Personal power involves taking responsibility for yourself—your thoughts, feelings, and behavior. You'll have more of it when you're self-referential. Connected to yourself, you'll connect to others. Thinking highly of yourself (being in good standing with yourself), you won't go into wacky contortions to be or do what others want from you. You'll speak freely what's true for you in a way that's clear, direct, and honest. You won't need to pretend or hide or in any way make yourself small. You won't reveal that you secretly believe there's something wrong with you, because you won't secretly believe that, or you'll come very close to it when any trace of such a thought bubbles up to your compassionate, dispassionate awareness.

The power zappers in themselves constitute a recap of all we've looked at so far, and then some. Here they are:

Unclear agreements
- Don't just assume they're thinking what you're thinking: *We'll meet where we met last time. "Some gardening" in trade means a couple of hours a week.*
- Don't leave out uncomfortable details, like dollar amounts, time boundaries, what you are and aren't willing to do. Step into any discomfort or awkwardness and discuss these things up front—it'll be more awkward later.
- New intention/affirmation: *I make clear agreements.*

Vague plans
- Not making a clear date with someone or a clear plan to make a date: "Let's get together sometime" or "We should have coffee," as opposed to "Would you like to have coffee sometime? Noon to two is good for me on most days—what about you?" Or, "I'll text you next Monday morning to set something up" (then text on Monday morning!).
- Agreeing when the other dangles a vague line. Better to say nothing or to counter their hazy words with clarity: "I don't seem to be scheduling much time these days for those coffee dates"—or whatever you've got that's true and direct and kind (i.e., not about something wrong with them).
- Being vague about details, such as time and place to meet, who will be there, cost, who's buying.
- Being vague about whether it's a date (the romantic kind) or not. Note this is no problem if you're curious and open and simply watching to see what's revealed. If you're stressed or feel awkward, ask if it's a date,

212

or say what you think it is, or make a playful comment about the ambiguity—get it out into the open, however you see to do that.

- New intention/affirmation: *I make clear plans with others or say no to a plan I don't want to make.*

Not keeping your word
- Forgetting you said you would or wouldn't do something.
- Changing your mind without proper renegotiation.
- Continuing to tell others or yourself that you'll do what you never do.
- New intention/affirmation: *I keep my word. I do what I say I'm going to do. My word is golden.*

Unnecessary explanations/Overexplaining
- Too much information or explanations that go too long or aren't solid (expressed with giggles, funny faces, or tones that imply you're a total flake).
- Using explanations to excuse or justify, to protect other people's feelings, to make sure they get you or don't disapprove of you.
- New intention/affirmation: *I explain only when necessary, only as much as is necessary. I choose how much I explain.*

Useless or ongoing apologies
- These boil down to apologizing for taking up space or for simply existing. Apologize once, make amends if needed, and then be done with it. Work out between you and you or with a neutral helper any discomfort remaining.
- A good apology goes like this:
  - It's specific about what you did ("I'm sorry I used the word *hysterical*; that was disrespectful and inaccurate").
  - It doesn't include the word *if* (Don't say, "I'm sorry if I hurt you").
  - It asks "How can I make it right?" or offers something specific in compensation.
- Any form of groveling is a sure sign you need to get clear with yourself before you take the conversation any further with another.
- New intention/affirmation: *I know when and how much to apologize. I know when and how to make amends.*

Fake laughter
- See if you can (kindly) catch yourself laughing for any reason other than thinking something is funny or absurd.
- Seek to identify typical discomforts that make you fake-laugh, and be still with those discomforts without putting sounds or more words or gestures to them. Examples of fake-laugh triggers include:
  - fearing you've said too much or said the wrong thing
  - wanting not to sound like you were complaining
  - feeling off about what you just said and worrying they'll think ill of you or disapprove
- New intention/affirmation: *I laugh freely when genuine laughter grabs me. I'm willing to kindly contain my discomforts and soothe myself.*

Forced smiles
- A Canadian woman at one of my workshops once told me that sociology textbooks talk about the "American smile" to denote any forced smiling that begins with the mouth—as true smiles are sourced in the eyes.
- Any smile is forced whose job is to manipulate how others see you (*I'm happy, I'm sweet, I've got it together*).
- Watch for smiles seeking to take care of others, to make sure they know you like them or see them in a certain way.
- New intention/affirmation: *I smile effortlessly, when genuine smiling grabs me.*

Self-deprecation
- Note that self-deprecation in your head is just as depleting and demeaning to you as the spoken version.
- There may be times when playful self-deprecation is okay—say, once a year, and when it's not mean. I remember once when I was among a small group of staff talking about oxymorons, and a coworker walking by—a tall, lumbering type—cheerfully threw in, "I feel like an oxymoron most of the time." We all knew he wasn't an idiot and didn't see himself that way, and it was just funny.
- New intention/affirmation: *I think and speak well of myself.*

Projected self-deprecation

- Telling others what they're thinking about you or what they think is wrong with you. They may or may not be thinking this; the point of a projection is that you're the one thinking it, and you're putting it on them:
    - "You must think my reaction's way over the top."
    - "You're going, 'Get me away from this lunatic.'"
    - "You think this idea's a crock of shit, don't you?"
- You may simply ask a direct question that allows another to tell you their thought, thus to speak for themselves.
    - "Do you think I'm overreacting?"
    - "Does that sound crazy?"
    - "What do you think of this idea? Is there a chance it'll work?"
- You may want to express the discomfort that's up for you (thus making your process transparent). In this way, you speak your own self-criticism, clearly making it yours:
    - "Ay, part of me thinks I'm overreacting and part of me thinks I'm totally justified in having a small fit right now."
    - "I'm hearing myself rant and I sound like a lunatic."
    - "I just got uncomfortable telling you this idea. I know it's kind of radical."
- You can combine the two above, expressing your own thought and discomfort, then asking, "What do you think?" or "Will you give me a reality check?"
- New intention/affirmation: I ask others what they think when I'm imagining or wondering about their thoughts. I stay out of their heads or choose to imagine they're thinking benign thoughts.

Presenting as broken

- How much do you identify with—and make sure others know about —the bad things that have happened to you or how broken you are? Stop telling about the time your attorney absconded to Mexico with your retainer and your ex.
- This is an especially bad idea at the beginning of a romantic relationship. You're not in your power if you think someone needs to know your harsh lot in life to fall in love with you. I once had a conversation with a strong woman I know during a difficult passage for her. When

215

we got to the topic of being single, she said she wasn't even thinking about finding someone in her current state. She wasn't opposed to feeling weak and vulnerable, but she was clear that the dynamic she wanted to be in with a lover wasn't about a rescuer swooping in to her damsel in distress. Further, this isn't the way she goes through life, so she knew she'd find the right partner—who would get her and support her at her best—if she started something new only from a place of feeling strong and solid with herself.

- New intention/affirmation: I present myself as powerful and whole. I connect with others through my strength and beauty.

Weak, troubled greetings

- On a smaller scale than the above, in daily chitchat, don't let people know in first greeting or small talk that your back hurts, you got a bad night's sleep, your spouse is mad at you again. Just say hello warmly, and process your problems in times set aside for that.
- You might redefine greetings to be about acknowledging another human being with the intention of welcoming them, meeting their face as the face of God, appreciating that you share (or being willing to share) space with them on the planet. I got much more comfortable with the question "How are you?" when I realized I didn't actually need to answer it; nor did I need to feel annoyed that, obviously, the one asking didn't really want to know. Now I just treat it like the American version of Namaste, and there's no stress around it.
- New intention/affirmation: I greet others freely and joyfully, honoring that we are one. [If you'd rather greet warmly, or peacefully, or with presence, go with that! Make any of these affirmations all yours.]

(Mindless) focus on what's hard or negative

- This could include any number of popular tiresome topics, like weather, money, the economy, traffic, politics, the day of the week, the way people or certain types of people are, and so on.
- Notice when you make comments or have conversations in this vein because you think you need to fill in a silence (not worth it—get comfortable with the discomfort of silence instead; try eye-gazing; watch your breath).

- Beware of using negativity as a way to connect:
  - you don't need to force a connection;
  - know you're already connected;
  - set an intention for solid and good connection and open to the moments to step into that.
- Notice if you're using absolute language that implies it can't be helped or we all agree. "Of course, I had to finish it over the weekend"; "I'm always doing more than I can actually accomplish—aren't we all?"
- New intention/affirmation: I live with effortlessness and ease. I look for all that supports me. I am in the flow.

Compulsory answering
- Answering a question just because it was asked. I've said this in direct terms to my children any number of times: "You don't have to answer a question just because someone asked it."
- Responding to a comment just to comment back. Silence is fine and in no way needs to be hostile. (Remember eye-gazing!)
- Unconsciously giving information you don't even want to give. (Where do you live? What income bracket are you in? What do you think of the new boss?)
- New intention/affirmation: I speak when it feels right for me to speak.

Puffing yourself up
- Overstating your skills, talents, accomplishments, or strong points.
- Under this is the fear you're not enough as you are. Remind yourself it's okay not to be everything or the best of the best.
- New intention/affirmation: I am not less than others, I am not greater than others. How I find myself to be right now is perfect—or perfectly acceptable for right now.

Seeking validation
- "Is this okay?" "Am I okay?" "Am I doing okay?" "How'd I do?" "How am I doing?"
- The subtext here is, *Do I have the right to think/feel/do this?* or *Should I be ashamed of myself?*
- New intention/affirmation: I am in good standing with myself. I have my own approval.

Wrongful responsibility

- Taking responsibility for what's not yours or for an entire situation that you couldn't have created all by yourself. "It's all my fault." "No, it was me."
- New intention/affirmation: I take full responsibility for what's mine.

Overstated gratitude

- Underlying this is the idea you don't deserve what was given, you're a burden, or you won't get your needs met if you aren't properly (overly) grateful.
- Too much thanking can take various forms, including going on and on in the moment, continually bringing it up at other times, or sending unnecessary follow-up notes, e-mails, texts, or even gifts. (If thanking feels depleting, you're overthanking!)
- Feeling and expressing being beholden to another. Instead, receive what's been given fully (this is an event between you and you), then carry on with no awkward invisible string between you and another. If you need to imagine cutting a tie between you and someone you feel indebted to, by all means, do that. If you believe someone gave to you with strings attached, have a conversation about that to clear the slate between you completely or to make a new clear agreement that makes explicit anything either of you still owes the other.
- New intention/affirmation: I express appropriate gratitude and feel it fully. I am nourished by my genuine appreciation.

Yes *as default*

- You've probably got a *yes* default in place if you don't check in with yourself before agreeing to things.
- You've definitely got a *yes* default in place if you say yes when you know or suspect you mean no.
- New intention/affirmation: I follow my true *yes* or *no*. I check in with myself before I say yes. I am someone who gives the right answer.

Being the seen, not the see-er

- Worrying about how others perceive you instead of having your own experience.

- Are you the subject or the object in your life? Are you the hero of your journey?
- New intention/affirmation: I am the see-er, not the seen. I am the subject of my life. I live with curiosity, connected to my senses, having my own experience.

Comparing yourself to others
- Such comparisons are usually focused on how you're lacking or less than, but it serves you no better to look for how you're superior.
- Live instead out of a personal-best model, in which you're only ever topping your own best past score.
- New intention/affirmation: I keep stepping into the next best version of myself. I release others to their lives, and I release myself to mine. (If you're thinking of a specific human being, use their name or the right pronoun for that one, as in, *I release her to her life, and I release myself to mine.*)

Being bored and checked-out
- Take agency for where you are, what you're doing, and how much you get out of it.
- If you don't want to be present, do you need to make a new choice? If you don't think you have choice, are you sure? You might research and engage others in brainstorming (radical) alternatives. If you literally have no choice (not often the case unless you're incarcerated or physically pinned in place somewhere, like the guy in *127 Hours*), then choose to harness your power of interpretation instead of going dull.
- New intention/affirmation: I am fully present and engaged with life, curious and full of wonder. I am willing to be present to this moment.

Negative self-talk
- Any unkind inner (or outer) chatter that's critical and demeaning of yourself, including literally calling yourself names.
- Constant predictions of failure or unlikelihood that you'll understand, make it happen, be chosen, do a good (or even decent) job, and so on.
- A perpetual focus on all that's not enough or undone, what you've done badly, what you're not master of, along with failing to celebrate completions, successes, what's good enough, what's good. Consider

ending every day in such mental celebrations as you fall asleep.

- New intention/affirmation: I address myself with kindness and respect, even inside my own mind.

Focus on right and wrong

- This applies to others as well as to yourself: Is this the right thing to do? Is this wrong? Am I wrong? Am I doing this wrong? I did the wrong thing. She's doing it wrong. He's wrong.
- All the *should* messages you carry around and deliver to yourself and others (including those mental lectures).
- Whenever you feel outraged, incensed, appalled, you might want to see whether you're out of your business (you probably are), and whether there's anything you can actually do about what's upsetting you. (That would be your business, and focusing on that would put you in your power.)
- New intention/affirmation: I am as right as I need to be. Others are as right as they need to be. I am accepting of myself and others.

Avoidance and procrastination

- Not dealing with things, which includes putting off unpleasant tasks or burying them so that they're forgotten; continually refusing to bring to the fore the thing that keeps tugging at your consciousness from that corner you keep shoving it into.
- Avoiding tricky people or situations.
  - Be someone who doesn't duck into another aisle at the supermarket when someone you didn't want to meet right now is in the one where you were headed.
  - Meet every face as the face of God, and get the benefit of the muscle that gets strengthened from the encounter. You may need to build the muscle of saying, "I'm not up for chit-chat right now," or "I'm staying focused on shopping—nice to see you." (Again, try using plain face to support you in this.)
- Failure to address or complete anything that lies unfinished between you and another or between you and you.
- New intention/affirmation: I am willing to meet whatever comes my way. I meet every face as the face of God. I face each task that's mine to face in good timing.

Not telling the truth

- Besides overt lying, this includes whitewashing, skirting around, omitting.
- Don't make it your job to take care of other people's feelings.
- Don't manipulate what they think of you.
- Let them have their reactions.
- New intention/affirmation: I tell the truth. My truth comes from inside me, however others receive it.

Disconnection from your body and weak physical stances

- Slouching; walking with your head down; unconsciously crossing your legs or arms; rounding your shoulders; standing in an imbalanced or flimsy position, with only one foot planted on the ground.
- Note that the best way to address a disembodied experience that keeps you from presence and power is to cultivate a practice that leads to physical awareness. There are any number of paths that can teach you to feel and monitor your own body—yoga, qigong, tai chi, Pilates, dance, various sports, working out. As with everything, good posture and physical balance involve catching yourself where you don't want to be and course-correcting toward what feels better. See if you can catch a slouch without judging yourself, and simply adjust your shoulders and spine.
- If you'd like to learn even a little bit more about how you experience and convey power or weakness through how you hold your body, you might begin with Amy Cuddy's TED talk, "Your Body Language Shapes Who You Are."
- New intention/affirmation: I am solid in my body. My physical carriage reflects my increasing alignment with personal power.

More than anything, I invite you not to use the power zappers to foster self-criticism or to beat yourself up. This would take your sense of personal power in the wrong direction! Use them to assist you in a kind process of moving from the level of personal power you have right now (at any given *now* moment) toward a level that represents what you'd like better. There's no problem in anything you see in yourself if you're willing to witness it with the compassionate, dispassionate witness, and start scooching.

chapter 30

Two Scooching Stories in Losing and Finding Power

Janine: Separating from a fundamentalist family

My client Janine has a memory of a moment when, as her seven-year-old self, she realized she could run out the door of her Iowa farmhouse when her father was yelling. She crossed the road and a patch of grass then climbed up a tree, where she just sat for a while in what became a safe zone, a space that was simultaneously containing and open, receptive of the elements. She looked all around—branches, grass, field, sunny sky. She felt the wind move through and around her tree. And somehow, in that moment, unexpected and unbidden, she had an experience of God that didn't match the rigid, oppressive fundamentalist teachings espoused and expressed ad nauseam in her home and church. The nature-centered God that met her in the tree, carried in the wind itself, held in the greatness of the open sky, present in the matter and texture and solid support of the tree—this force had no language attached to it, no rules, no requirements for merit, no bullshit. She articulated none of this then: only experienced the deep (and it would be lasting) impression of a truth that comes in whole and known and apprehensible, on the personal and universal levels at once.

As an adult, Janine moved westward. She became a spiritual seeker exploring various traditions and open to universal concepts of truth that weren't attached to and limited by denomination or even Christianity. As many people raised by fundamentalists (or cults) have experienced, despite much distance from family and a great deal of self-chosen exposure to other worldviews, it took her many years to feel safe (or even okay) in fully shedding the religion: it was taught her as Truth. In life's larger moments, when core fears came up, it could happen that she got sucked in again to her clan's model of flawed, sinful people needing to be reined in by a schizophrenic deity, partly gracious, partly punitive, reliably capricious, whose spokespersons were mean, demanding, hopelessly hypocritical people with ugly secrets hidden behind a posturing that couldn't be exposed, because everyone went along with it and called it good.

What made it harder for Janine to extricate herself from the clan was that it was important to her to stay connected to family. She had ongoing phone relationships with many of them, and her defaults for holidays—including chunks of summer, as she was a teacher—automatically placed her in their midst. She wasn't in choice with any of this: it was unquestioned, predetermined, elemental. As an Enneagram Two, Janine was deeply motivated by needing her family members to love her and know without a doubt that she was there to love them, support them, be of service, offer whatever help was needed. They made much of her self-sacrificing, ever-available, giving ways ("Neen is such an angel"), and she thrived on this. Since she never married or had kids (suspect behavior indeed), she became the aunt whose money was made available when other family members couldn't handle some unexpected expense, especially related to the care of the next generation. Still, in the day-to-day of it, Janine lived away from her family, created home that felt safe to her (and beautiful and sweetly containing), handled her love life away from their scrutiny, and pursued activities and friendships that allowed her to develop an eclectic, heart-based, nature-oriented spirituality without dogma.

Fast-forward to a time in her forties when Janine was going through a painful break-up (think earth-shattering—betrayal in both heart realm and financial, and a move that involved drastic downsizing). Cut to the scene when she felt panicked about where money would come from to meet her needs. Ay, though she and I had done some work together at this time (we were on hiatus), she forgot to mind the pain body and tend the mind. She lost track of the fact that a sense of urgency is almost always false (curtains on fire might be legit) and that it tends to yield unclear, wrong action. In that moment, distressed and urgent, she called Lea, her cousin's daughter, who owed her a huge chunk of money. Janine had taken out a loan to help the girl get through college, and while they'd agreed Lea would repay her gradually and with no interest, through regular payments, the terms were largely unclear and unenforced: some months no payment happened at all; sometimes it was as low as twenty-five dollars. Janine had definitely contributed to this lack of clarity. (You'll remember "unclear agreements" is one of the power zappers.)

Lea counter-panicked in response to Janine's distress and sent her a desperate e-mail drenched in victim mentality. Without full awareness of the tender button she was pushing, Lea accused Janine of not caring about her safety and well-being and of putting her in a position where she'd have to work ridiculously harsh hours to pay back money she should never have accepted—and, by the way, she was pregnant so this would happen at the baby's expense.

Again, Janine did not pause to mind the pain body and tend the mind. Her break-up (unknown to Lea) was so grossly characterized by uncaring treatment from someone who had professed to love her and whose latest choices placed her in a frightening financial position—a place from which she currently couldn't see how she could comfortably organize her life while rebuilding it—that she couldn't stand feeling this was what she was doing to Lea. (She wasn't.) Further, she was deeply conditioned to see a new baby (the domain of other women in the family, who were making a supposedly more valid feminine contribution) as trumping all—certainly anything she needed or wanted or felt. In the swirl of old beliefs and unquestioned thoughts, she simply swallowed whole (believed) her young cousin's take on things in a moment of stress. Guilty before even considering a possibility of innocence, Janine was horrified that she could be *this* awful to Lea.

In reality, her list of crimes might look something like this: she gave too much too unconsciously over time, so that a sense of furious resentment and feeling ill-used reared its ugly head in a moment when things got rough. She had made unclear agreements and then, when she got scared, tried to demand that this be set right at once. (Not likely to work in most cases. The undoing, too, must run its course.) She had communicated with another human being when she was distressed and feeling urgent, which simply means that she wasn't kind in that conversation and she didn't create an atmosphere of calm or of trust that all would be worked out for the good of all concerned. Further, this way of communicating had taken her out of her power—so she had no solid footing for moving in a powerful way (or in any way) toward a desired outcome.

Beyond that, she hadn't done anything wrong. She had certainly committed no monstrous atrocity. She had not been entirely careless toward her cousin over time (far from it). Nothing she'd said or demanded at the peak of her distress required that Lea make self-destructive or baby-harming choices, but in Janine's response to Lea's accusations—which she didn't pause to consider, never mind refute—she entirely agreed to view herself in monstrous terms.

It was summertime, so Janine happened to be visiting her family, staying with her brother and his wife, who tended to be the most accepting of her liberal ways. She jumped into her car and drove the country mile to her aunt's house (her aunt being the clearly dominant matriarch of the whole clan, now many years after her husband's death). Janine waited alone there for hours, sobbing and despairing, not yet able to question or in any way clearly look at what she'd been accused of. Once having been seen in a bad light, she was entirely caught up in believing herself to be guilty and to need exoneration.

Her whole identity might be summed up at that moment in this way: Janine was selfish, careless of others, unconcerned with the well-being of family. She had proven herself to be ultimately unloving and had, through her carelessness, hysteria, and general base, vile nature, created a rift, perhaps unbridgeable, between herself and someone dear to her, perhaps the whole family.

By the time most of the family gathered after work hours in the matriarchal hub—and gather they did—everyone knew Lea's version of what had happened, and this version was firmly established as what had *actually* happened. Janine may as well have put a gun to her cousin's head and declared she had to work her fingers to the bone throughout her pregnancy to pay the whole loan back right away. Janine wasn't even thinking about contesting this story, now being treated by the whole clan as objective truth. (Another way to say this is that she didn't harness her power of interpretation, as she wasn't yet aware that anyone was interpreting here—and, likely, neither was anyone else.) She was a weeping mess, which gave a clear external marker of her assumed guilt, and the family surrounded her in tough-love mode, offering messages of both utter guilt and ample forgiveness. *Yes, she was sinful, and kept making choices over the years that willfully kept her from God's grace. And yes, that grace was still available, ever renewed, and in keeping with that, they forgave her.* Not without speeches cataloguing her sins, though. Not without harsh, painful statements directed her way—which began, for one example, "If you ever treat anyone in my family this way again. ..."

Janine actually missed what came after that one, because she got sidetracked wondering about family. If she was outside of "my family" in that sentence, whose family was she in? Who were these people and what did she owe them? More important, could she be sure they were telling the truth just because they all agreed to it? She was years into knowing the answer to that one, but had momentarily lost track of it—and lost track of choice—in the thick of current crisis. Janine stopped listening to what was being said and simply moved through the motions as talk led to prayer, as the women moved to gathering food, as things settled back down to normalcy and she was able, finally, to leave placidly. She didn't make a statement of defense or offer another take on the situation—she was just on the edge of understanding anyway—but neither did she leave in tears as she had in last recent memory (a good decade old) of a time they'd all gathered in prayer around her sinful soul.

After this scene, Janine headed back West earlier than planned and kept much more distance even by phone from her family. When Thanksgiving time rolled around, she chose not to go to Iowa. At Christmastime, she made an agreement with her brother to stay with him for a couple of days and hang out with his nuclear family, but she would go to her aunt's only for the big holiday meal, wouldn't set foot in church with any of them, and would go on to visit a friend in another state during the rest of her holiday time.

Her entire family objected to this plan. Someone tried to reel her back in by calling her unforgiving and declaring that she always was one to hold a grudge. Janine felt the sting of that but also remembered to check out the truth of it—and landed squarely in feeling sure that these choices weren't about that. Even if forgiveness was hard for her (it's pretty hard for people in general), even if she'd held grudges in her life (who hasn't?), this was about choosing into her well-being instead of doing what her family expected in order to please them. In short, Janine checked out what others told her about herself and came back to what she thought, to being in good standing with herself.

Letting go of her family's approval—not needing to be the angel anymore—was key to Janine's freedom. Note that in regaining power, she had no need to exert power *over* anyone else. She had no need to drag anyone to her camp or stake down their agreement to look at things in a new way with her. She simply had to get her own clarity about who she was and what she was up to, and proceed to make her best choices from that clarity. This is personal power. When she thought of her family members, she blessed them, but she didn't organize herself around what they thought or what they wanted from her or even what they declared they needed. In healing herself, Janine has truly learned how to live (how to keep coming back to) "I release you to your life, and I release myself to mine."

Kyra: A cushy lab for a grand experiment

When Kyra took in the full extent of the mess she found herself in, she came up against the dead-end hopelessness she felt about her finances. Irksome irony: here she was spending most waking hours amidst luxury and good taste, working with wealthy customers in this highbrow interior design and home-furnishing store, and yet the business was discreetly going under. How was it possible she'd landed again in wall-to-wall scarcity—and in her mind was plunging headlong into some personal abyss as fast as the business headed south?

Mystifying, how they could trek in opulence daily while on the brink of failure. Find anything cotton in the store (sham, throw, bedding), and you could bet that cotton would be brushed or Egyptian or in herringbone weave; find a mirror—easy to do, with more on the floor than chairs— and it would be framed in antique silver leaf or bone. But tucked away under plush cushions, silken drapes, and sumptuous bedding was the threat of going out of business—customers grumbling, orders on hold, no money to pay the companies that had stopped delivering the goods until further payment was tendered.

When Kyra called me, she laid out the story of how she'd used all her savings to pay for a Master of Fine Arts in sculpture (not a practical degree!) then gotten this job at Posh Quarters to make ends meet. She figured if she worked four days a week, she could find time to advance her artwork and at some point start to sell it to get past her hand-to-mouth existence. Well, it wasn't looking good.

It did before: the store was close to her home in San Diego, she loved the wares and how it felt to be there, she got along beautifully with Elsa, the store owner, and they were compatible in their ideas of design. She enjoyed the people who came in for help in redecorating and furnishing rooms, and her natural talents and sensibilities plus her education in art—despite the fact sculpting didn't figure in this reality—allowed her to truly serve the Posh Quarters clientele. Not to mention that Kyra was about as personable as a person can get.

By the time she understood how far gone the store's finances were, she and Elsa were the only designers left, she was sorely needed, and she couldn't imagine leaving Elsa on her own. It was getting seriously uncomfortable, though. A typical workday included putting off clients asking for the furnishings and accessories they'd ordered months before, so she made up bogus reasons, bought them little gift baskets or a nice bottle of wine, smiled until her face ached. This detracted from working with new people—how could she be in integrity promising anything?—but new orders were the only way to bring in enough money to move along old orders standing by so the women could send a few more semi-satisfied customers on their way. This was not fun.

It was beyond not fun. It felt like punishment, and Kyra's reckoning of her life suddenly boiled down to a lot of wrong choices. Perhaps she could deal with it better if she really were working four days a week, but she always brought home any number of tasks—especially the calculations required so customers could have accurate numbers to make final decisions (she was slower at this part and needed to work uninterrupted, fairly impossible in the store). Some of her time off, she just needed to drop out of the buzz and hum and bring her heart rate down. She needed to sit and stare.

Why was this happening?

I asked Kyra if she believed in a punitive Universe. This is a question that comes up often enough in my work. Crazy how many people walk around thinking they're being punished. She briefed me on her religious upbringing, the long indoctrination on slow-drip IV, the daily messages about her sinful nature and the vigilance and self-denial required to smash the ego (like a vile, crunchy cockroach under your little patent-leather Sunday shoes). We kept coming back to the question. What about now? Now did she believe in a punitive Universe?

It was hard for her not to interpret her current difficulties as a clear message she'd been grossly extravagant to lose her savings to an arts degree. A detour at the casino would have been wiser! How could she make that money back? Who was she to take herself seriously as an artist? No, the best she could hope for was being a glorified salesperson helping people put together some nice colors and fabrics and shapes to feel better about their living rooms. But the store hosting her modest efforts was hanging by a thread.

The more I listened to Kyra, the more I knew that she was fine. I saw her as going through one of those periods I call "when life pushes you to your walls." I define those walls as the place where you stop applying your own belief system. Because she'd had to deconstruct the beliefs handed down by her parents, she'd given a good bit of thought to variant ways of conceiving reality. She already loved Abraham-Hicks as much as I did. She knew The Work of Byron Katie. By and large, she had come to live with the trust that she could step into her dreams and show up for whatever was happening without fearing the heavenly lightning bolts. That had gotten her to art school—and despite her terror that current signs meant she'd somehow exceeded her allotment of grace, it had been a great experience. So now life had her in that place where she was squeezed again. Here—with money tight, time overfull, all her not-good-enough buttons being pushed—was she still willing to believe? Could she still find the support of a friendly Universe?

Besides reminding Kyra of a bunch of things she already knew (my job is often to remind), I helped her understand that she was going to get through this better if she treated Posh Quarters like her lab for a grand experiment. She needed to claim her power, and this was not only as good a place and set of circumstances to do that in as any other: it was perfect. There were a number of things she could work on to move toward joy and ease, with the following representing some highlights:

- Not believing something bad was happening (certainly not that she was being punished)
- Telling the truth, without providing unnecessary explanations
- Not manipulating customers to see the store or her in any way
- Showing up and being fully present to the gifts in this situation:
  - there was so much she might learn (about anything, from setting boundaries to cataloguing daily how the friendly Universe keeps supporting her)
  - she got to not only offer service, but serve at the right level (not as a martyr)

- she could play with the design tasks and creative collaborations with customers (as long as they kept coming in) and actually enjoy the people and the creation of beauty (in other words, love it—which was all she wanted)

We reviewed the three kinds of business to help Kyra get clear about how she could support Elsa appropriately but not take on daily agony over whether her store would make it or not. If Kyra chose to cast her lot with hers and stay with the store until it folded or, by some miracle, took a turn toward a new level of solid operations, then Kyra could do just that. She did need to stay conscious of choice. She also needed to keep in view she wasn't rescuing Elsa, and it wasn't her job—never mind obligation—to do so. She had certain support jobs to do and some skills and natural inclinations she may want to lend, but she was out of her business if she took on Elsa's troubles and strained against whatever life gave her to meet: Elsa had a valid journey here, and Kyra didn't need to get in the way.

As for Kyra's personal future—definitely not her business. This included how and whether she'd make it as an artist or even have this job or any other to ensure basic security. Today she had a job. She was also showing up for it with all her heart, and would end up with good experience and a fabulous reference; if Posh Quarters dwindled away, there would be another place for her.

Checking in on her clarity, she found she was clear she didn't want to leave Elsa and the store now, so she committed to a consciousness of choice: she wanted to hang in there. She took in that it would feel better if she got 100 percent behind that choice and loved the work and people, let go of the future, gave her time willingly when she gave it (presence!), and let go of the store mentally when she wasn't there.

We talked plenty about nonresistance and letting go of outcomes. As long as she had a ferocious grip on the idea that Posh Quarters had to stay in business, she was resisting reality. She could vote for that, and show up doing her part, then she'd best let go. That letting go would enable her to enjoy today, right now, and to work with customers and Elsa in a way that actually constituted a good life.

Thus, the store became Kyra's lab. There, she witnessed in a heightened set of circumstances what she'd done all her life, which she boiled down to people pleasing. She sought to accept that if the customers were let down by the orders not coming in, this had nothing to do with her. It had nothing to do with her even if she was the one telling them they had to wait, even if their frustration or anger got directed at her. She started truthfully letting them know how open-ended the wait would be and apologized appropriately (once) and stopped giving gifts and compliments and strained smiles. Let me insert here that anytime you're doing your job (whatever's yours to do) with greater ease, you're on the right track.

As Kyra shared her process with her partner in crime, Elsa began to look into Abraham-Hicks herself. The two women discussed the teachings, especially the emphasis on navigating in the direction of what feels good. They made a pact to prioritize feeling good at Posh Quarters and making it a place where people felt drawn to come in and linger. They filled it with love. They laughed with clients and focused on their joy in designing spaces with them. They gave the best service they could despite the extra wait time built in, so that people had a great experience choosing furnishings and designs with them; they loved coming in, they loved being there. The two women found it didn't take long to create just that.

Still, businesswise, it felt like Posh Quarters was a sinking ship. Elsa went in and out of worry, and Kyra kept seeking to help her locate what she could do and where she needed to let go of the process and outcome, which served as reminders to herself to do the same. Kyra met her discomfort when she had to put someone off or tell a hard truth, and kept meeting it, and kept meeting it, now and now and now, and found she could get through those moments and move on—not carry guilt and worry around.

The design was fun! The interactions with customers were fun. Sometimes she'd realize she'd been working with someone for hours and really needed food. In the past, this would have meant pushing through until the task was complete. Now she let them know she needed to pause or invited them to order pizza with her—in other words, she took care of herself so she could continue offering her service, instead of shoving down her needs to keep pretending and overextending to please the customers. All of this made a tremendous difference in her day-to-day experience. It also allowed her to see that she could think of this whole reality as a friendly-Universe construct: the angels truly had outdone themselves in setting up the perfect gym for building her weak muscles, the perfect lab for experimenting with all she wanted to keep playing with in a friendly Universe.

At some point a sailor appeared to try to rescue the sinking ship. He was considering buying the business and Elsa was open to talking to him. Funny that he happened to be someone Kyra had known some two decades back in time, when she'd categorically classified him as a slimeball. Wanting to clear her old thinking before he came into Posh Quarters, she questioned her thoughts about him. She ended up acknowledging how much she'd changed and grown in the past twenty years and decided to stay open to the very real possibility that he'd done the same. The day he came, Kyra told me, "There was nothing but love in the room." They met with an easy embrace, and her inner sensors didn't cringe in his presence. Kyra held down the floor that day while Elsa spent hours with the sailor and came out with a plan that involved his investing in the store, but not buying her out.

The relief that came in for the two women was palpable. The store shifted again to another level of feeling like a great place to be. But here's the part that I think is actually funny, and full of juice. Nothing happened right away, and in fact the sailor was called away (far across the seas) on business, and it wasn't long before Elsa was looking at the very real possibility of being right back where she'd started. Except she wasn't. And she wasn't willing to be, which was a very good idea: no going back. Remember that it's important not to insist on specific interpretations. The message from the sailor wasn't that he was the savior. The message was that things could keep shifting, that there were options, that it was a very good idea to stay open to various possibilities and scope them out. It was a great process to be in.

Elsa had a dream that they were on a ship with winds whipping up and waters splashing into their quarters. They scurried to shut the windows, then as she gazed out into the ocean, she was struck by a vision of three massive horses standing there—in just a few feet of water, with a lush island behind them. They were so close to shore! Not there yet, still in the thick of the storm, but so close. ... Kyra, having more of a connection to horses than Elsa, took the dream to heart as well. I don't know that much about totem animals, but I do love looking up creatures for their symbolic meanings for both real-life and dream sightings. (You can just google *animal totems*, or the critter in question plus *totem*.) Horse is one I've got down: it's all about power.

As I write this, the verdict on the store is still out. Kyra and Elsa are having fun and developing their skills in retail, design, customer service, and trusting life while letting go of outcomes. They know that down the road there will be work for them and wonderful adventures using their talents and skills—maybe at Posh Quarters, maybe not. To be sure, they're living in their power.

As I've said, if you're going to experiment at all, make it a grand experiment.

PART 4

Your Power to Create:
Scooch from Vision to Fruition

Having a crazy-smart hyper-dyslexic son with a wacky sense of humor and a love of fun facts, how could I not read Gary Larson comics to him? One evening as we read, I came upon a particular cartoon during a time when I was already fully engaged in articulating with clients this idea of getting from vision to fruition. I was so delightedly blown away by what Larson had depicted in one image plus caption that I momentarily became one of those tiresome parental units who forget their job in favor of some private agenda. I stopped reading because I couldn't stop laughing, in between pauses to shake my head at his pure ingenious expression of this concept: you'll start with a vague understanding of where you're headed, then as you move in what looks like roughly the right direction, life will guide you to the precise place for you—that place where you're both truly fulfilled in yourself and able to offer your gifts to others in the highest way. Until you get there, in order to stay open to guidance and to the evolution, don't attach to the outcome or to any particular form along the way. You'll try out some possible forms of the vision that won't be quite right, but they'll move you along the path. Let life (the friendly Universe, the Divine—whatever you've got) call it for you.

When I seek to explain this, I have to go on for a few sentences, as I just did. Gary Larson nailed it in one pithy cartoon depicting a Robin Hood character kneeling in the woods next to a porcupine, offering the creature a bag of gold. It would appear that our hero of Sherwood Forest was initially slightly off-point, robbing from the rich to give to the porcupines. Brilliant. (Still shaking my head over this.)

Cartoonists are like poets, elegantly capturing a lot with a little. They distill what is grand and vast and profound and hilarious and absurd into something succinct you can absorb in seconds. This was never my way. I bow to Gary Larson and his wacky weird gift.

My gift, perhaps, is to walk you through a process for making things happen or bringing things into your life that aren't yet in place, with attention to how the friendly Universe surrounds you with guidance and support. I'll encourage you to scooch and keep scooching toward your goal, or vision, because whatever comes up from inside you that you're drawn to move toward—there's a reason for that draw.

There's no grand music or hype accompanying this section of the book. No Secrets will be unveiled here. No magic wands will be held just out of reach or proffered. Please note that I'm never saying you get to have whatever you want just for the wanting. The gifts may be in the journey, not the outcome. The gift may be in a redirection you couldn't have imagined when you set out with a very different idea in mind. There will most certainly be a gift in your relinquishing all expectations and disappointments along the way in order to find that what you get is always more beneficial than what you thought you wanted.

In short, life gets you where you need to go, and this may or may not be where you thought you were going. So beyond the realm of magical thinking, I'll champion you to aim for what you want, while trusting that what you get every step of the way and in every outcome is perfect—perfectly crafted for you to get what you need for your growth, healing, and evolution and for sharing your gifts with the world. Robin Hood progressed from the porcupines to the poor: what else could have happened?

If, like my sister Denise, you're allergic to any New-Age talk of visioning or manifesting, no sneezing attacks will be triggered by this material. If you're a truly no-nonsense scientific type, you can fully apply all the sensible advice here about moving persistently toward your vision with choices, actions, thoughts, and language all aligned with what you say you're seeking to do. If you're Tosha Silver or one of her devotional fans with your own love affair going with the divine, you will see how my presentation encompasses the idea of aligning with divine order, because that's the way of nonresistance and that's how I live.

Are you willing to head boldly (or take tiny, tremulous scooching steps) toward your heart's desire, holding your intention with a loose grip and allowing life to keep directing and redirecting you? Will you yield to life or to a friendly Universe that'll get you to the right actual place for you—but not by giving up before you begin, staging a false yielding that comes of some self-defeating idea that you never get to have what you want? Will you experiment with this to see what else is possible for you?

If so, the only way to know how it all turns out is to start moving. So for those who want the longer version of what Gary Larson's cartoon delivers instantly, several chapters on the topic follow.

chapter 31

Loose-grip Visioning Basics

Wanna make something happen? Get a vision. Anything you create or accomplish in life begins with a vision. This isn't true just for doing great things or achieving your soul's purpose. It's equally true for when you'd like a few more pairs of nice socks or some live green plants in your living space. Your vision is whatever you imagine experiencing in reality that you're not experiencing yet. It's what you want to bring into being, from fantasy to reality. Your vision is the *what* that begins with *what if.*

What about the *how*? How do you get from vision to fruition? People often stop themselves before they even begin by lamenting that they don't know how. They may even feel terror in not knowing how. They may scold themselves (even viciously) for daring to have the vision if they don't know how, and shame themselves right out of it. I invite you to the tremendous relief (and the release of misplaced focus) from this fact: You actually don't need to know how. You never have to know how.

Check out your own past experience. Is there anything you've ever done a first time that you knew how to do before you began? When you learned how to ride a bike, you didn't know *how*. But you knew *what*, didn't you? You had the vision. You could see yourself fly on the thing, right over that asphalt ribbon. You didn't know how to place your hands, how to pace a stop, or how to take off from that moment both feet touched the pedals and for a weird, precarious instant, all balance was lost to the random wiles of gravity and the four directions. You didn't know who your teachers would be or how that snide sideways comment by that crooked-nosed kid named Ricky would get your eyes looking ahead in the right place while you rode, so that somehow the whole game snapped into place. But all of this came clear because that's the thing about *how*: the *how* reveals itself along the way.

I can just hear someone thinking, *But I don't know the way.* You don't need to know the way. You need to know the *what*. All you need is a vision.

For any visioning (from new socks to new career), here are your three jobs:

- Have a vision
- Hold the vision
- Move toward the vision

If it sounds too easy, that's because it is—and you've been thinking it's too hard. What's hard is allowing for all we can't control, which is (have you got it?) the *how*. And that's in the Universe's realm of control—the Universe's job, not yours. What's hard is staying in your business and showing up for your job not only day to day, but moment to moment. But that job itself isn't hard. Your job is to have a vision, hold the vision, and move toward the vision.

Have a Vision
People often ask, with furrowed brow, *What if my vision is vague?* Start with as clear a vision as you've got. That's enough. The vision is the far point on the horizon. You can see something shimmering there, but you may not see exactly what it is. Or think of it as the painting across the room. You may see the shapes and colors or get the gist of the content, but until you move in close, you just can't tell that pointy thing poking up behind the wheelbarrow is a pig's ear.

When you get to where you're going, there will be details you couldn't have begun to imagine if left to your own devices. It's fortunate that you never *are* left to your own devices—the Universe, with its marvelous organizing intelligence, is filling in the details as swiftly as you move toward the vision. It will come up with particulars that will delight and amaze you to color in the whole canvas. (Haven't you experienced it before? Could you have thought of the details of your lover's or child's face back when you were simply thinking, *I want a lover, I want a child?* Would you have come up with that quirky twisting of the mouth in moments of impatience?)

It's not just a matter of getting okay with the unfortunate vagueness of your vision in its current state: you actually benefit if the vision isn't too specific in the beginning. When you home in too quickly on something overly precise, you keep a multitude of possibilities from coming in to surprise you with their unexpected brilliance and their appeal to various parts of you. If you declare, for example, that you want to be a registered nurse, now you're on a nursing track, and all that's left is for you to sign up for the right nursing program and get a job as an RN. This is great if every cell of your being is in love with nursing and you know without a doubt that's exactly what you want to do. But if that's not the case, and you start with a vision that's more open, then there's all sorts of room for any number of specific manifestations (or forms) to suggest themselves as you move toward that far point on the horizon.

Let's look at this more closely. Your broader vision behind the idea of nursing might be to help people heal, or at least feel better in their bodies. As you explore this (move toward the vision), it might dawn on you that you've always been a teacher of sorts and that you've been into whole foods since your early twenties—and isn't it funny that your favorite documentaries are about food? You end up working as a nutritional counselor and helping people heal and feel better through food and herbs. Or life might direct you (beginning with that aromatherapy class your college roommate dragged you to) to explore alternative energy-healing modalities, or mastering an ancient Eastern tradition with marvelous modern-Western application—acupuncture, shiatsu. You might find yourself suddenly becoming your sister-in-law's greatest supporter in hanging in there through some harsh challenges in the first weeks of breastfeeding her baby, because you had a hell of a time getting the right help when you went through something similar; you remember out of the blue that you used to ask pregnant women if they were going to nurse or bottle-feed before you even hit puberty, and it's so obvious: you're a lactation consultant. Who knows what it might be? You've got to start vague so the journey can guide you to the best super-specific expression that fulfills that larger thing you're after.

Lorraine: Progressing through levels of specificity

It's so beautiful (fun, satisfying, sometimes mind-blowing) when you land in the particular thing that just sings to every cell in your being. Lorraine Faehndrich is a life coach practicing, like me, out of Ithaca. Unlike me, or hardly anyone else on the planet, she works with women suffering from pelvic pain! How precise is that? Obviously, those who find her are desperate for her services, and they bask in her warmth and clarity. She's positioned right where she can do the most good while thriving herself

(Lorraine is quite passionate about her work).

When she began, her intention was to be a life coach. It wasn't even as specific as *wellness coach* in the beginning. She got to her current level of hyper-specificity by moving toward her vision and attending to all that life brought her way, both personally and professionally.

One specific detail she was aware of, when she began, was that she wanted to use the law of attraction in her approach. She earned a life-coaching certification through Martha Beck's life-coach training program (she loved it), but it was after that, in a forum on LOA, that she met someone whose work in mind-body coaching got her attention. Something resonated at once. What Lorraine then embarked on with this woman represents more than the next training: it was the next level of specificity.

In the course of this second program, the practice clients she kept interfacing with were women with pelvic pain. She had no idea why they were drawn to her or why, in return, she felt so compelled to work with them. Only in the flimsiest, most fleeting way did she connect this to a physical malady she'd once experienced herself. It didn't last long, in her case, but long enough to bring up loads of frustration and turmoil of various kinds: it had an emotional component, affected her sexual relationship, chewed at her self-esteem, brought up old painful memories, and highlighted her challenges in self-care or the maddening overwhelm in learning to balance self-care with the care of others, to name a few. Add to all this that her dis-ease was never properly diagnosed, never mind addressed—an all-too-common experience for women with pelvic pain.

Thus, it took working with this population awhile (only because they kept gravitating her way and she kept welcoming them) for Lorraine to realize that what she'd dealt with herself those years back fell under the same rubric of pelvic pain! She was able to help women with this issue because it was in fact deeply personal to her even before she was fully conscious that this was so. Perhaps more important, she could help them because, in her own experience, she had learned to let her body's pain be her guide into overall well-being. In short, she had faced this problem herself with the mind-body approach she now brought to coaching others.

About her coaching, she wrote me this excellent articulation:

I *really* love working with these women because it incorporates everything that I am passionate about helping women with—helping them *love* themselves, work with their thoughts, connect to their body and inner wisdom, find and follow their passion, and create outrageously joyful lives. But I had no idea it would—and I never could have figured that out on my own.

In other words she did not, of her own devices, directly think to take her experience with pelvic pain and translate it to a super-specific coaching niche. Perhaps she couldn't have thought of such a thing even with far more clarity about her bygone malady plus all her best smarts rubbed together. More to the point, she didn't need to. That's the Universe's job. Life *wants* to guide us to just the right place, and it's more super-specific than we're taught to expect. Thus, Lorraine traveled from life coach, to mind-body coach, to mind-body health coach for women, and finally gorgeously landed on pelvic pain–relief coach. (If you think your problem matches her expertise, I highly recommend her! Find Lorraine at radiantfeminine-dot-com.)

What I find again and again with clients actively engaged in creating something new in their lives is that they don't like the vague stage. It's not as fun when the vision is the far point on the horizon. It's so wonderful to find yourself standing in the midst of that fabulous final form, ooh-ing and ah-ing over what's come to be. Please don't rush to specificity out of discomfort with the vague. Sometimes I have a funnel handy to give clients a visual: the top, widest part is where you are now—yeah, it's a bit roomier than you like, it's nonspecific, it's an edgy, uncomfortable place to be. But whatever you drop into a funnel will end up down at the super-specific point at the bottom, and without your having to force anything. Stay awhile in that wider circumference of so-much-possible until life swirls you down to the fine point of the specific version you get to live out. (You'll assist and participate in this process simply by moving toward the vision, to be covered below.)

So start with as clear a vision as you've got: that's all you need in order to move toward the vision, following what beckons to you, watching for how the details fill themselves in. As they say (I, for one, have heard them say it), Let the Universe take care of the details. That super-achieving student with the nose ring looking for a prestigious school with a liberal atmosphere had no idea that how wrong and weirdly stifled she felt in the Northeast (Why is everyone here so ramrod-uptight?) was part of her guidance system. She couldn't know that this unease would redirect her to a smaller campus in Ohio (seriously? the Midwest?), where she felt like she'd come home before she first got her car parked on Oberlin's middle-of-nowhere grounds. It felt so open, so green, with the perfect mix of older and more modern buildings. It hit the sweet spot between respectable and antiestablishment, with non-cookie-cutter students she recognized at once as her tribe. All the marvelous details are evidence, by the way, of the *how* revealing itself. Your delight in or recognition of the details, your relief when you locate them—all serve as evidence that you're on track.

Hold the Vision

Your second job, holding the vision, is important to stress because people have visions all the time that drop off into oblivion; they lose track of them altogether. This is why we have those dreams (the sleepytime kind) with some compelling character (oh my goddess, the baby!) that we've forgotten somewhere and must somehow get back to—if only we knew the way. ... Isn't it strange that it's even possible to forget your most cherished dreams? How could you lose track of that ingenious idea about hula-hoop fund-raisers? How could you misplace that thought of *doing something* with that love of dance combined with your weird gift of getting people who hardly know they have a body to hook their hips into the rhythm and discover the astonishing thrill of how the music moves them?

Our fears and perceived limitations are powerful agents of psycho-chemistry, brewing up potent distractions, soporifics, and coma inducers. Excuse my heavy hand, but I kind of want to point back to the (already weighty) last sentence and emphasize the word *perceived* in front of *limitations*. If, knowing the Universe is in charge of the *how*, you stop being the doer or playing God and just show up for your completely manageable three-part job of minding the vision (have, hold, move toward the vision), then you can drop your ideas of limitations. This isn't about you; it's about something much bigger than you. And that something doesn't entertain the same limitations you love to pour tea for (or meet for coffee, or propose a toast to with one more drink, and then you'll have to put it all off again till tomorrow for sure).

Something I do routinely with clients is have them write a potent personal manifesto that articulates a vision for their entire lives. The manifesto blueprint I've created, including language specifications and the rationales behind its various components, appears separately in its own chapter later in this section. It will guide you to create a beautiful document to support you in living intentionally if you're interested in playing with that tool.

But you don't have to write out some exhaustive (and for some, exhausting) personal credo to benefit from putting a vision into words. Especially when people start out feeling overwhelmed or when they need to focus, for now, on one particular aspect of their lives, I have them write up no more than a sentence or two or a brief paragraph to express what they know about that far point on the horizon they're after in that one realm. To carry on with our health-care example above, the brief articulation of the vague vision might go something like this: "I love going to work every day to help people heal and feel better in their bodies." That's enough right there. (Note that it's written in the present tense, as if it were already happening.)

As you move toward the vision, and start to learn more about the details, you might amend the statement accordingly: "I love my job helping people heal and feel better in their bodies. I have fun educating them to take full responsibility for their well-being."

You might also make the statement more about the journey, if that feels better to you than articulating the end point. For example, "I'm in a fruitful and fascinating process of locating the best professional venue for me to help people heal and feel better in their bodies."

You know you've got the right statement if it sings to you. To hold this vision, keep repeating your statement. Post it in a visible place, and change the note to a whole new look when it starts to blend in with the wall or the fridge. Other ways to hold the vision are: Talk about it (to people who aren't naysayers). Daydream about it. Write about it. Find an image that epitomizes this vision and set it as the background on your computer's desktop. Actually take moments to sit around (or drive, or do dishes, walk the dog, nurse the baby) imagining various scenarios of how it might look once those glorious details do get filled in. You can hold the vision—no sweat, no striving—if you simply create ways to keep it in the forefront of your consciousness.

Move toward the Vision

Then there's your third job in visioning: move toward the vision. Even if you're persistently holding the vision, it's equally possible to forget to move (or to avoid moving) toward it. The *how* can reveal itself along the way only if you're moving along that way!

But how do you know which way to go? Just do anything you see to do that looks like a step in the right direction: aim roughly that way. Follow your guidance, your hunches, the thing that gets your attention. Have a conversation, look something up, read (or even leaf through!) that book whose title keeps coming up; call the person who popped into your head (after which you saw someone with an uncanny resemblance); sign up for the training, join the club, unpack the box, block out time on your calendar for the next step. ...

Let me flag that last one for you, in case you missed its import. Sometimes you can't do something right now, but the vision pops in, along with that familiar longing to do that thing you're not getting to or to get out of this thing you're in that keeps feeling off. Take the action of making a date with yourself to explore what needs exploring. You can write it into your daytimer just as you'd write in coffee with the friend who just texted you or block off a weekend for the conference your boss just mandated. Cordoning off time for things counts as action taken. (But do teach yourself you're reliable by showing up for or, if you must, properly renegotiating those agreements with yourself. Review "Keep Your Word" if you must!)

The Universe will best guide you—reveal the *how* and fill in the details—if you're in motion toward your vision. My most vivid of few positive memories from the Baptist church, back when my upbringing had me sitting on its pews, was hearing a minister say, "God can't steer a parked car." (Actually, he didn't merely say it. He sing-song-yelled it, the way those evangelists do, and it rang and reverberated and hung there vibrating and, yep, it made an impression.) I actually love *God can't steer a parked car*. I live by it and give it to my clients to use, however they might define *God* or whatever substitution they might use for the G-word. Move, and life will direct and redirect you. If you don't believe in external guidance, believe in internal guidance (it's all the same anyway). Call it intuition or divine intervention, it's still the voice of uncanny and effortless wisdom that comes up from inside you and gets echoed in the outer world and says, with clear, quiet authority, *Go that way*. (All things guidance are treated two chapters hence in "Accessing Guidance in the Moment.")

Follow that voice with no expectation that it's taking you to your final destination. (How much in life is final anyway?) Remember, your job is to move toward that vision. Forget about getting there—whether, when, and how you'll arrive and what it will look like when you do: that's all the Universe's business. A very liberating thing to keep in mind about moving toward a vision is that you don't need to map out the whole journey: just take one step at a time.

I used to cringe when I heard the term *baby steps*. I remember how discouraged I got once in my twenties when a therapist told me I could change something with baby steps. I heard this as, "It'll take forever and you'll be graceless and ridiculous all along the way." I translated that to *Forget it* and shut down for a few more years.

I've since had babies! I'm pretty sure that their capacity for change and growth is unrivaled by anything in the adult world. Watching them learn to walk is truly inspiring. Every day, many times a day, they bring all their energy to bear on doing as much as they've figured out to do so far and upping their game again. They don't care how often they fall down. No one needs to explain to them that repeatedly landing on their bum is part of the process. No pep talks required! And it may well be that they're graceless and ridiculous sometimes; but even more than that, far more often, they're beautiful, focused, fearless, fearlessly emotive, quick to shift, funny, and incurably lovable.

I've noticed babies tend to get upset about falling down when grown-ups turn sad, poor-you faces toward them and use oh-no voices to reassure them that they're really okay. Have you seen this happen? The babies knew they were really okay before reactions like that threw it all into question! On the other hand, when the mirrors around them are confirming that it's a marvelous journey from point A to point B no matter how many bumps along the way, there's truly no problem.

Apply this to yourself: it really helps to remember that you're always okay.

The main thing about a baby step is that it's doable: it's doable here and now. The key to moving forward with baby steps is to keep taking them. It doesn't matter how often you fall down. Like a good baby (or you can be a bad baby if you're feeling peevish), get back up and take another step, or if you're done for now, pause—but don't even think about forgetting what you're up to; watch for the next step to take in just a little while. Baby steps create true change, and much more quickly than anyone thinking too hard about it might imagine. And single steps shift (often unnoticed) into real walking, running, leaping, bouncing, soaring.

Your job is to move toward the vision until it becomes clear beyond the shadow of a doubt that it's time to let go. That moving includes asking for help, applying for positions and programs and funding, seeing if others want to invest or contribute or collaborate with you, asking people to share what they know with you. That means you'll need to set yourself up for any number of *yes* or *no* answers, and you'll hear *no* plenty. "*Yes* lives in the land of *No*" is an idea that comes from BJ Gallagher and Steve Ventura in their book by that name: it's par for the course to hear *no*, perhaps many times over, before you hear *yes*. Just expect it (and they teach how to prepare for it), and there's no problem.

We looked at valuing *yes* and *no* equally in the chapter "Yes or No: Be Someone Who Gives the Right Answer." See if you can divest yourself of negative interpretations of *no* as they apply directly to what you're trying to make happen or create. Write them down: "I've been rejected"; "I shouldn't have asked"; "I asked too much"; "They think I'm out of my element"; "They don't see the value of what I'm doing." These thoughts can be questioned using The Work of Byron Katie, or you can turn some or all of them around and look for reasons why those opposites are true. You can also ask yourself with each one, "*So what* if that's true?" That's kind of radical, and very worthwhile. *So what* if they think you asked too much? People think that sometimes. You've thought it. And that doesn't make it true, or absolutely true, or a great sin on your part. You're on a journey; ask for what you want or what you perceive you need. If you see *no* simply as guidance, showing you the way as clearly and helpfully as any *yes*, you can move on down the road with ease, following your guidance as you go.

Sometimes we stop ourselves from moving forward when we have disappointments and perceived setbacks. My personal belief is that there's no such thing as a setback—but there sure can be a standstill if you stop moving. A so-called setback only means that you thought things were going in a certain direction or following a certain timeline and then it turned out they weren't. Or it could be you thought you should have a clear direction by now but you find you still don't.

What if you trusted that there's no problem? Let life show you what's happening instead of insisting on your way. As you move toward the vision, you'll do better (way, way better) if you hold any idea or direction you're trying out with a loose grip; and by all means, detach from the timing (the Universe's business every time). Let life direct and redirect you. Trust that you're better off going the other way when the road barrier rises before you.

How many times have I told my client Sandra during her fertility adventures (one month strung upon another, and still not pregnant), *the obstacles you encounter aren't random!* (Mental note to rename myself the Broken Record Coach?) You always get the precise challenges you need. For Sandra, the patience required of the fertility process is sometimes maddening—and won't she need patience with the colicky infant and the terrible two-year-old? She can hardly stand the anxiety churned up for her in those interminable stretches of waiting for the latest verdict—and won't she need to master her anxiety when that wee one keeps her up through the night?

Imagine this: a panel of angels has come together to set up the perfect circumstances in which you can heal and grow and build muscles where you're weak—but only the muscles you'll need in order to function beautifully in that next level of life you're moving into; only those needed to have a great adventure on the way. Those circumstances are the ones you're living now. (As far as I can tell, that's the most empowered way to interpret a perceived setback or cluster of obstacles.) So when it feels harsh, come closer; don't shove it down or run away. Come close, believing you may be on the point of breakthrough, and all of life wants to support you in your expansion.

Dawn: Swift redirection

My client Dawn came up with a brilliant interim step toward creating the family she wanted. She invited a younger friend, Kendra, who was in transition, to move into the extra room (she thought of it as the baby's room) in her apartment. Together, they created a vision of being family to each other for now. They declared many things about what this would look like and how long it would last. They were wrong. Dawn's head was kind of spinning as she watched how quickly everything somehow devolved into a bit of a mess, and Kendra moved out prematurely, leaving Dawn with unshared rent again and a deep disappointment in herself. How could she have chosen so badly?

It took me lots of questions and some inspired talking to help Dawn scooch away from her self-judgments: She should have known better. She wasn't getting it right. Did she have to make every mistake in the book before she learned enough to get to what she wanted? I asked her this: How might you view the story if you had no judgment about what you did? What if it couldn't even occur to you to judge any of it? Let's say it all happened just as it should: it must contain some gifts; it must offer some further clarification.

Really truly, there was no problem in what Dawn had attempted to set up. She concocted an interesting vision with Kendra, and it deteriorated swiftly. Friendly Universe! What if she now thought in terms of how quickly life redirected her when she misstepped? None of it was evidence of how badly she managed things. It simply revealed to her, counter to what she'd imagined, that life with Kendra was not, in fact, the best interim step.

Again, hold any idea along the trail with a loose grip. Keep your eyes open to let life show you what's actually happening—with no judgment toward yourself or any other player in the game (by which I mean, notice and clear the judgments—not, don't have them). Dawn didn't need to be angry with Kendra for not playing things out with her as they'd planned it: that's how life showed her Kendra wasn't the right one to fill that room. Nor did Dawn need to find fault with the wisdom of her choices. With all that out of the way, what's left is simply: *Oh, I'm not doing that. I'm doing something else.*

This requires a basic trust in life. Nothing is ever going wrong when you trust that only the right things stick; what drops away is in fact what needs to be shed. For Dawn, this could have meant getting excited about what was coming next. Kendra's dropping out of the picture could even mean that the family Dawn was after was closer than she thought. But truly, it's not so important to figure out all the whys and wherefores. It's crucial, on the other hand, to hold any vision loosely, and to test any potential version of a vision that life brings into your field with curiosity, allowing life to show you what you will and won't be doing. Whatever you learn from the exploration will make it well worth your while no matter the outcome. In the realm of dating, I notice, people frown and say, "It didn't work out" when they don't land in a relationship after a few dates or a few months' dating. But it worked out just fine, didn't it?

If you don't create unnecessary attachments and get lost in a lot of bogus judgments and expectations, then you can simply let life direct and redirect you, trusting it's all forward movement. I don't know all that Dawn was meant to get in this episode with Kendra, but she must have gotten it quickly. Time to move on—toward the vision.

Uma: Perseverance in action

When Uma was twenty, she took a gap year that she divided between the small seaside village of Mbodiene in Senegal and the sparkly city of Paris. It was an intense and important time for her, during which she made a clean break from the prior track she'd been on (which devalued her academic abilities and failed to point her toward her potential); she thus set herself up to start anew on a much more solid path much better suited to her. The day she was set to travel from Senegal to France, she found out at the airport in Dakar that they had no record of her being on the flight—despite the itinerary she'd received by e-mail when she changed her travel plans. She suddenly needed to buy a ticket all over again on the spot but had no cash. This would have been fine, except their automatic teller machine (ATM) was broken. Without the cash, she couldn't even get on the plane. At this point in her stay, some political unrest was stirring, and she didn't want to stick around to watch it rev up.

Perhaps more important (and mirrored by these external disturbances), she was emotionally ready beyond ready to leave Senegal—along with the attention she drew there as an attractive young white American blonde; the rampant poverty that kept brushing up uncomfortably against her sense of privilege; the strangeness of living in a convent of Catholic missionaries (whose belief system she didn't share) and of working with them in schools (whose old-fashioned ways of teaching and treating children created any amount of discord inside her).

You know that edgy feeling when you're Ready. Uma could hardly imagine not flying out that day. She felt surly even momentarily considering a night spent in the unfamiliar convent in Dakar, though the nuns would graciously welcome her as one from their sister convent of

Mbodiene. Was she a hopeless ingrate? Ay, but missing this flight would mean missing the connecting flight from Morocco to Paris, too, and she didn't *want* to figure out plan B on that end to boot. In other words, she really, really wanted to be on that plane: that was her vision.

Uma recounts that she was basically running around looking distressed when an African man got involved: Ask them to hold the plane, he counseled firmly in the French language they shared. Hold the plane? This was one of those weird perks of being in a developing country. It's not like there were a number of Morocco-bound flights for her to just hop on later: this was it. So she did ask, with her impromptu helper tagging along, and the decision-makers were actually willing to stall departure till she came back with cash. Then, despite her accrued experiences after some months in Senegal (dubious help offered from the male contingent with possible strings attached), she made a quick decision to trust her helper as he now offered to get her to another ATM. His energy was kind and consoling, not forceful, and she felt him to be one of those human angels who show up when you really need one. She threw caution to the wind and jumped with him into the taxi he flagged down.

The ATM wasn't that far—except that she mistakenly punched in a sum that exceeded the limit and promptly shut the thing down. Ay, the whole setup was nerve-racking: the machine was ensconced in a metal grate with a big armed security dude sitting next to it. Now what?

No problem, conveyed the angel. Onward they went, to the next ATM just a few blocks away. Third try: out of order. The journey Uma describes of navigating the streets of Dakar in search of a viable cash machine features alarming speeds, a harrowing instance of taxi-going-the-wrong-way-up-a-one-way-street, a ticking clock in her chest, and the weight of a stalled plane full of passengers on her shoulders. Too much adrenaline! By the fifth malfunctioning ATM, she called the nuns back in the village (her helper handed over his cell phone; the ever-meticulous Sisters had written their number down in case of emergency before she left). Uma told them, in tears, that they'd have to come get her.

This was the point when she first felt she needed to resign herself to not going—it wasn't happening. The good folks back at the airport would hold the plane for how long? Was it even still there at this point? Even if the nuns came with money to buy her ticket, it would be a good half-hour before they arrived. And still, Uma and her intrepid hero kept questing for cash. ATM number 6 yielded none. Number 7 spat it right out.

On the way back to the airport, Uma canceled the nuns with gratitude and held her breath—please let the plane still be waiting on the runway. Nothing in her life's experience made such a thing likely or even possible. But it was there, actually really truly waiting for her, as if her being on that particular flight mattered. She hugged her angel hero with all her heart. She forked over the money, was whisked past security (oh, Africa!), jumped into a little cart that delivered her to the plane on the tarmac. Uma got to Morocco for her next flight and landed in Paris right on schedule.

I love this story. When I tell it to clients, I like to add: Be someone who tries seven ATM's. If you really want to be on the plane, keep going till the plane leaves without you. If you need an angel, one will appear. Hold the vision. Until life shows you it's not yours to have, move toward the vision.

Your guidance may take you through some unexpected territory along the way. If that includes perceived setbacks or disappointments, don't let them stop you. If a door seems to have slammed in your face, you can give double thanks: phew—wrong door, and you almost went through it!

Do you worry you can't tell the difference between persistence and pushing the river? I find this comes up for many clients. How can you tell when to keep going and when to let go? Is it time to try the next ATM or to throw in the towel?

As long as you still really want something, and you still see something to try, try it. Invite the Universe to go with you, show you the way, stop you if it's time to stop. Then as long as there's any momentum for you to ride, if the energy comes up to do something else, if you feel a spark or even a blast of fuel from the inspired thought of that one-more-thing-to-try—go for it. Always move toward the expansions. Conversely, if you're starting to feel contracted—exhausted, hopeless, heavy; if you're trying to push through those feelings with increasingly frenetic urgency; if your thoughts say it just has to work or you can't possibly stop—now you're pushing the river. There's no detachment in any of that.

If you're having a strong emotional reaction to the thought of letting go, you've lost track of that loose grip! You've probably gotten attached to one particular manifestation of the vision. Remember, if life doesn't give you one specific version, this doesn't mean you don't get to have what you were after at all. Go back to your broader vision; look away from the particular form. It's been known to happen that, once someone releases a death grip on something specific, that very thing comes around again. But if something else appears instead, consider this next form the better thing, the right thing for you.

Finally, I'm not implying that you can't have something if you're attached. You can (though you may have more stress on the way to getting it). Uma was quite fixated on that particular flight—according to her, she was pretty much hyperventilating—and no punitive Universe kept her from it to give her a good lesson in detachment! Would you like to scooch toward holding the vision with a loose grip, toward trusting that what comes to you is just right, and what eludes you is best let go? Tosha Silver puts it simply, "Let what wants to come, come. Let what wants to go, go."

chapter 32

Line It Up: Four Things to Align with Your Vision

There are four things you must consistently line up with your vision—or just keep bringing back into alignment as soon as you notice you've gone off-kilter with any one of them:

1. Choices
2. Actions
3. Thoughts
4. Language

When I say this to people, they sometimes say, "That's so obvious." Except they say it in a voice of wonder or even dismay, realizing the plain weird truth of it: they aren't doing the obvious. They didn't even recognize the obvious. But once you see it, it's not hard to take this on as a way of life to apply to visions large and small. Truly, it helps with starting up the organic vegetable garden or the new online business; it'll support you in getting down a habit of a daily walk or weekly accounting.

Think of these four components as belonging in two groups of two: Choices and actions go together because actions enact choices. Thoughts and language go together because language speaks thoughts aloud. Think of them as the four wheels of a car: if they're misaligned, you may still get to where you're going, but it won't be the most efficient or quickest trip, and it may cost you more or wear something out.

Living in upstate New York, I like to use a metaphor of going to Santa Fe when I speak about pursuing a vision. Let's say you're going to Santa Fe: that's your vision. It's such an amazing place, Santa Fe—desert and mountains, the presence, color, and culture of beautiful Native peoples, amazing food that values and fully validates the wonder of green salsa. ... So you get in your car and you head northeast.

Ah, but going northeast will get you to Maine, won't it? Maine is an amazing place, too, but it's not Santa Fe. It's pretty much the antithesis of Santa Fe—ocean, rocky beaches on a scraggly coastline, lighthouses and lobsters (no green salsa to be found). You said you were going to Santa Fe. Why didn't you head southwest?

Your vision means nothing if you don't hold it and keep heading in the right direction—toward the vision. This means pointing your choices and actions that way. Choices and actions are the most obvious and easiest to get into alignment with your vision once you decide to do so. Let's be clear: it's just as easy not to, so bring this choosing-and-acting thing to consciousness. You can even ask yourself a simple question to keep yourself in check as you make decisions (choices) small and large: *Does this move me toward or away from my vision?* If the answer is *away from*, this would be a Maine-bound choice: choose toward Santa Fe instead.

What pulls you to Maine? Some people are particularly vulnerable to choosing in the direction of what others want from them. They may even be so conditioned to *help* that they hardly see it as a choice if someone presents a *need*. You need me, I'm there—never mind my energy level, my prior plans, or anything I, myself, might need in the moment. And my vision? Can't even see it. I'm heading toward your lighthouse with a great big new light bulb just for you (and I took time I didn't have to wrap this pretty colorful ribbon around it). Others fall prey to flattery and being honored in community. If they're asked to be on a board, they can hardly think clearly if it's a good cause and a prestigious appointment to boot. Of course they'll make time for that! And they've just traded chili peppers for lobster traps.

Whatever it is that gets you—your particular downfalls, distractions, and defaults—all will surely show up presenting you with choices you need to make toward or away from your vision. If you're the life of the party and love that social thing, any number of large and small opportunities may come up to squander away your time for organizing that community center or setting up that mentoring program in local schools. It could honestly be nothing more than a series of coffees, drinks, lunches, parties, and movies keeping you from your vision. Note that these may sometimes be great choices—that is, when they point right to Santa Fe: when the coffee date means face time with someone who has something to teach you; when the party is about networking; when you've worked enough and that off-task dinner with friends is the very thing you need to be refreshed and ready for the next Santa Fe–bound step.

Small choices do count too—if you have twenty minutes before it's time to get ready in the morning, you could default to checking e-mails and Facebook the whole time or—let's say you have a vision of living in a clear, well-ordered space—you could use that time to clear clutter and start setting up that filing system you only fleetingly picture in moments when you can't actually take it on. Getting on the internet, answering the phone, going for that more labor-intensive dinner preparation (de-seeding the tomatoes, because won't the guests be wowed!)—any number of small choices can take you to Maine in the moment and ultimately affect the ease and efficiency in your journey to Santa Fe.

Keep track of the question: *Does this move me toward or away from my vision?* Use it often.

Thoughts and language are trickier to get into alignment with a vision—or perhaps they simply require more diligence. Let me remind you that nothing you decide to do gets set in stone just for having decided it. Remember that meditation metaphor? Something about the clear, still, Zen, Bahama-blue-water pool of the mind? Ah, no, it was about catching yourself in one random thought after another from bungee cords to revenge plots and simply bringing yourself back to the breath. Applied here, as you move toward your vision, you will most certainly catch yourself in Maine-bound thoughts.

Think of all your mind drivels on about in attempts to stop you from moving toward your vision: *I'm not smart enough; I'll never get in; they won't choose me; I don't have the money; this is a pipe dream; I won't stick with it; others can have that—not me. …* Why would you sit around thinking you can't have what you want or aren't equipped to create what you imagine putting into the world? It's about as counterproductive as thinking gets, but people do this all the time.

If you're having the thoughts, you're probably speaking them aloud. How many people have declared they want to be in a relationship and even take excellent steps to invite it in (they've got well-crafted profiles up on three dating sites, they're active in their communities doing things they love to do that attract other singles), but their speech is a constant listing of obstacles—either about the problems out there (*All the good ones are taken; They're nice but not attractive, or they're attractive but not nice; If they're single at this age, they must be sketchy*), or about their own perceived personal flaws (*I don't know how to date anymore; I just attract the crazy ones; I'm not lovable; my body isn't what it used to be*).

When you catch yourself in Maine-bound thoughts or speech, think again; speak again. We love to bring thoughts and sentences to completion once begun, but how often have you already noticed you're on the wrong track as you keep going? Stop! Stop mid-thought, mid-sentence. Tell yourself what's true instead. In a conversation with another person, depending on the context and the level of intimacy, say more or less to make your process transparent: "Hold on. I've got a whole project going to steer away from thoughts like this. What I want to say instead is …" and speak again. "Wait—I'm clearing out this particular line of thinking. Let me start over." Then do.

When you drive a car, your hands are never still on the steering wheel. Even if it appears you're moving forward in a straight line, your hands constantly make minute adjustments left and right. You can do this too with your choices and actions, your thoughts and language. Just keep bringing them back into alignment with your vision as quickly as you catch yourself veering off. Sometimes this involves a major shift and some hard decisions—a divorce, a resignation, a move. Sometimes all you need is a small or medium tweak that's pretty effortless: *I'm not having dessert tonight; I'll just unpack one box while I talk to my brother on the phone; I won't go away this weekend even though it's super tempting; I'm putting these chips away now, even with just this many left.*

It all gets easier the more you practice it. As you consistently line up your life with your vision, moment to moment, you train your entire being to better stay in alignment—that is, to keep realigning quickly when you catch yourself heading Maineward. You'll love how it feels. You'll find it allows for the most streamlined (the most effortless!) journey toward the vision. Line 'em up: choices and actions, thoughts and language, all pointed in the right direction.

chapter 33

Accessing Guidance in the Moment
(No Matter What Your Belief System)

You are guided. Whether you're working on achieving something on a large scale or simply proceeding through the banal aspects of a human day, it's empowering to move through life with the awareness—the conviction—that you're guided. When you're traveling from vision to fruition, you'll move much more quickly and with far greater ease if you believe something bigger than you is fueling the journey, directing and redirecting you, inspiring and guiding you, protecting and supporting you. And in your third job of visioning—moving toward the vision— guidance is what reveals to you each next step, a plan (not at first, but when you're clear enough to make one), the thing to try next when what you thought was going to work didn't (or the door you thought was opening just shut, or the initial *yes* from a reliable source somehow still morphed into a *no*).

We all know those impulses (we feel them *physically*) to put down the book, pick up the phone, open the envelope, close the account, check on the baby, turn left, keep trying, stop talking, sign up, drop out. People seldom think of these as guidance, but those who operate by their inner signals navigate life with more ease; the word *effortless* may even apply (at least some of the time).

Guidance abounds. It comes up from inside and out through any number of channels—ideas, hunches, images that pop in; memories that pop up or get triggered; the thing you suddenly think to google or ask; people, books, films, songs, all things seen, heard, perceived in any way; animal encounters, stories, and sightings; the thing you just know, because you just know it. Then there's the magic of synchronicity, which could involve anything coming up in unexpected pairs or threes (remember toorthrees?), or showing up all over the place, especially in a narrow time window or with that what-are-the-odds kind of charge. Whether it raises goose bumps or seems like no big deal, it's all guidance nonetheless.

Your guidance is unconditional, ever accessible, and operating entirely in your favor—as well as for the good of all concerned. (Following your guidance won't ruin anyone else's life, even if they accuse you of that initially.) Guidance comes in all the time, out of the blue, in the moment. In order to best access guidance in the moment, you'll benefit from having a few things in place.

Believe that you're guided.

You must have an overarching sense of connection in place. That is, you need a sense that you're connected to Source or simply to your higher self or inner wisdom; however you conceive it, you need to believe that you're connected, you're guided. The more consciously you hold this awareness, the more connected you'll feel.

Note that I said *feel*, not *be*. You're always connected; you may think you're not (and therefore you'll feel you're not), but you're never separate. One of the 12-step precepts is about improving "conscious contact" with Higher Power, or what guides you. Bring it to consciousness. Get in touch with it. For some time I've repeated every day, sometimes several times a day, "I am guided. I follow inspiration and guidance. I follow magic and synchronicity." Since reading Florence Scovel Shinn's *The Game of Life and How to Play It*, I've added her phrase "I make right decisions quickly." This supports me to stay connected—or rather, to stay aware of being connected.

Believe that your guidance is you-friendly.

It helps to believe that guidance isn't tricky to access: it's not such a still, small voice that you have to strain to hear it and half the time just won't. It's not coming to you in code—some code you can't crack that's always testing your incompetent skills for deciphering all things cryptic. (Your guidance is not the *New York Times* Sunday crossword puzzle.) Wherever guidance more obviously requires interpretation (say, dreams or synchronicity), trust that unless some super-clear meaning emerges along with a vivid knowing that it's right on, you probably don't need a super-clear marker here. Just let it contribute to your sense of veering left rather than right, or watching for your tendency to let money decide it as you proceed or to go for what will look more impressive to others (or whatever tendency you know to watch for and counter). A cool coincidence or compelling dream may serve as no more than a reminder that you're not alone: you're in a rich ongoing discussion with the Universe, and when you're not sure what you're talking about, there's no problem.

Play with synchronicity, but beware of interpretations.

What I mean may best be illustrated by that lovely insanity people fall into when they meet someone who initially looks like a good potential romantic partner. Amazing synchronicity keeps popping up to compound the bliss, and many, at this juncture, make the mistake of false interpretation. They go straight to *We're meant to be together.* To my mind, there's seldom a solid objective *meaning* to apply to the magic of synchronicity. I see it as on-course feedback from the Universe, but not necessarily as in *You've found the one, so hold on tight!* Go for a broad interpretation, as in, *Something important is happening here. Pay close attention.* Then you don't have to fear the red flags or be all bereft when you find this wasn't the one after all. And you won't end up shaking your fist at the Universe, like it was just toying with you—*What about that exact-same fucking brownie recipe both our great grandmothers handed down?!*

So having been alerted by synchronicity to pay attention, you can simply open your eyes wide (get curious!) and see what you get to learn next. It could be to watch yourself so clearly this time that you notice the moment you stop saying what you think and start saying what you think she wants you to say. Or you stop checking in about what you want and start acting on what you think he wants. Or you stay and let her leave first or leave when you first notice it's time to go or ... whatever it is the gift will be this time. Loosen your grip and stay tuned.

Ask for guidance!

Truth is, guidance will come whether you ask for it or not. It's like air, the element you live and breathe in (or as I once eloquently put it talking to a friend, the fishy-water you swim in). But when something is up for you and you're obviously in a position of wanting clarity or needing to make a decision, do ask. Then do these two things: expect answers and show up to listen for them. You may want to be still and practice some form of meditation/contemplation. This could look like sitting down with a journal, sitting in meditation with the intention of getting a clue, or doing some activity (walking the dog, washing the dishes, taking a shower) while watching for what will show itself. It could also look like going about your life and noticing when anything happens or comes to your awareness that's related—or even that might be.

In some way or another, input your question and expect answers to emerge. It's a lot like entering data and letting a software program organize it and crank out some specified output. It's a lot unlike that too—because you really don't need any particular program, and the guidance computer may do something totally unexpected with the data you put in. The boundless intelligence of the Universe, able to coordinate any amount of data, is available to you. Consciously give it your questions and concerns and watch for what comes back to you.

Note that there's an important component of pausing and looking away in here. Some of us remember when computers were big hulking machines that didn't belong to ordinary folks, weren't companions in coffee shops, and didn't pop out instant output following input—as opposed to the most commonplace search that any random person might currently engage in on a multiple-times-daily basis. Now, you can hear Paul and Phil in a Saturday Night Live skit say that they hail from the Hawkeye state, and in seconds learn this means Iowa. (You can read right here about Paul and Phil in the Halloween 2014 SNL graveyard skit and instantly find it on YouTube so that you, too, can fall in love, or fall over laughing.) Let your guidance system take whatever time it takes, which could be nanoseconds or may involve some lag time.

Once you've taken care of input, your job is to look away. As long as you're brooding and figuring, you haven't released it to what's larger (and smarter) than you. Quit believing the answer comes from the workings of your mind. I'm not saying the mind won't do what it does. If it keeps reaching to check for what's happening (like the kid opening the oven door while the cookies are baking), just gently release it again, again, again.

Operate out of self-trust.
Guidance comes from both inside and out, but what comes in from "out there" does need to be perceived and processed by your own inner receptors. This means it's all inner guidance, and it's all about you—what gets your attention, what resonates with you or just doesn't, what strikes you as *on* or *off.* You need to believe that you're trustworthy to read the signs, evaluate, prioritize, or just feel for that gut response and choose

with little weighing of pros and cons.

I once had a memorable talk with a client in which we looked at the fact that both the intuitive and rational, linear-thinking parts of you can weigh in, and both are willing to stay present for the whole conversation. Don't treat these parts of yourself as if they're at odds with each other. Just because we can separate them out and give them different names doesn't make them inherently separate. All of you works together as one. Your intuition isn't some right-brain character smirking with disdain while the careful, left-brain part of you sits there listing pros and cons. If you think of these two as two different characters, since you're making it up anyway, also make up that they're not only on speaking terms but excellent collaborators.

You can trust yourself, and all the different aspects of you, to decide well. If you feel like you're confused, you can't read the signs, or you're getting mixed messages, then don't focus on confusion; don't think there's something wrong with you. Hold a consciousness of questing, not of being confused. Stay open. Acknowledge that you're in a process, and you simply don't know yet. (It helps to love not knowing—not to think it's a problem not to know. Byron Katie likes to say that don't-know is her favorite place to be. Anything is possible from there!)

Honor the power of intention.
If you're both clear about your intentions and committed to holding them, they will assist you tremendously in receiving clear guidance. Another gem for me from Deepak Chopra is the idea that intention invites synchronicity. If you're not sure about your child's schooling, your clear intentions about what you want for your child and for your home life will guide your process in evaluating the options and choosing minimal versus radical change (and noticing events, people, dreams, or signs of any kind that point to the right answer for you). If you have clear relationship intentions, it gets a whole lot easier to take in and process information about whether you want to keep dating or living with someone (are your intentions being fulfilled or neglected, even violated?). Clear intentions about where you're headed professionally will make it much easier to say no to the better but less-than-where-you-see-yourself-next job opportunity. Have and hold intentions and have a healthy respect for the power of intention. You may also want to watch for (and enjoy the fun of) synchronicity that

obviously relates and responds to what you're holding as a clear intention.

Get your concepts out of the way.
When we have very clear ideas about how things should be and adhere religiously to preset existing structures, it's hard to get guidance in the moment—we're just not that open to it. If you must always follow the same route to go home, you'll disregard that sense to go another way this time—an intuition that could keep you out of danger or delay. Don't let the clock decide your timing when the inner voice urges, *Get up now.*

On a small scale, a concept could keep you from wonderful encounters with various human beings: you've declared as truth that you don't hang out with homeless people, or people dripping in money, or pretentious academics, or skateboard punk rockers. A concept could rob you of brief glimpses of hummingbirds: you've nailed yourself down to a task you must not budge from, so you ignore the impulse to step outside. A concept could cause the scorching on the bottom of the pot: you thought *Get up and stir the soup,* but you were wed to winning one more round of that game.

On a larger scale, if you have a strong belief (concept) that the way you've set up your family is the way you should keep it, you may spend decades in a straight life when you're gay, because the clear guidance you're getting to explore your sexuality and create an alternate lifestyle keeps getting caught in the but-I've-already-got-the-family-that-looks-like-this filter. You may not go for what you know to be your true calling because that would violate your concepts of job security, the imperative of insurance, or the level of backing you believe you need in order to start something new and potentially radical. As a coach and as a human being, I love using The Work of Byron Katie to question any of these concepts so that the channel can be cleared for guidance. (At the risk of repeating myself, it's the most effective tool I've encountered for that purpose.)

Don't talk back to your intuitive impulses.
This is closely related to getting your concepts out of the way, but important to present as a separate point—especially since we seem to love talking back. A brilliant little example of this happened during a session once when I almost pushed away the impulse to silence my cell phone because I had the fleeting counterthought that my client wouldn't

feel listened to if I reached for my phone. Instead, I pushed this concept away in favor of the first impulse (guidance) and grabbed the phone to turn off the volume. The second it was off (it was an old model that required pressing downward through the volume scale to one beep then to silence), a call came in noiselessly—just one second earlier, it would have interrupted the session. It still did, actually. I got all excited and told my client about what had just happened—because we were talking about guidance in the moment!

When you talk back to your guidance, you're treating it like some bothersome authority figure that's getting in the way of your fun. Reacting from this inner-kid place, you may reach for your actual adult status to respond with entitlement, as in, *I can bloody well have one measly glass of wine, I've earned it.* If your intuition is telling you not to drink tonight, there's a good reason for it, and it's not to keep you from pleasure, or give you a dry, boring life, or deprive you, or punish you, or anything else you could come up with that has any sort of keep-you-down spin on it. Actually, your inner voice isn't that of a mean teacher, tyrannical boss, or controlling parent. Treat it like the voice of your dearest and wisest friend, the one who wants the best for you in every sense, fun included, and knows the most efficient and fulfilling ways for you to simultaneously get your needs met and offer your best service to the world.

I connected to this idea on a deeper level when I was working with a client who responded to his wife—especially her requests of him—with a sort of knee-jerk resistance. Geoffrey knew that the resistance had been cultivated during childhood when his mother (who was an addict) asked too much of him too much of the time. Still, despite this understanding, he couldn't stop responding to his wife as if that level of self-protection were still needed; as if his wife were also some uncaring authority figure using him to get her needs met. His ongoing resistance to her was misplaced and created disconnection in the relationship.

Somehow it came to my awareness that he was doing the same thing with his own intuitive impulses! Messages would come in to ask again for the payment, end the conversation, invite So-and-So to lunch—and instead of following them, Geoffrey went into instant resistance, as if intuition were some internalized version of the demanding addict mother.

See your intuition only as a parent if you make like you're old school and honor and obey it without question! My generation, give or take a few years, fell into the tail-end of that era when *why* was largely considered an inappropriate and defiant word to put to a parent. You just did what you were told. Apply that to your intuition. As soon as you reach for a rational reason for ignoring your intuition, you'll be sure to find one, or plenty of them. You'll then ignore that knowing that has no logic to give you in the moment when it simply directs you here instead of there. How many times, following accidents or thefts or other misfortunes, have people declared, totally baffled but equally sure of it, "I *knew* I shouldn't have …"?

Forget needing a reason to follow what intuition dictates. Florence Scovel Shinn, who wrote about the power of the mind in the 1920's, offered this affirmation: "I am always under direct inspiration. I know just what to do and give instant obedience to my intuitive leads." I love the *instant obedience*. (Hey, you can look up more affirmations from Florence online.)

I mentioned *Get up and stir the soup* in the section on concepts above because that was my personal training ground for following intuition. I used to get lost in writing activities or editorial tasks (my bread and butter for years), and I started noticing that whenever I found the soup was scorched (ay), I could mentally go back a few minutes to a wordless sensation that had most obviously meant *Get up and stir the soup*. As I take good eating very seriously (and make soup from scratch!), I started paying attention.

Let me address here the fact that what we typically call the voice of intuition is often no kind of voice at all. I was first struck by this when I heard Deepak Chopra describe how the Universe guides us through sensations in the body. I instantly flashed back to high school when I would sometimes keep reading late into the night even though I knew I had to get up at what would feel like a brutal hour. As I kept reading, knowing it was time to turn out the light, I'd feel in my core a sensation that had a fascinating crescendo effect, gradually increasing in intensity as I persisted in ignoring it. I could go back even farther in time to playing in the woods as a child and feeling (as a sensation in my body) that I should really go home now. I'd known about this for years and years and years, and still wasn't responding to it appropriately! I wasn't making use of this amazing resource right inside me.

I certainly hadn't been taught to pay attention to any such thing.

Like most everybody I ever talk to about this, I was taught rules, rights and wrongs, any number of concepts, but I wasn't taught to monitor and respond to my inner directives. What an egregious cultural lapse! As far as I can tell, this one still prevails. Few and wondrous are those who point their kids to their own guidance system.

Note that sometimes the intuitive sensation's meaning isn't precisely clear in the moment, in which case I've come to respond with a pause. This usually lets in the needed instructions. I may get up and wander around, stretch, step out to gaze up into the sky, or make that the moment for a tea break—anything that pushes the reset button. I say, *Show me.* (Best prayer for non-praying types: *Show me.* Or, one notch up: *Show me, I'm open.*)

Your training ground for connecting to intuition can be anything that suggests itself to you. The thing is to simply notice what you notice, and respond. Beware of selective listening where your intuition is concerned! My client Aubrey told me about those moments when she just didn't want to listen, especially when procrastinating to ward off some odious task. The nonverbal message would come in to put down her colorful quilting cloths and go work on the drab document, and she wouldn't budge. (It's that misplaced response to the pushy or punitive parent again.) In any number of realms, she was delighting in following whatever impulses came up (one of those clients who opened fully to the challenge to experiment with a friendly Universe), and she was richly rewarded with greater peace, increased well-being, and lots of cool synchronicity. So ... what would happen if she never talked back?

How do you want to play this? By what criteria do you decide or justify what you follow and what you don't? At what cost do you say yes to some intuitive flashes and no to others? I have no scientific evidence for this, but I'm pretty convinced that your intuition will more consistently feed you clear, powerful signals that you're equipped to interpret if you offer consistency in responding to those signals: try that instant obedience Florence suggested.

Go for Joy!

I've already discussed the importance of scooching toward joy in "Why Joy Now?" in part 1. To quote myself (this is fun!), "We're supposed to feel good and—it's really quite miraculous—life guides us by what feels good." This bears repeating and expounding on now. Definitely go for joy, as it's one of the primary ways life guides you. You're on the right track if joy stirs inside you.

While I'm quoting myself (told you I was having fun), let me repeat something from the "Two Liars" chapter: "Your guidance system speaks to you through sensations of expansion and relief and pure, simple knowing—never by making you feel bad about yourself." Never by making you feel bad, period. Ultimately, it's about going for what feels better.

How does this thing you're doing or this option you're considering feel? Does it make you feel heavy, contracted, burdened? Just the thought of it puts you in overwhelm? Head the other way. (Head the other way even when your mind inserts every logical, sensible, responsible, people-pleasing, stay-in-your-place, [fill in your] reason you really should plow through.) When it feels better, lighter, expansive—when your breath naturally opens into something greater and easier—now you're on it.

If it makes your heart sing, you're aligned with your guidance system.

Yes Yes Hell No! (The Little Book for Making Big Decisions)

Brian Whetten, the coach I had the good fortune of working with for a season, wrote the wonderful, truly helpful book by the title above. For any decision, but especially at those major turning points in life, he advises checking in with three inner voices to get their yes/no votes. Brian says you need a *yes* from the voice of intuition—that gut knowing without many words attached. You also need a *yes* from the voice of reason—which will approve the idea when logistical concerns and the weighing of resources are dealt with: overall, this choice fits with the rest of your life (or properly displaces something ready to go); it makes sense. As for fear—which balks at being taken out of your comfort zone, which does not appreciate the stretch, which remains perpetually baffled over whether fight-or-flight is in order here or not—that voice will say, perhaps scream, "Hell no!" With that trio in place—yes, yes, hell no!—you know you're good to go.

I think his model is brilliant, because people routinely sit around waiting for the voice of fear to get to *yes* before they move. This could mean a long wait. You may talk yourself right out of what the rest of you knows it's time (sometimes high time) to do. Fear will try to hold you back, and it may very skillfully masquerade as the voice of reason, listing all the very good and sensible-sounding reasons this thing you're proposing is a bad idea. There are always valid reasons not to do something. Do you want the voice of fear to call it?

I talked to my client Nigel about the idea of *yes, yes, hell no!* when he was thinking about quitting his (well-paying) day job to focus on an entrepreneurial adventure. Let me back up. He had decided to quit his job a week before in the wake of a coaching session, and then he undecided it. Ah, because he called his father, who very kindly, very calmly, very firmly counseled against it. The pater-figure proffered all the most reasonable arguments on behalf of the voice of fear, until Nigel was sold again on waiting. Fear (mimicking reason) declared that Nigel didn't have much of a cushion in the bank, had no guarantees about how quickly he'd make the first sale, and didn't want to get himself in a bad position financially. The true voice of reason argued that it would take just one sale in his new business to move him along both personally and professionally. There were no guarantees, true, but there was enough proof it looked promising that reason voted yes.

Of all that boded well, the most relevant bit was that Nigel had recently found the ideal business partner, who was savvy in areas he wasn't, and—no question—the particular brilliance in the merging of their strong points seemed greater than the sum of the parts. It was a match made in heaven, serving him not only in obvious practical ways but in emotional bolstering as well: Nigel felt so much less alone in the venture and this inspired him toward bolder action. So, he told me, he would still take that action of quitting, but later, once ducks X, Y, and Z were all in a row. The plan, in the meantime, was to continue to exhaust himself running this separate full-time venture around the edges of a full-time job. (A recent violent cold had already chimed in with what his body thought of that.)

Catching me up on all this from a place of pure discouragement, Nigel started reminiscing about the night a week before, when he'd decided to quit. A sudden great burst of energy (that very night!) got him going on an important marketing task he hadn't been able to get to with the full-time job still in place. That's a quick expansion (Hello, intuition). He described the lightness that came in and how his breathing expanded as he worked on this task—only to shut it down the next day after a talk with Dad reversed his decision.

Nigel! That was a *yes* from intuition. Let's go over all the *yes* evidence from reason! Now, would you look over there at that chap cowering in the corner whimpering *Hell no!* You're going to let him veto these other guys (who are way better looking)? Nigel gave me some grief over what he calls my golden flyswatter, then tendered his resignation later that day.

If the voice of fear says no, while intuition and reason agree it's a go—what are you waiting for? Go!

Telling the Voices Apart

Someone asked me recently, How do you tell the difference between reason and fear when fear can sound so reasonable? For starters, the voice of reason speaks in a reasonable tone, while fear is high-pitched, urgent, adamant, talking way too loud with too many hand gestures. Fear has an agenda and is glaringly obvious in trying to talk you into his way; his way is very black-and-white, right-and-wrong. Reason, on the other hand, is neutral—interested in fact-checking, in reality, in what actually does or doesn't work, in risk assessment, in probability and likelihood, degrees and shades of gray.

Reason is the gal with the sexy-geeky glasses who's going to present a thorough, well-researched report and tell it to you like it is, without pretending to know what can't be known. If there's a balance of pros and cons, she'll present the balanced view. Whatever she's presenting, she won't sound scared or urgent; she won't make any predictions that feature your personal doomsday just up the road. The bottom line, with Reason, could be one of three things: this really could work; this just won't fly; or this could very well go either way—and here's what you'd be risking on each side. Note that Reason doesn't care which way you end up calling it—just wants you to be clear about what's what. Reason knows you'll be okay either way.

Okay either way? Fear, with his fixed agenda, predicts it will not be pretty if you don't do as he says, and tells you in detail (even reasonable-sounding details) just how ugly *ugly* can get. Here's a position Fear would never take: "Go ahead and take the risk! If things don't come out right, there'll be nothing lost, and plenty gained." Fear just wants you to play it safe and will seek to persuade in drastic terms of failure, loss, insufficiency, homelessness, utter disgrace, what a fool you'll look like, how you won't get your old life back if the new plan doesn't come through, and so on.

Fear tries to scare the bejesus out of you, so when you're attuned to that voice, you will feel scared. The voice of reason is more likely to be calming, perhaps sobering, encouraging you to get curious about looking dispassionately at the whole picture and breaking down the parts, futurizing only to hypothesize where different paths could take you. Fear sees the future as a dangerous place and reaches into the past for ugly stories with the wrong morals gleaned to use against you as cautionary tales. ("You saw what that got you in college"—when, you might point out to Fear, you were a different person, at a different stage of life, in different circumstances, with fewer lessons under your belt, with different characters playing the scene with you, and so on.) Fear isn't open, watching for what's possible; he wouldn't think to say, "Show me," as he's fixated on one viewpoint. Finally, Fear makes no room for trust—not in yourself, not in the people who show up as reliable helpers, not in a friendly Universe showing you the way.

But now that I've said so much about fear versus reason, let me remind you of intuition, because decisions aren't just a matter of sorting out fear from reason. Let Intuition have its voiceless say. If you're getting an expansive, sigh-heaving, load-off sort of feeling from that sector, watch for the good reasons that go with it. Where reasonable-sounding factors just make you feel frightened of risks, of the future, of your likelihood to get basic needs met—don't accept that line of thinking or let it make the decision for you. Do not put Fear in charge of your decisions. Do question the thoughts that scare you on the way to deciding.

You are guided. Trust yourself, and trust your guidance. This guidance is unconditional, ever accessible, and operating entirely in your favor—as well as for the good of all concerned.

Jess's vision board: Guidance in action

Jess was working with me on what to do with herself professionally. She was actively questing for a time, then sort of came to a dead halt: stuck. I knew it was bad when the primary topic in session became how to manage those addictive serial shows (watch the little arrow spin for fourteen seconds ... and on to the next episode!).

Jess had clear passions, solid experience, obvious strengths—all of which should have yielded some obvious jobs to pursue. Naturally gifted in creating programs, she'd been honing this skill doing underpaid work with underserved youth. This in itself had the effect of depleting her energies a bit, and somehow devaluing the worth of what she was doing. But some days it was clear enough. Thanks to Jess's networking with any number of cool community organizations, the kids in her care got to work in a variety of spaces (for an ongoing project or just for a day), learning hands-on in a variety of spaces while they actually made a difference: they weeded city-owned flower beds, cleaned up the boat docks, processed returns at the public library, cleaned and fixed donations at the ReUse Center. The kids loved it. Their growing self-esteem was palpable.

A natural leader with easy people skills, Jess not only established solid rapport with the youth she served, she also earned their respect (they knew not to give her any shit). Further, she loved being outside and doing work that kept her moving and interacting with earth and tools. That fueled her success in getting passive, media-saturated youth digging in dirt and making things happen outdoors!

In searching for possible new directions, Jess didn't lack for inspiration. She found her spots to watch for job listings, targeted particular companies and outdoor-oriented organizations, explored various educational options across her wide scope of interests—but each new idea fizzled into a dull *no*. Often, something or another felt just enough beyond her reach—money and distance were the top troublemakers—and it just wasn't worth the stretch.

Further education did seem to be a stronger draw than available jobs. She got super excited when she found a program at the Naropa University in Boulder that combined transpersonal psychology and wilderness therapy—wow, did this really exist? But the school required a visit as part of the application process, and (fizzle, fizzle) she couldn't find it in herself to invest so much money with so much uncertainty. Another school she was drawn to was Antioch University in Seattle, but (ugh) all the way on the other coast—and how would her dog Tater Tot fit into this picture? (A valid nonnegotiable!) All in all, nothing seemed to truly call forth that easy, full exhale that says, "I've landed." And although her work with the youth still currently yielded some good adventures and excellent results, she couldn't shake the feeling she was done there. She was getting depressed. (*Why am I lying here watching TV again?*)

Something had to give. At the time I had vision-boarding materials elegantly worked into my living-room decor, as I'd recently held a string of daylong visioning workshops at my house and kept thinking I might do some more. (Besides, what could give offense in a bookshelf stacked to the gills with magazines, colored labels dotting the wall above?) Vision boards figured in the program to get participants into right-brain mode—plus for the pure fun of art and art tools. I decided that's what Jess needed too, and invited her to stop by so I could literally hand her a vision-boarding kit: a collection of magazines, a foam-board poster, some rubber cement (won't warp the cut-outs as do glue sticks), some Mod Podge (don't get me started on the glories of this nontoxic finish), and a humble fifty-cent brush to apply the latter. If she failed to complete this project, it wouldn't be because I neglected to set her up for success! She seemed excited about the idea of trying this—at worst, it would be a fun, if pointless, art project to immerse herself in for a few TV-free hours.

My philosophy around magazines to use for vision-boarding is to go for variety to the point of absurdity, including content that has no apparent bearing on you or your life, as you may come upon unexpected images and words that give you a zing and take you somewhere interesting and seriously appealing. So Jess found herself interacting with and drawing from an array of magazines that I purposefully did *not* tailor to her: fashion, lesbian, sports, nature, entertainment, science, technology, architecture and design, home, health, yoga, travel, and more. It was fun to put it all together—kind of like throwing Martha Stewart, Oprah, and Ellen into a bag with an orange panda and a handful of squid, then tossing in a sesame kale stir-fry, a lacy dessert, a fix-it project, and a rainbow of meditation cushions.

The first step, then, is to simply gather images, and possibly words—more than could cover the board. The main instruction I offer in the initial choosing of cut-outs is to go for whatever gets your attention and appeals to you. Don't require a rational reason for including it; in fact, don't think about it at all. You know what you're drawn to. It's also nice to tear instead of cut in the beginning: it's less persnickety, and you can later trim with scissors the clippings you actually use or contemplate using.

That's next: take your time drawing from your gleanings to arrange and rearrange various configurations of cut-outs on the board. It's good

275

to be detached about what ends up on the board and what gorgeous tidbits get redirected to the recycling bin. The arranging can be done in a deliberate, organized way (sectioning the board into themes—for example, people aspect here, money aspect there) or by simply letting the clippings land where they want to be. My current joy is to set up four sections according to Florence Scovel Shinn's Four Squares of Life, the four areas in which she believed we're meant to thrive: health, wealth, love, and perfect self-expression (see *The Game of Life and How to Play It*). I prefer to think in terms of an invisible X drawn across the board, so that the four sections are roughly triangular, meeting at a point in the middle that may even contain an image or phrase to encapsulate the whole—like a coiled snake does on the latest one I made.

Even if you choose some more deliberate pattern of arrangement, it's best not to be in thinking mode but to simply let yourself be guided, within the framework you've chosen, by what feels good and right to you. Watch for those on/off signals in your body. By all means, don't sit around making up what each image means and why you must put it right there. You'll trump right-brain function completely if you do this. Put your intuitive self in charge of this process, and play dreamy music without lyrics, if you will, for further support. Ask for guidance and inspiration and let the results surprise your left brain.

Jess was fascinated to find, as she looked over her spread of chosen images, that she was apparently obsessed with certain kinds of landscaping and architectural structures. (I'd managed to procure some gorgeous architecture and design mags from interesting Ithaca epicures.) Her mind took her back to some bygone work she'd done in ecological restoration—a stint in New York City with AmeriCorps right out of college. It was the first job that placed her outside and taught her she thrived in weather, working away from the comforts and constraints of ceilings and walls.

Jess didn't feel indifferent or uninspired when she next turned her attention to researching design schools. The Conway School in Western Massachusetts came right up and got her attention with its emphasis on ecological design and sustainability. Could it be true that they were hosting an introductory program for potential students within two weeks? Quickly reorganizing her calendar, Jess got herself there with her supportive mom in tow, and completely fell in love with the place and program. It's a small school, and to her this felt intimate and containing. Her sense was that she'd found just the right comfort-to-challenge ratio. A few months later, she was established there, starting the fall program with a great sense of possibility and curiosity, renting a room in a house that welcomed Tater Tot.

Jess's experience with the vision board is of particular interest to me because it had such an unusual outcome. In most cases, the gathering of images and sometimes words (in mine, lots of words) results in a completed board that evokes a certain sense of joy, fulfillment, and possibility. You've got the right vision board if looking at it just makes you feel good and open to all that could come in at any time. Staring at your board, you actually believe your life could rearrange itself into something that looks and feels this lovely to you.

For plenty of people, something happens in the making of the board, during the actual process: new insights stir up, ideas come in. There's often that element of surprise, that odd and wondrous find that inserts itself out of the blue or comes in with an exciting twist or heightened sense of relevance. Jess took it to the limit, actually landing in that elusive thing she couldn't locate before then. Without meaning to, she stumbled on her next career direction. It was a cool way to get there. Not unusual, though. Guidance will ride in on any breeze, drop through pure stillness, bubble up from murky waters. Get your concepts out of the way, stay open, and give attention to whatever gets your attention. Move toward what feels good, saying, "Show me. I'm open."

chapter 34

What's Your Weird Gift?

We're all healers. There's a way, I'm convinced, that every single person's presence on the planet provides healing for others. Stay with me. When you were a kid, you knew the house to go to where it just felt right and safe to be, and the mom had this uncanny timing for pulling baked goods out of the oven or offered anytime sandwiches with ingredients that might not even taste good at your house. That mom was a healer to the neighborhood children.

Think about all the weird, often beautifully idiosyncratic gifts people have that are really, in the end, their way of healing others or the planet. Could be their way of listening, fixing and refurbishing, explaining in pictures or symbols or songs; capturing absurdity or shaping anything into art; bringing folks together, telling it like it is, communicating with angels or animals; using their bodies like the rest of us dream about; inventing or innovating, making dolls or furniture, concocting herbal blends or French pastries; knowing a piece of land from its flora and fauna to its heart and soul. Could be their sense of humor or irony or their connection to the beauty in pathos. Could be the way they seem to land where people or creatures need help dying or giving birth or finding their footing in a passage.

The thing about your weird gifts is that they don't necessarily correlate with career paths—though they might, and can be directed that way much (much) more intentionally than most of us believe. Culturally, though, we don't yet think in terms of each having a weird healing gift, never mind organizing ourselves around it. But what's to stop you from getting to it individually?

This begins with identifying and honoring your gift. Honoring a weird gift is an ongoing process: you need to hold the conviction of its value, and use it wherever, whenever, however you can, so that you build the muscles that support it, so that you and others think of you in terms of your gift (they may already), and so that you're gradually evolving your understanding of how this gift fits into your whole life—work included.

I've known for years that my sister Denise has developed her love affair with her two cats (Faith and Hope!) through an animal communicator who's a friend of hers. She recently told me the story of how that friend established her footing in the field. Cathy had always had a connection to animals and, in keeping with that, used to pick up a few dollars through pet sitting. Sometimes, when caring for critters in her charge, she thought she heard them say things. It was a wacky phenomenon, just ideas from the animals' perspective that popped into her mind—and which she immediately discounted. Nothing in her reality had prepared her for a psychic connection to animals: she had no context for any such thing. So when she was wrapping a dog's pill in cheese as the owner had instructed, and the thought came in, "Gee, he gives me a lot more cheese than that," why would she do more than laugh and bat the thought away?

It happens that Denise read and loved Amelia Kinkade's *Straight from the Horse's Mouth*, a book on communicating with animals, and when she learned the author was holding a workshop in her city, she signed right up. Following a strong inner urging, she invited her friend Cathy to come along. While Denise had the typical participant's experience of picking up a few cool tidbits, Cathy found her life's calling: this thing she'd always done that came to her effortlessly had a name, could be cultivated, was valued by others who needed that service. She was launched with her weird gift. (If you need her services, you can visit her site online at coolaideclinic-dot-com. She communicates with both current pets and ones that have passed.)

If you like no-glitz, low-budget documentaries that inspire, you may want to watch *Buck*. It's about a man called the Horse Whisperer, who worked closely with Robert Redford on his film by that name. I saw that movie a while back, and enjoyed it, but I'd choose the documentary for a second viewing any day. Buck, in his low-key cowboy way that sets the tone for the whole film, reveals the heinous way he and his brother were treated in childhood until they were taken from their father and put in the kind of loving, healing foster care you read about (*Ellen Foster!*). He could have become a victim and excused himself to be a shut-down human being behind closed doors for the rest of his life, and we all would have nodded, *Of course, who can heal from such abuse?*

Instead, he found in himself a particular compassionate way of connecting with other beings—first and foremost, with horses—a way of approaching them that he wouldn't have been so singularly drawn to if he hadn't experienced exactly the childhood he had. (Please note that I'm not recommending, condoning, or excusing abuse. I do, however, highly recommend a response like Buck's to having been on the receiving end of it.) Not only did this man learn how to interact with horses in a way that allows them to thrive in cooperating with human beings, he taught and to date continually teaches this way to other people. In the end, though, the most fundamental and fascinating thing is that he's healing the people he comes in contact with, helping them to know themselves through the negative behaviors they've unwittingly created or reinforced in their horses.

It's pretty amazing to see footage of Buck in action. I was moved by the (sometimes weeping) people talking about coming to see they'd been mistreating their horses—out of a simple, wrong belief that how they were taught to tame and control them was the right and only way. There was so much redemption for them in adopting Buck's compassionate and connected way of interacting with these elegant power beasts. Beautiful.

Everything in a life's journey contributes to making human beings who they are. If you truly believe this (or experiment with believing it), you can find that the stuff of what you're here for is all right there in the story, in the best and the worst of it, in how you got thrown off and how you found your way, in what got you through, in how you connected to your own particular ingenuity despite getting dragged down by the particular ways you give up on or stop believing in your own best self. What you're here to do is definitely contained in the things you've loved even when all of life has seemed unlovable, in the topics of endless fascination to you even when you were too cynical to pursue them, in the thing you were naturally good at even though you feared or kept putting off getting the training to make it official. All the time, I listen to people arguing for what they can't do, or how what they can do isn't legit. I'm asking you to look at it another way and take this lens seriously: whatever has had your attention ever since it got your attention, whatever you could always do and have always done or even recurrently thought you could do if given half a chance—follow it. That's your thing, or some version of it, or some part of it. More will unfold as you experiment and explore.

In *Book Yourself Solid*, Michael Port recasts how to think of your career when he recommends avoiding labels when you tell what you do. Instead, offer more descriptive and anecdotal ways of presenting your work to others. When you give a known label, people don't hear beyond their preconceived ideas. For example, if I say I'm a life coach, someone may assume that I help people switch careers. And while I have done just that with certain clients, the actual thrust of my work is to guide people out of suffering and into living by their own belief systems, whatever their presenting issue. More than anything, I guide them into that two-part process of minding the pain body and tending the mind. I help them question their limiting and self-defeating thoughts and change their relationship with their thinking. I often work with them to create a clear vision of what they want in life, or in one realm of life (sure, it could be career), and then to move consistently toward that vision, clearing any thoughts, beliefs, or tendencies that get in the way of reaching it— or of even groping in its general direction. Once I've gone through my description along these lines, someone might make a little frowny-thinky face and tilt her head and say, "So, you're like ... a life coach?" People do love labels. So I laugh and say, "Yeah, I'm exactly like that. A life coach." But by that point they're open to new meanings, including what I mean by that.

There's no denying the forceful prevalence of the idea that what we do to earn money must fall under some neat, preexisting, carefully labeled and defined rubric. But that doesn't make it true. Whether you do or don't have such a tidy label for what you do, you must *know* what you do—know your weird gift. Because if you're a yoga teacher, for example, you probably have a lifelong connection to your body and the energies that move through it, or you made that connection at some point and got a rush and rebalancing from this that no hard drug, fast ride, or raw cacao nibs could equally effect. In your work, you correct lifelong posture problems; you awaken body awareness and move chi; you call in deep stillness through conscious movement: you're a healer, pure and simple. In Jyoti's case (she's based in Ithaca), teaching yoga means bringing her ministry and music to people in a hatha yoga context. She even offers some Body Bliss events that combine yoga and live devotional music with her band, One Love. Brilliant. Can all that be captured by "I'm a yoga teacher"?

You must validate your own weird gift—your whisper, your way of healing. You must own it. You must value it whether our culture notices it or not, never mind assigns it worth. You must value it whether the people close to you value it or not, or even begin to entertain its wondrous potential. Unless you come upon someone whose weird gift is to point out to people what and how important their weird gift is (I get to do that sometimes!), you're going to have to do this for yourself. How do you know it actually has value? Because it's here, it's yours, and it just moves through you, not only without your effort, but without your consent. It's the thing that has buzz and crackle to it and no apparent off-switch.

This isn't to say that you can't resist it or squash it or limit it or even forget all about it. You can do all of those things. Perhaps you have. But be sure this all comes at a cost, and that cost is this: you won't fulfill your potential, your mission, your whole purpose for being here. Do I speak too grandly? If you think so, you may be thinking too small, both about your weird gift and about yourself.

So how do you tap into your weird gift and its immeasurable potential? How do you turn your (possibly secret) whisper into a whisper that you get to use at full volume, and perhaps even get paid for? Consider this: the evolution is in progress; you've probably already seen your gift evolve. Look back over the trajectory of your life and see how it's been there, in one form or another, all along, and how it's grown either despite you or because you've consciously given it your good attention, or whatever scraps of attention you could muster during loaded times. So what could happen next if you gave it its full due and allowed it to become what you haven't even begun to imagine? Who would you become allowing yourself to claim your gift, step into it fully, use it at every opportunity for your own fulfillment and the greater good? I'm thinking you'd probably be a healer, even if the unlikely kind. You'd also feel aligned, expansive, and just plain right with the world.

Aria: Following the clues to your weird gift
A newly single woman in her forties, Aria was trying to understand where to place herself and what to do to make a living that would keep her out of drudgery. She had a number of skills and found she preferred working outdoors (most recently in a vineyard!) than sitting in an office managing tasks and deadlines—though she'd successfully done that too.

As she pondered making her choices more consciously, she could never get very far into dreaming up one path before she switched to another: the food truck would segue into an organic herb garden, which yielded to a bakery, then bookstore, then coffee shop. She really wanted a clear direction, because she'd chosen a place to live in another region across the map and couldn't see how to make the move happen without knowing how she'd support herself and what she'd be doing.

At some point, I suggested that Aria might read (and would love) Tosha Silver's *Outrageous Openness*. It's a great book for steeping in the idea that life will guide you to what's right for you, the perfect outcome has already been selected, and you don't have to sweat the details—all of this delivered in Tosha's warm and humorous style, two parts devotional to one irreverent.

Armed with this new perspective, Aria took to asking for divine guidance, but she could see no evidence that any was forthcoming. When she felt stupid with discouragement, she would spend hours watching a TV show called *Rehab Addict* in which a woman salvages historic homes. She found the show utterly absorbing. She also noticed the Day-Glo green envy it stirred up in her. Aria didn't like this. As she sat in it one day, she allowed herself to feel it. She let in the frustration of zero gains in the divine-guidance department and watched the whole picture. She suddenly saw recent visions of herself scraping plaster off old brick in her room. This was a new-to-her room in an old farmhouse, where a friend had invited her to stay. Yep, a historic home in need of some salvaging: that was the temporary lodging the Universe (divine guidance) had opened up for her during this time of transition.

It then struck her that within a two-week period, someone she worked for in an office setting had offered her extra cash for gutting the upstairs of her 200-year-old farmhouse, and someone else she'd assisted with landscaping in the past asked her to come help with a construction job. Aria wrote me about her epiphany: "All of those instances hit me upside the head with a wallop! Was this the encouragement I was looking for??!!"

Looking beyond those two weeks, she connected to her love of re-purposing materials and the satisfying work she'd done to refurbish the last house she lived in. What if she organized her move and new life plan around buying a little old house in the Southern realms she felt drawn to? She could redo the house herself—and go from there into helping others with their homes.

For some time, in moving toward her personal emancipation, Aria had been piecing together odd jobs, prioritizing environments she felt good in and factoring in how the work itself made her feel rather than following a prior career trajectory and opting for higher-paying jobs. (She came to moving toward what feels good quite apart from me.) These choices laid the stage for a deeper understanding of the precise thing she wanted to do and the ideal setting to do it in. Who knew that a call for divine guidance would yield an addictive TV show and a sequence of events not immediately interconnected in life or in Aria's mind? But there it was, all pointing to her weird gift and greatest passion and how these could translate in very practical terms to income-producing work, while also providing the structure she sought for how to drastically change her life.

Chris: Gifts of life and death
Weird gifts can get really weird, to the point that you don't see them or can't initially identify them as the gift that they are (they're just too weird). Chris, for example, started privately thinking of herself as the Finder at some point because she was always the one who came upon the remains of her chickens when the occasional hawk caught them. Since hawks drag their prey into concealing bushes, it's easy enough for them never to be found. But Chris had some sort of private, peculiar radar that allowed her to locate what was left of her feathered friends. This closure was important to her.

The chickens were important to her. (Is it too much to say that Chris reveres chickens?) She worked for a time at Farm Sanctuary, an organization with three different locations (one in upstate New York and two in California), where abused farm animals or animal victims of factory farming are cared for and sometimes placed in new, healthy homes. Over time, the rescue animal she's gotten closest to, hands-down, was a white Bearded d'Uccle bantam hen named Lola, who came to live with her for a season (and is gorgeously memorialized as a black-and-white tattoo on her forearm). Chris sums up their relationship with the words, "I was her legs, she was my heart."

I don't think I can (or want to) tell about Chris's weird gift without giving some background on her mysterious and crazy-sweet connection to a chicken who fit in the palm of her hand. Lola was among a fancy clutch of thirteen that Chris saw in a cage at a farm-supply store she popped into on an innocent shopping mission. The chicks stopped her in her tracks. They were not thriving, to understate the case, one lying beak-down in the chicken wire. Chris boldly asked to be given the chicks, as they were visibly unwell, and upped that to an offer to buy them, but they had already been purchased—request denied! She then downsized her request to taking the frailest one to the veterinary hospital for help, and the minder of the store agreed, throwing in for good measure, "He'll never make it to Cornell." (The chick did make it that far, but not much beyond.) Determined to help the others, Chris asked again to take them and was granted a sort of delayed permission—yes, if they were still unclaimed a few days later. That's how she ended up with the seven survivors, Lola included.

Typically enough, the chicks had been given hefty doses of anti-biotics, and this can sometimes impair neurological function. Lola was thus affected, and the damage devolved into paralysis. Life with Lola and her mates, in Chris's own words, looked like this:

This clutch was my family. I took them with me to the Farm every day, worried about them being alone for a whole day. Susie Coston, my boss and the director of Farm Sanctuary, once said to me, "Dude. You know, most normal people take a brief case to work. Not you. You bring your peep case." This pleased me greatly: my peep case.

When Lola and I were out for a walk, she would ride in her backpack and would alert me by trilling when "somebody" was flying overhead. Often, it was a heron. When I heard her trill, I would stop, or at the very least, pause. So in many ways she was my temple bell, calling me home to the moment, inviting me to pause, to stop my hectic living and tasking. She also needed me to take time-outs to place her in her sling so that she could be a chicken. The sling would allow her to stand, peck grass and dirt, dust bathe, and be in the company of other chickens. In the wintertime, I had a kitty-litter box filled with dirt from our yard so that she could dust bathe in the house.

One evening, I was outside picking up bowls for our regular

flock. Suddenly Lola trilled a long alert trill and stretched her neck out as far as she could. When I looked to where she was pointing, I noticed that I had inadvertently stepped on the tail of a snake, who was pulling with all of its might to escape me. I lifted my foot and the snake slithered hastily away. Lola's eyes were like none other for clear seeing and taking many things in.

Our connection was deep. Before other human, dogs, or anyone else could hear or sense that I was coming home, Lola would make her "Here comes Chris" sound and flap around. Within minutes, the truck became audible and visible to everyone else.

At some point, I developed a panicky feeling that would often come when I put Lola in her bed at night (a huge dog crate with towels rolled up for her to roost and nestle upon). I would be overcome with a fear that she would die, and found it difficult to leave her for the night. I began saying a mantra, "I will love you all of your days," followed by her nighttime lullaby. Being able to say this mantra helped me let go in those fear-filled moments. It wasn't until some time after Lola's passing that I realized that the real mantra is, "I will love her all of *my* days."

Chris could hardly wrap her mind around it when Lola disappeared, and wanted only to find her alive. All the obvious and unlikely places she looked yielded nothing. When she finally dropped into a place of surrender and declared she wanted to find Lola alive or dead, her Finder radar kicked right in. Bittersweet, to be sure, but infinitely preferable to Chris over that endless wondering. Turns out a hawk was responsible for Lola's parting from Chris's world.

But what was it with Chris and dead beings? The word *curse* did suggest itself more than once. It's important to note that, before working at Farm Sanctuary and collecting foster chickens, she'd had the painful and shocking experience of coming upon her father-in-law lying dead in his yard. Her instant initial response, typically enough, was a sharp *no!* This wasn't only for the loss, but for *more* loss. Only three months before, she and her then-partner had come to the end of a conscious experience of helping Chris's mother-in-law, her father-in-law's wife, die at home. This was preceded by an extended period of home-hospice care, in which Chris and her partner served as the primary caregivers. They had held the coming and passing of death so closely, so consciously, right through the end of the journey. Now this crazy, unexpected addendum?

Grief, then, was already present and raw when Chris dialed 911 for her father-in-law. The emergency dispatch operator gave her instructions on CPR (which she'd been trained in before but in that moment needed to be walked through), but truly, her father-in-law was gone. After Chris finished that school year (she was a teacher then), she needed quieter, more heart-centered work in a containing space, and that's when she retreated to the kind fields and barns of Farm Sanctuary. She was a perfect fit. Part of the farm's mission is to promote a vegan lifestyle, which Chris had already adopted. Effortlessly in love with all the animal residents, she couldn't learn or do enough to contribute to their well-being and the peace this brought her. (Enneagram fans? Yeah, she's a Nine.)

When Chris's life choices shifted her work to a library at Cornell University (the veterinary library, of course), she stayed involved with Farm Sanctuary, occasionally going to volunteer or just to breathe in dung-and-hay magic. Sometimes the creatures there are taken to the famous Cornell vet school to be treated for what ails them, and damned if it didn't start happening that someone from the Farm would call Chris to say an animal wasn't gonna make it, and none of them could get there. Would Chris go be with their dying friend? Of course she went: nothing felt more natural to her. She was lucky to have a supervisor at the library who supported these brief time-outs in the work day.

Once, she was visiting Farm Sanctuary when a goat named JT had just been loaded to the back of a truck for transport to the vet school. One of the workers came running in to where Chris was and asked her to come quickly. There it was again: she was the one with JT's head in her lap when he died. She sat there shaking her head quietly to herself. At this point, her supportive supervisor at the library had gently pointed out the possibility that this curse was in fact some kind of gift. (A weird one, to be sure.)

Then there was the time, quite apart from the world of Farm Sanctuary, when Chris had just put her kayak into the water of an inlet on Cayuga Lake. A woman appeared out of the woods, asking if she'd seen a deer come this way—the woman was agitated, worried that the beast wasn't okay, as she hadn't seen him reemerge after he ran for the water. Instantly in high gear, Chris quickly located the deer, fully immersed where it got deeper. (Who does this? Well, the Finder does.) She even started trying to get the creature out. She was in full adrenaline-driven rescue mode when she heard an inner voice say simply, clearly, *Stop*. She listened. She stopped. She noticed that the deer's back leg was mangled and obviously wouldn't be okay. It was a moment of death, not rescue or revival, just as it had been when she'd found her father-in-law, already dead when she didn't want him to die.

Can we say this was one of those moments of pure redemption? This replay with the deer allowed Chris to make space for the rightness of death, the quiet, complete appropriateness of it, ready or not. She was able to sit in that witnessing thing she somehow knew how to do, holding space as the deer's life ebbed to a close. Because by now it was clear that this weird gift wasn't merely about finding what was left behind where death had already passed, but also standing by, before, during, and after the passing, for all the mysterious, profound, beautiful stirrings in those movements.

May I just point something out here in the how-weird-gifts-work department? I've hung out in nature any number of times, and I've even come upon hurt or dying animals over the years. But the heightened, almost dreamlike quality of Chris's scene with the deer isn't likely to come up too often for too many people, even through miles and miles of outdoor adventures over time. When you have a particular mission, a purpose, a weird gift—it will find you. You will land (life will land you) where you get to experience it, express it, apply it, learn more about it. There's nothing random about the random woman calling to Chris on the edge of a lake: "Did you see that deer ...?"

Chris and I did some work together for a time, when she was thinking about easing out of library land and felt baffled about where to place herself next. She felt no draw to go back to teaching. She vaguely wondered if there might be more she could realistically do with her drawing/cartooning that could actually be income-producing. There was also the fact that she was already occasionally making money on the side by performing the magic of her gourmet vegan cooking at lovely Light on the Hill, a beautiful retreat center in Van Etten, New York, with seemingly more window than wall. (It's my own favorite place to hold weekend programs!) The atmosphere there is sweetly sacred, and it gave her great pleasure to spend some of her weekends cooking for groups of peaceful retreatants, who, as a bonus—all doped up on good vibes and away from life's stressors—truly appreciated being well fed. Maybe she could find a way to provide vegan meals for people who didn't have cooking time? Or those cofuddled folks just learning vegan ways?

At some point in our discussions, Chris found a faltering, hesitant way to tell me about her weird gift. How to even put words to this, never mind think of getting paid for doing it? It sure wasn't featured in any job description she'd ever read. She found dead creatures and people? She somehow showed up or got called in when they were dying? What's fascinating is that later, when we were looking back on our journey together, her memory was of seeking to understand what she might do with either art or cooking, while I had a clear memory of a triad-vision containing those two plus that death-and-dying thing we couldn't quite name.

Not to put too fine a point on it, the weird gift can be so weird—or may seem so unlikely in terms of being something to commit to and get further training in, to shape into some clear money-making con-figuration—that people sometimes can't seem to go there mentally, or can't hold on to it, and may thus even slow down the process of letting it come to fruition. Let me hasten to add: you don't have to figure it out; but you do need to honor it and allow it to unfold. It's certainly true, too, that people manage to keep it at bay an entire lifetime.

There was a lot going on for Chris at the time of our coaching and beyond, including the slow dissolution of a long-term relationship, and she needed to move into the next career venture slowly anyway. Good thing, as life revealed on its own terms the application of her weird gift and how to organize herself to best use it. Still, life did reveal it. I want to stress that Chris didn't have to strive and strain or blow a brain valve to crack the thing open. Nor did she have to wait forever (more like two years) before she could see where it was headed. Note that things happened and clues dropped in all along the way to direct her, though she couldn't possibly have been aware of a start-to-finish journey as it was happening. There never is a map-itinerary-schedule-budget-with-feasibility-study provided.

I can only roughly relay here the confluence of events with gorgeous synchronicity woven in that got her to where she is now. I'll aim for giving the highlights. At some point Chris noticed, advertised in a Buddhist publication, a Contemplative End-of-Life Care certificate program. It was a 15-week online class with a week-long residential finale. Finding it totally appealing, she immediately suggested it to a hospice volunteer she was close to. Next time she saw the ad, another friend came to mind—a woman who had lost her partner to cancer. This friend had taken to hosting viewings of the film *Griefwalker* to make space for hard-to-come-by discussion opportunities for others moving through grief. When Chris noticed the ad for the third time—*oh!*—she applied it to herself.

It was a huge financial commitment to sign up, but committing was crucial here, though she didn't see the import of that at the time. (Nothing like a down payment to register commitment. A conscious buy-in will always change the game and stir up the energy, even if you're committing to just one piece, or to something small.) The weeks of virtual classes and homework felt doable (she got excited at the thought—always a go-for-it sign), but it wasn't clear that she could get the time off work to participate in the one residential week. She most certainly wouldn't be granted a week off with pay. How would she manage this? Would they let her go for just part of it?

She really, really wanted to be there, though, not only because it was the real-time, real-life component of the course, but because of the location. While the overall course, at the time, was hosted by the Naropa Institute in Boulder, the residential finale was to be held not only in upstate New York where Chris lived, but more specifically (ah, synchro-nicity) at the Light on the Hill retreat center where she sometimes cooked. When Alice, the head of the center, learned that Chris was slated to come stay as a student in this contemplative class, she generously offered her an unexpected hefty discount on the room-and-board fee.

The course also required that Chris work for a stint as a hospice volunteer, so this again brought her close to people in actual transition between life and death. Needless to say, she loved it. The experience further deepened her sense that she was on the right path, despite ongoing lack of clarity as to where the path actually led, if anywhere.

Around that time, she also lost a former beloved colleague from Farm Sanctuary, and a friend involved in burial plans asked Chris for her support, as this colleague had wanted to have his body brought to Ithaca to be interred at Greensprings, the relatively new eco-friendly cemetery outside of town. The place allows no chemicals in any form (thus, no embalming), requires natural materials in the burial sites (wooden coffins or cloth shrouds), and practices minimal grooming of the grounds to allow nature to run its course all through and around the space. Situated on one of the many beautiful mini-mountains in the area, Greensprings offers a quintessential vista of the Finger Lakes region. Chris had no actual connection to the place at the time, but who else would someone call for help in getting a body to the right resting place?

Greensprings, functioning as a nonprofit, is overseen by soulful, intelligent people with a missionary zeal about creating an environmentally and naturally coherent opportunity for people to bury their loved ones. It made sense in the Ithaca area, where so many people are working toward sustainability on so many levels: we take low carbon footprints seriously here. Why not die the way we live? A friend of Chris's (of course) had gotten herself onto the board of this phenomenal organization. And did she invite Chris to join them, because it was a no-brainer? You bet she did.

This quickly and naturally led to Chris's shadowing and then assisting the burial coordinator in actually holding space during funerals. Chris was in her element. She remembers the first time she stood on that breezy hill for the first funeral she assisted, taking in the sacred grounds there so minimally touched by the usual unnatural human interventions in death. Every cell of her being said yes to this place and this peaceful group experience of a soul's send-off.

Each time she repeated the experience thereafter, she found she was struck more than anything by the oneness called up for her in joining a group of people where death had brought them together. The level of loss and grief we meet in death is such a basic common denominator for human beings of all kinds. There was something about this that Chris loved (and loves) tapping into like nothing else.

When the cemetery's director announced an intention to step down, Chris had an idea that felt instantly right and, simultaneously, sat uncomfortably with her tendency not to assert anything with a strong fist or elbow anyone out of her way. Of course none of that was remotely happening. She merely saw a reconfiguration: what if the woman currently in the position of burial coordinator became the director and Chris stepped into her position? She did find it in herself to speak this to her friend (the one who beat her to the board), and the friend relayed it to others in a moment when it made sense to do so. The elegant perfection of it was clear to all concerned. They came up with a plan to gradually bring Chris in as a part-time paid staff member to do what she was doing already—assisting the burial coordinator—so that within a couple of years the position could be fully and rightfully hers.

When Chris and I talked about all this, she kept slipping and saying *spiritual* coordinator instead of *burial* coordinator. Of course the slip is perfect. In her peaceful, non-assuming presence, holding the spiritual truth that we are all one, Chris will get many opportunities to stand on that wind-blown hill and give her blessing and support to grieving people as they seek more or less gracefully to make sense of the natural place of death in the rhythms of life.

So beautiful. So respectful. So Chris.

I hope no one is reading this chapter with the idea that it doesn't apply to you. When I made a post on this topic on my Jaya the Trust Coach Facebook page, someone commented that she derived a strange comfort from the notion of a weird gift. Ah, I think that's because, while we're all one, we're also all so idiosyncratic, when it comes down to it. To think that there's actually rhyme and reason to the weirdly particular thing that comes up from inside and captivates you, that moves through you and touches others, that expresses in some singular way not only when you allow it but sometimes entirely despite you; to think you can harness that and let it direct you into and through a life you love—very comforting indeed. Would you like to play with that?

chapter 35

The Sprawling List: Ingredients for the Chef

Want to change jobs or career tracks or find an avocation that blows anything you've called a hobby out of the water? This exercise of making a sprawling list is meant to take you beyond what you typically think of when you grope for your next job (or project). It could usher in awareness of your weird gift and even its perfect expression. More important, the sprawling list invites you to lay out all together in one space the many aspects of who you are, the pieces you tend to think of in categories that really all belong to one whole. So you might consider loving and admiring the pieces as you play with them, and feeling fond of the whole. (What I really want to say is, the sprawling list could be your chance to fall in love with yourself—but I don't want to scare you off.)

Ideally, create the list in more than one sitting. The finished list will include components that describe who you are as a worker, what you're most interested in, how you and others think of you, and much more. Whatever comes to mind that seems in any way relevant to who you are, what you've done, or how others perceive you—by all means, toss it in. You'll be including the normal stuff, the impressive stuff, and the unique, even idiosyncratic traits that make you who you are.

Some of my clients have enjoyed using some format that feels more creative and free-form than a linear list in a typed document. They might make bubbles, clustering together things that fall under the same category or somehow call to one another. They might use colors to code categories or to keep themselves entertained and right-brained while they flesh out their list. Make your list however it comes to you to do it.

Most important, be thorough. Keep adding over time as things come to you. My client Leanne uncovered in a session how supremely meaningful it was for her to give kind, careful listening to other parents who, like her, had intense, special-needs kids. It especially felt great when she got to guide them to resources and mindsets that might serve them better. This kept coming up in her life, brought her deep satisfaction, and turned her particular life experience with her own child into a way of offering help and solace to a population she felt kinship with and compassion for—a sprawling list item if ever there was one! Somehow, she hadn't thought to put it on the list, perhaps because it matched neither the career track she'd been on for years nor the line of work she was toying with moving into next. Leanne went in post-session, weeks after she thought her list was complete, to add this very important piece.

Typical resume stuff
Include jobs, education, degrees, special trainings, certifications.

Particular skills
Include people skills, tools of any kind, computer savvy, skills in cooking, sewing, writing, editing, acting, building, sketching, facilitating, speaking—*anything* you do well, whether you've had formal training in it or not, whether you've used it in vocation or avocation, whether you've hardly used it at all, or not in some time.

Experiences
Especially include peak experiences and anything particularly joyful or profound, fraught with learning and growth, or in any way peculiar or exotic or fun to tell about. Note those adventures you take pride in, keep coming back to mentally or conversationally. Note what seems odd even to you, though you lived it yourself.

Ways others (and you) think of you
Record the qualities people automatically think of when they think of you, what people bring (perhaps always have brought) to you, what they say about you when they introduce you or tell about you. You can cover the gamut from throwing together a mean curry to building bikes, your wry or corny sense of humor or particular way of listening intently, your constant, effortless networking that's as automatic as a reflex—whatever you've got that would spur a number of people to nod together in unison if someone spoke it aloud. If it feels like it would add something, include what you think about yourself on top of that, or what you wish others would see about you that they don't seem to (or that you hide!).

Things you're passionate about

This could include ideas, random topics, fields of study, places, specific populations you love to hang out with or serve, politics, social issues or causes, animals, games, sports, art, food, publications—you name it. Include even things you've always wished you knew more about or wish you'd done by now—whatever you haven't gotten to yet that continues to feel compelling to you.

Job musings

Write down missed callings, jobs you've never had but have thought about wistfully ("I would've been a great X" if only you'd started earlier, if you were good at math, if you could afford the training—whatever). Include anything you still wonder about even though something has stopped you from pursuing it directly.

It's likely that concepts are what's stopped you: *I'm too old now, I'd need too much training, It would take me away from my family too much, I'm not smart enough, I don't have the right connections, They wouldn't approve.* Write down even the things that your concepts would tell you are out of your reach.

Work needs and preferences

Add every detail you can come up with to describe optimum work conditions for you.

- Time structures (9-5, flex time, summers off, manage your own schedule)
- Place (move about locally, travel, work from home, work in an atmosphere that feels good to you—windows, plants, spaciousness)
- Supervision (want it, don't want it, prefer to be your own boss, like to manage others, feel curious about peer supervision)
- Independence/interdependence (work alone, collaborate, be part of team, work with public, have clients)
- Money (regular paycheck, commissions, passive income, opportunities to take on extra projects for extra pay)
- Benefits (are you sure these are nonnegotiable?)

Service

Include any service work you've done or thought about doing or keep returning to in life or even in musings—whether you've done it, or done it recently, or not. Play with answering this question: "If you could be of the greatest service to the world or other sentient beings, and didn't have to think about money or time or what anyone else thinks, what would you do?" (Note that by *greatest* in that question, I don't mean that the answer must be grand. It could be gorgeously humble, brilliantly minute.)

Cherry on top

In a similar, but more decadent vein, what would you be doing with yourself if you didn't have to worry about money or even about making any sort of contribution? Go crazy here—it's just an exercise of the imagination and obligates you to nothing. It won't put you in the poorhouse or soil your track record for being a good person. Go for something (or things) that you'd feel great about (just not necessarily in terms of money or service). Go for joy!

Anything else!

A client of mine offered the following categories:

- Things you're most proud of
- Inherent qualities or traits/gifts you were born with
- What makes you feel alive
- Things you've always wondered about
- What you like to do in your spare time or on vacation

Feel free to take off with whatever comes to you.

You're Not the Chef

This is important, possibly the most important aspect of using the sprawling list in the most fruitful way: think of the sprawling list as an ingredients list that you put together for the chef, but you are not—don't get to be, will never be—the chef. That role is filled by the marvelous organizing intelligence of the Universe, your Higher Power, Divine Order—whatever you want to call it. Connect to the force that's bigger than you and far better equipped to weave together any number of seemingly disparate components into a whole that's in gorgeous balance and harmony, and that truly resonates with every aspect of your being.

When people seem to think that, in their case, it's just too big a job to pull it all together into something cohesive and workable, I tell them to upgrade their Higher Power. (This chef heads up the top culinary school of all time.) The Universe is more than capable of synthesizing your past experience with your new awareness of what you want, what felt or feels off that you'd like to correct, who you're becoming—all of what wants full expression. Apply this to job, love, health—anything. It's just evolution, plus the fact you don't have to figure it all out or force it into being (you're not the doer). Don't wonder how it will happen; don't believe fleeting or prevalent thoughts that you can't have it (even if such quite-universal thoughts are there, or move through, or drop in weightily when you're down and discouraged). Just give the next articulation of your vision your best shot and keep moving toward it. A force much bigger than you can weave together into reality more imagined components than you can imagine.

The chef metaphor allows you to think of the sprawling list as your list of ingredients. It's your job to gather those but not to make the dish. You don't even get to choose what kind of dish it will be, or which ingredients will ultimately make it in there. I once told someone that he might be thinking he'd get a stew, but it would turn out to be a soufflé. (Then I burst out laughing: This was a gay man I was talking to, and I think I got those backward. What self-respecting gay man thinks *stew* before *soufflé?*)

Nonnegotiables
While you don't get the final say on what goes into the pot, or what the final dish will be, you do get to declare some nonnegotiables: both what must and what absolutely may not be included. Be clear about your nonnegotiables, and be sure to declare only what's truly nonnegotiable—not just preferences, however strong. (Your list contains one preference after another.) Note that this idea of declaring nonnegotiables in no way counters the idea of yielding to divine order. If they're true nonnegotiables, your own guidance system has brought you to see them as such. If you're wrong, if they're actually still up for negotiation, life will show you. But in the meantime, once you've declared something a

nonnegotiable, don't consider any job or endeavor that violates it. Do not negotiate a nonnegotiable!

So once you've got your list, that's the first thing to do with it: mark your nonnegotiables. Highlight them, make a separate list of them—flag them however you like.

You don't want too many, or you limit the field too much. That said, if they're really, truly nonnegotiables, there they are, however many. See if you can stake down just a few as parameters for the chef to adhere to, but not so many that you're seeking to control outcome too much or being too specific. Remember, the *how* is the realm of the Universe; the Universe takes care of the details.

Move

Once you've got the list in place (and you can always keep adding as more reveals itself), go toward anything that seems to evoke or contain more than than one list component at once. Notice what you notice and follow that. Notice the people who come into your field and talk to them; ask them to meet you for coffee or lunch, even if you're not sure how they can help you. (People love to give a hand up when they can.) As you follow leads and hunches, remember to value the open and shut doors equally. Trust that something greater than you guides you. Let the chef pull it all together into a dish whose textures, colors, and aroma will delight you beyond your current wildest imaginings.

Recognition

You'll know you're on the right track when several components from the list marry together, often in unexpected ways. Remember Aria from the last chapter? When she came to realize the import of her fixation on *Rehab Addict*, she quickly came into contact with a woman in the right geographical spot who had a cottage in need of renovation and who was happy to have Aria live there in exchange for the needed work. On top of that, this woman wanted organic gardens planted around the cottage (another area of interest and experience for Aria) and needed further help maintaining vineyards on the land (ditto!). She even owned another property for Aria to turn her attentions to once the cottage was in shape. A perfect match is a *perfect match*: it's just not that subtle.

chapter 36

Blueprints for Your Personal Manifesto

"Alice laughed. 'There's no use trying,' she said. 'One can't believe impos-
sible things.'

    'I daresay you haven't had much practice,' said the Queen. 'When
I was your age, I always did it for half-an-hour a day. Why, sometimes
I've believed as many as six impossible things before breakfast.'"

            — *Lewis Carroll*

What It Is and How It Works
(and What I'm Most Certainly Not Proposing Here)
A personal manifesto is simply a written articulation of your vision that
allows you to keep it in view through daily repetition. It's the best means
I know of to hold a vision. In creating a manifesto, you must clarify what
you want your life to look like enough to put it into words and writing,
which process results in a document you can have, hold, and hold on to.
As with everything, I invite you to hold it with a loose grip, allowing it to
evolve as you go, allowing life to show you what you're doing, which may
not match what you thought you were doing. Think of the manifesto as
dynamic, not fixed. Keep changing the words to match your vision as the
vision shifts; keep tweaking so that the content feels current and fresh
and the language sings to you.

    I suspect that if anyone's going to accuse me of being hopelessly New
Agey, here's where they'll do that. I invite you to read on with beginner's mind and take in what I'm actually saying, not what habitually gets
evoked for you when you hear any version of the word *manifest*. I'm not
putting this forth as a way to make magic or to guarantee an outcome. To
be explicit, here's what I'm not saying: declare anything you want every
day and you can have it! Nope. Again, what I do offer here, above all, is a
way to hold the vision. This tool also provides another way to work with
the mind, lining up your conscious thoughts with your vision, making
it more likely you'll choose into that vision to bring it into areas where

it doesn't yet match what you're living. Thus, in pure practical terms, the manifesto encourages your deliberate and conscious movement toward what you say you want for yourself by keeping the vision clearly in the fore.

It's important for me to clarify, too, that the manifesto best includes and could even focus exclusively on states of being or what I think of as your stance toward life. For example, it could articulate that you love your life; you live in the present moment, connected to breath and senses; you feel connected in community, giving and receiving support; you meet every face as the face of God; you live in ease, in flow, with confidence; you're at peace with yourself and all beings; you're a child of the Universe, a steward of the Earth.

What happens with the manifesto is that as you repeat it again and again, you begin to believe that your life could actually look and feel the way you keep declaring it to look and feel every day. Note how different that is from occasional fleeting thoughts along the lines of, *Wouldn't it be great if* ... or *Someday I'll figure out how to* ... or worst, *Why is it I never get to* ...?

Through the repetition, you're likely to notice where you're already embodying and living your vision, and you'll thus expand this reality by giving it your focus. Further, because you're repeating the words of the manifesto so often, you'll feel a certain discord when you choose or behave or think or act in opposition to the vision you keep articulating. You may find that the discord is or becomes intolerable; you may experience it as a call to action. For example, if you say in your daily manifesto recitation that you live in integrity and tell the truth, it can only hit you wrong when you get into some verbal whitewashing. You're more likely to catch yourself in it and you'll course-correct sooner rather than later. You cannot keep declaring that you're loving your easy relationship with food and allow yourself to unconsciously shovel it in at high velocity while vaguely hating yourself. You can't continually reiterate how well you get along with the people in your life and grumble about how irritating your coworkers are with their tiresome little cute-pet stories around the coffee machine. In short, the manifesto keeps you on-track, moving in the right direction.

In essence, your manifesto is one carefully crafted, highly personalized, big fat affirmation. Don't like affirmations? The thing is, you use them all the time. Everyone does, whether they call them that or not. Whatever you walk around believing and repeating to yourself about your worth, how life works, what you can and can't have, all that you're stuck with and can't seem to work out or all that you're good at, no question—those are your affirmations. You may as well fill your mind with a few potent ones you've thought through and consciously chosen, those that you truly want to make your reality.

Perhaps what you don't like about affirmations is the same thing I don't like, which is that shoving-down thing, in which you might use them to stuff what you really think and believe, then try to gloss it all over with pretty words. It's like masking heartache with a cheer-feigning, tooth-baring grin: that wretched pain in your chest remains, and your face looks weird. Detestable. For me, that's a great use for The Work of Byron Katie: expose any ugly, habitual thoughts that are detrimental to your peace and well-being; question those thoughts; come close to them to see what they do for you and to consider what else is possible. Then, if you like, you can use affirmations to help your mind create new mental habits of your choosing that counter the old stressful, self-defeating thinking.

Using the Manifesto

Once you have your document (many suggestions for creating it follow), read or recite it unfailingly (or as close to unfailingly as you can get without being a tyrant to yourself) morning and night—first thing in the morning and last thing at night. This is when your subconscious mind is most suggestible. I wrote in "Got Self-love?" (part 2) about the importance of how you put yourself to bed, and the impact this has on how you sleep and wake up. The personal manifesto is a brilliant way—providing a structure solidly in place when you're still shaky and bleary-eyed in the morning, or completely spent at night—to consciously reach for thoughts that feel good and emphasize why you love being alive, what supports you, where you're headed, and so on.

If you try the manifesto, notice how it affects your last thoughts of the day and your morning mindset. How does it inform your overall feeling about the new day? You may find that the manifesto keeps your mind from dark or dreary places that don't serve you or that it helps you move away from such thoughts much more quickly. You may feel more equipped than ever to meet each day. Feel free to repeat the manifesto more than once in the morning or while drifting off—or repeat your favorite paragraphs or phrases—especially if your mind tries to go somewhere you don't want it to go (kind of like distracting the toddler from the forbidden fruit with something benign and still compelling—car keys!).

Here are five simple and important guidelines for the recitation of the manifesto:

1. It's best to say it in bed. This isn't obligatory. (A steamy shower's a pretty great setting too.) It just helps to fix your vision in that liminal place between consciousness and unconsciousness.

2. Before you begin, focus in on your breath for a moment, with awareness brought to belly and chest, so that you're present here and now in your body.

3. Speak out loud so that you hear it; whispering counts.

4. Attend to the words with your conscious awareness and your emotions: picture what you're talking about as you say it and do your best to feel the emotions you'd feel if all that you're declaring were fully operative in your life. If you're just not in that space, see if you can generate some image from the past (could simply be your child's or dog's face, maybe the moon's)—something that most makes you feel how you want to feel. (More on this under "Emotional Fuel" below.)

5. During the day, line up your thoughts, words, choices, and actions with what you're repeating morning and night. Don't beat yourself up when you don't; just notice lapses, and bring yourself back to the vision and language of the manifesto. This process happens anyway just by dint of the repetition. You can choose to make it more conscious.

Directions for Creating Your Manifesto

Simply follow as closely or as loosely as you like the guidelines outlined here to write out your statement of what you most wish to experience in your life. I strongly suggest that you type it into a computer document so that you can easily make changes and print it out as needed. If you're a fan of longhand, there's nothing to keep you from composing initially by hand, or from writing out the current version to post or keep nearby. Still, an electronic file allows you to keep succeeding versions, if you like, and to more easily edit or revamp the latest.

This chapter culminates in two blueprints or templates that you can follow to a tee or amend to any degree. As for all the guidelines offered, take what you like and leave the rest. I tend to believe that the language specifications are important.

Length and Scope

Your manifesto shouldn't exceed two typed pages. I don't recommend making it longer than one. It could even be a single paragraph. You need to like the length and be willing to recite the whole thing morning and night, or at least one of those times daily (see "Short Version!" just below). Ideally, it'll be short enough that you come to memorize it after a number of repetitions. What matters is that you have in place all the pieces of your best current vision laid out in language that sings to you and at a length that feels manageable.

If you find that you dread repeating your manifesto, shorten it. If it feels difficult to fit into your day, shorten it. Sometimes my clients who've enjoyed using it but catch themselves drifting away have identified the length as the problem. A brief manifesto will do you much more good than no manifesto at all.

Note that you can use the format of the personal manifesto to lay out a vision for one realm of life or even for a single project. At certain times or for certain people, this may be both more useful and more manageable than an all-encompassing declaration about your entire life. Apply everything here to your career change, or your upcoming trip to Haiti, or your decision to bring a child into your life. Craft a written statement about any vision you're serious about bringing into being.

Short Version!

It's good and helpful to have a short version of the manifesto that you can scale down to when you're especially tired or discouraged. Better to repeat it in brief than not to repeat it at all. Some people opt to recite the whole manifesto on one end of the day and the short version on the other. My preference is to recite the long version in the morning and the short as I drift off at night; that said, you'll know what's right for you. The short version can take bits from the whole, or it can be the first sentence or first paragraph or two, or the beginning plus some "I am" statements—you'll find what works. The point is to choose the best part or parts that can stand for the whole.

Language Specifications

I suggest that you adhere to the following parameters for putting your vision into the most effective words:

- Use the present tense (so the vision isn't perpetually cast off into the far-off future).
- Write as if what you describe were already solidly in place; don't write about what you want, wish, or would like.
- Use positive language (what you're moving toward, not what you're moving away from: don't say, "I don't hang out with negative people" but "I hang out with creative, life-affirming people who make me laugh").
- Use strong, emotive words that evoke feeling great, loving life, thriving. Be in love with the words you use—keep tweaking them if they feel like someone else's language or in any way hit you wrong as you speak them. Note that because the manifesto is dynamic and impermanent, something may come to sound wrong that sounded right before. Respond to how it feels now and tweak again.

Move Away from the Specific

Leave the text more vague where you don't (and don't need to!) have the specifics worked out. Let the Universe mind the details. For example, you may know for certain that you want to be a teacher but don't need to fixate yet on a third-grade classroom at Belle Sherman elementary school (even if you just applied for that job); leaving it open, you could end up teaching wilderness survival skills to teens. Or if you're teaching now but are open to changing or actively want to change your subject, venue, or student population, then leave the statement broader; this allows life to guide you into some new specific manifestation that you may not be able to dream up right now—something that will surprise and delight you. However, where you have specific details sharply in view, then name them as precisely as you know them. Be clear about where specifics matter to you (and feel good to you!) and where they don't—that is, what's fixed and what's flexible.

Here's an interesting and important application of this concept in the realm of love. If you're using a relationship affirmation when you're married (or otherwise partnered), you may well want to insist on the particular person already in your life. However, if you want an upgrade in your love life, you might use the word *spouse* or *lover* or your generic word of choice instead of your established partner's name. I understand that this is potentially scary or could feel disloyal. The beauty of it, though, is that it leaves you equally open to two possibilities: changing the state of the current relationship so that it more closely matches what you want; or dissolving the current relationship to let in someone new who's better suited to who you are now and who you want to become and are becoming. Never imagine this as harming another. If things reconfigure in your life, anyone else in the equation can also land on their feet somewhere else that's better for them. Your personal manifesto can and should align with the good of all concerned.

Abraham urges people to be less specific *especially* when they're wavering in trust or faltering in the belief that they can have something. The more uncertain you feel, the more it behooves you to stay out of precise forms and details. The idea is that you'll trip yourself up with the stress that the seemingly tricky, unfathomable specifics bring up for you, and you'll basically ward the vision off instead of drawing it in. Whether you believe this or not, why allow any language into your manifesto that sets off a vague or sharp alarm inside you? Better to stay with or come back to the broader vision.

Pan out and remember the ballpark thing you were after all along: living in the cozy, well-lit house in a part of town that feels good—not making sure this specific bid goes through; having a wardrobe that feels and looks great, suited to your body and your sense of style—not purchasing a closetful of expensive threads from Alexander Wang; making the health benefits and joy of organic gardening accessible to more people—not making a grand success of this community garden in Southside. Can you feel in these examples the relief and relaxation that come in when you move from specific to general? When it's hard to believe you can get to where you're going, find a nonspecific version of the thing you're after—the broader vision you're fully able to believe you could attain. Drop the details of what it might look like or how you might get it, and hold that broader vision.

A Side Note for Couples

Let me throw in here that I've had some couples in my clientele create manifestos for a joint vision. This allows two people to get clear about such things as what they're doing together, what they appreciate about their shared life, what they'd like to create that isn't present or sufficiently vital in their world, and what they've always meant to do together that they haven't gotten to—which lack they see as now undermining the health of the relationship and therefore as important to address.

A shared manifesto is a great way for a couple to get on the same page, as the saying goes. It provides them with a way to check in on a deep level while creating the manifesto and leaves them with a document to refer to for further check-ins to stay on track. One couple made the manifesto one of their main tools when they felt they were at a huge turning point in their marriage, equally considering scenarios that could place them on two separate paths and ones that could yield a stronger partnership. The manifesto supported a fruitful process that allowed them to identify the best city to move to and to get the right jobs in place there and go! They report coming closer together as a result.

Emotional Fuel

Napoleon Hill (author of *Think and Grow Rich*, a book that greatly informed my thinking about the personal manifesto) insists that the fuel for bringing things from mind to matter is emotion. A number of teachers emphasize the primacy of feeling it: really want what you want—ardently, passionately, with great conviction. So repeat your manifesto making pictures in your mind as you say the words and, as much as possible, feeling the feelings that would go with having these things in place. When you don't feel it, say it anyway. If the best you can do is find even a single image that makes a tired would-be smile pull just a bit at one corner of your mouth, then in that moment, it's enough. You can even honestly tell yourself and the Universe (which are not separate entities), "Hey, today I'm not feeling it. You hold the reality for me. You hold that place in the Universe where it has already come to be. I'll just repeat the words."

But do look for the feeling. Muster up any fragment of what you want to feel in your life and expand it—even if it's unrelated or has a flimsy connection to what you're actually after (like my fun on the sidewalk greeting Sadie, the flirty neighborhood cat, to start letting in the energy of flirting!). I've heard Abraham explain any number of times that the Universe responds to the meaning and intent of your words, not to the words themselves; so align your feelings with your manifesto recitation. Notice if you're not backing your words with desire and emotion, and consider that you may need to say something different; or look into how you might infuse your vision with more emotional fuel. Imagine it, talk about it, find other people whose experience can inspire you and perhaps render a vague possibility more tangible.

A Note on Sssstttretching

When something you want to bring into your life feels like too much of a stretch, you may want to acknowledge this in a way that doesn't negate your positive statement. You might do this by making a statement about process instead of product. For example, when I first set an intention about public speaking, I had no experience with that whatsoever and little idea of what it could possibly look like or how I might even wade into the shallow end. So after a general statement about public speaking, I added these words: *I'm now actively questing about and getting answers as to what I have to say, where, and to what audience. I let the Universe take care of the details and the* how *and follow guidance in each aspect of the journey.*

I was amazed at how quickly I did get answers. The quest began with just these words, which kept the idea of speaking to groups in my consciousness as an active intention. That's how I caught the moments to talk to the right people about this vision and to follow the inspirations to try out topics, test venues, invite audiences. I asked people to host me in their homes and invite friends; I rented a room set up for that purpose at the public library and put fliers around town to call to the curious; I held a regular drop-in class for a season at a local business that provided a space rent-free to most anyone offering most any program, especially one relevant to new parents (Thank you, Jillian's Drawers!). I kept trying things (even when nobody showed up!) based on any scrap of confirmation I got that I might be on the right path: topics that kept coming up when I sat down with people; folks telling me the good results they were getting in applying what I'd given them; an inner sense of joy and connection when I was speaking even to a tiny crowd—and the crowds and opportunities grew.

Mind you, I was picturing talking to a large roomful of people from the stance of zero experience, and that's what I got. My favorite experiences have been giving those outdoor workshops I've already referred to in the woods of Michigan, plus the sweetest retreats at Light on the Hill in upstate New York, where the great meeting room has a pyramid-shaped skylight way, way overhead, and more window than wall, with a sweeping view of hill and dale. Who would've thought of such gorgeous details?

I haven't put energy into expanding into bigger venues and groups from there (my focus has been on writing), and my manifesto has gotten more general, not more specific, so I'm currently not inviting this actively. I expect I'll do more and bigger public speaking, just because I love it and because it's likely to naturally ensue from what I'm doing now. It also exists as a previously held intention that I haven't nullified just by looking away from it. So I still invite it if that's what's best for me and others, if it wants to come. Should it crescendo for me mentally before it does in actuality, I'll reinfuse specific language on that count into my manifesto and direct more mental energy that way, then start choosing and acting into the renewed intention. From there, either my experience of public speaking will expand or I'll come to the clarity that it wants to fall away, and I'll let it go. That's how this works.

I have a client who, following this idea of writing in a process statement to support the stretch, included these words in his manifesto: *I am now actively searching and getting answers as to what kind of agent/manager is most fitting for my artistic career. I let the Universe take care of the details and the* how; *and I follow guidance in each aspect of the journey as I'm being guided to him.* We were both in awe of the amazing, gifted human being (a *her,* not a *him*) who showed up within six months to fill that role, offering the most solid support from a stance of completely *getting* my client and his body of work and seeing so clearly where and how to place it to be seen by the right sets of eyes. He contacted her following an inspiration while groping toward a number of possibilities (moving toward the vision), and there was nothing subtle about the recognition between the two or about how beautifully their partnership fell into place. (Let me add that a certain boldness and willingness to be told *no* was definitely required in his initial query to her.)

The statements in your manifesto may well seem like outright lies to say in the present tense, but as you continue to repeat them, your entire being gets behind them and calls you and the Universe to action. Synchronicity and signs line up to show you the way and confirm your chosen path, shift important components, or redirect you altogether. It's downright fun!

Again, if the stretch is too great and creates discord inside you; if it leads you to doubt or get cynical; if your mind starts composing lectures to you over what bullshit this all is—get less specific. You might leave out the details in the recitation when you feel that way, or if you keep feeling thrown off, delete them from your current manifesto. The broader articulation will then serve you better to keep you moving without resistance. Keep reading: the next section treats clearing out of the way any beliefs that actually oppose what your manifesto declares you want.

Clearing Out Contradictory Language and Thoughts

If you catch yourself saying or thinking anything, ever, that contradicts this daily recitation of intention, negate it and replace the errant thought with something that actually matches what you're after. It's not that you need to fear that whatever you think or say will come into being (that's such a stressful belief!), but that the more you assert and keep coming back to what you want to create, the better. What you hold and habitually reaffirm will most influence your visioning journey—hence, the power and effectiveness of the manifesto.

One thing you can do when you catch yourself in thinking or reverie that isn't what you want (like envisioning your kid's funeral instead of seeing them make better and better choices that lead to thriving) is to release the vision. Simply say or think, "I release this vision," then use your manifesto statement to affirm what you do want instead, and take some time to picture that. Part of what the manifesto provides for you is ready-at-hand language to assert what you're consciously creating anytime your thoughts or words stray to what you don't want.

Do ferret out any conflicting, undermining beliefs that you could get out of the way using The Work of Byron Katie or some other system. Find where you believe you can't have something, or it's not okay to want it, or you're not capable of getting to this or of sustaining that. Question those thoughts. Get help to believe something else. And you can always keep saying it till you mean it, and gently witness (without judgment) how much you believe it today. You could even put a number to it every once in a while, gauging the movement along the spectrum of belief (e.g., I've mostly been at a drab 3 with imagining a job I actually love, but today it lifted to an optimistic 6). Again, you can also remove something from your manifesto for a while if it feels like you're just giving it lip service, then focus for a time on things that feel better and truer. Seek to reintroduce it when you feel stronger and capable of believing one more impossible thing before breakfast.

Think in Terms of *Now*

Anything that comes to be in your life as you keep using the manifesto (or holding the vision in some other way) is coming to be now, for now. I invite you once again to hold all that comes with a loose grip, allowing it to move out again if it wants to in order to make way for the next, better-fitting reality. People get excited about the job offer and don't tune in to whether or not they actually want to say yes to the job; or they lose track of negotiating details or of making sure none of their nonnegotiables are being violated—because, a job offer! People get excited about the great, sparky chemistry they stir up on a first date and go straight to wanting a relationship that sticks. Better to show up in each new moment for what's actually happening, willing to notice that the evening of great connection has yielded to a week of missed connections and that life has revealed, despite what's truly lovely about the other, that it's truly not a match. Don't project a future from what's happening now. If it looks like things are happening, like the energy's stirring, like the Universe is bringing in concrete real-life options—that's fabulous! Love it, revel in it, have fun with it—but don't latch on; hold loosely this current form that your vision's taking. Right now, for now, just enjoy watching your manifesto come to life. As for the form, it could shift again anytime without notice.

Remember the artist I told about in the section on stretching? That divinely ordered relationship with his agent went south just as suddenly as it came into being, and he was initially a bit in shock—even felt it as a betrayal. But the agent had come for a season and a purpose and, once those were over and done, moved right along. Then, once my artist was able to find the gifts in all that had passed between them, he resolved to carry on representing himself, following his own intuitive guidance—which is what he had wanted to do all along, but he'd taken in an external message that it wasn't possible to navigate the art field without an agent. Anything that happens is happening now, for now. Flow into the next manifestation as it reveals itself. Offer no resistance!

The Power of "I am"

Something resonated for me when I heard Harrison Klein say that "I am" statements tell the Universe what we want to bring to completion. "I am" statements are powerful and rife with creative potency. "I am" is a name of God in some traditions, Judeo-Christian included (Moses asked for the name of God, who answered, "I am that I am"). Just as it's great to create a few consciously chosen "I am" statements to repeat regularly in the manifesto, it's also a very good idea to notice when you carelessly use "I am" in negative ways in daily speech: *I'm exhausted, I'm such a loser, I'm a techno-idiot.* When you catch yourself, rephrase on the spot: *I feel exhausted, I'd like to get better at this, I need more support with technology.* Eventually (keep rephrasing as often as you catch yourself), you can cut out the habit altogether.

Trust and Perseverance

Believe that this manifesto will bring you the right manifestations of what you want—or experiment with trying out that it very well could. Keep it real, keep it alive: amend and rewrite anytime something rings false or feels incomplete. Since you're writing about some things that haven't yet come to be, in a sense it's all false. What you may want to tweak will likely fall under these categories: you come to realize this isn't what you want to create—or you don't want it enough to include in the manifesto; you're being specific where you don't need to be (limiting the outcome and triggering disbelief); your language is still broad where your path has led you to specificity (so follow that, and revise to express it here). Again, the manifesto is dynamic, always a work in progress: keep tweaking as needed.

Further, keep repeating it out loud twice a day every day. I've heard that it takes twenty-eight days for the brain to start believing what you tell it over and over as fact. *The Abundance Book* is structured around a model of forty days to create a change of consciousness. Keep going! Whatever the magic number is, it doesn't take forever; it does take persistence.

Believe that everything that happens to you every day is connected to your intentions and wants to either fulfill your intentions or change them to bring them into alignment with what's truly best for you. I love Tosha Silver's emphasis on divine order. If you like the idea of being guided by the divine into what's right for you, you can always hold your vision—compose and speak your manifesto—from a place of yielding to divine order. It will be crystal clear when you want to change your intentions—life will show you. Keep aiming toward where you think you're going, and life will let you know where you're actually going. Take everything that happens as good news. Value *no* as much as *yes*; value closed and open doors equally: it's all good information to have, directing and redirecting you along your way to manifestation. Act as if you believe the Universe is conspiring in your favor. Experiment! The personal manifesto contains the stuff of a grand experiment.

Consider It a Blessing

Bless yourself with this manifesto you're creating. It has the power—if you imbue it with that power—to change your life. I find that my clients who have the most success with the manifesto make it a point to notice where it's coming to life. They honor and celebrate changes in their lives or even small happenings and moments that align with their manifesto. This helps to keep it alive and increases its momentum.

My client Lindsey wrote me about an event in which she felt like she was watching her manifesto in action. As she was driving to a retreat getaway in a rental car, she lost control on the icy wintry road and landed in a ditch just short of entering a creek. Protected and guided by a friendly Universe, she was fine, and the car seemed undamaged, if temporarily stuck off-road. While the car was taken care of by the insurance systems in place, Lindsey still needed to get herself to the retreat center. She almost called a cab, but all the content in her manifesto about friendship and community was tugging at her, so she called a friend instead, who was happy to drive thirty minutes to pick her up and get her to where she was going. Because the accident prevented her from driving, the rental agency took a day off the price of her trip, supporting her in an ever-improving relationship with her finances, as per the money statement in her manifesto. "I feel like a kid who believes in magic," she wrote. "I think the manifesto helps me focus on things that are already in my life and then they expand further. I am definitely full of gratitude."

The Manifesto Blueprints

In what follows, I provide blueprints to create two possible kinds of manifestos. The first is the basic, all-purpose blueprint, while the second takes its structure from Florence Scovel Shinn's concept of the Four Squares of Life, the four areas in which she believed we're meant to thrive: health, wealth, love, and perfect self-expression (See *The Game of Life and How to Play It*).

I offer the blueprints with examples and explanations, then follow each with a template that simply lays out the categories (headings in place, with the examples deleted). When your manifesto is done, you'll take all scaffolding out so that only your words remain declaring your beautiful vision. Note that, while you may have a preference for one blueprint or the other, you could still draw on aspects of or examples from each.

You may also depart from them entirely with a gorgeously idiosyncratic concept that comes to you. (I'd love to hear about what you do!) Make it personal. If you're a planning type, you could even include a plan of action if you like—but mind the specificity; keep it at the appropriate level for where you are in the journey. More than anything, make sure you love your manifesto. The language and content of your manifesto should sing to you.

Onward to the blueprints!

BASIC MANIFESTO BLUEPRINT
(with examples and explanations)

Write an overarching statement of what you're creating in the realms of life you wish to emphasize. You may wish to include something about your stance toward life or Higher Power.

I, [Name], thrive in my beautiful balanced life. I enjoy a loving, connected family life, including time to focus on a love relationship with my spouse. I have lucrative work that I'm passionate about, I enjoy vibrant good health, and I have time for social justice work and political pursuits [or creative expression and spiritual growth, or environmental work and time in nature or ...]. I trust that the Universe always guides, protects, and supports me in my total well-being.

Add specific statements of what your thriving will look like in each life realm you wish to expound on.

[Use as many bullet points or paragraphs as you wish in order to lay out more details about each category. Be sure not to put in more than you're willing to repeat at least once a day every day. You may want to include statements only for the categories you're currently most focused on creating or recreating, or you may opt to have more text for those. For some aspects of life, all you need to say may be contained in the overarching statement above. My first manifesto had a long series of bullet points related to work matters, a shorter but notable list for love relationship, and brief, succinct statements for children, health, friendships/community, and my stance toward life.]

⊙ *With my children, I practice loving what is. I practice pausing instead of reacting. When something seems to be wrong with them, I look at what I could do differently. I ask them questions and listen to them. We laugh together and prioritize fun.*

⊙ *I have fun and satisfying group and one-on-one time with my spouse. Together, we cultivate humor, passion, adventure, and also honoring the beauty and joy in the mundane aspects of everyday life.*

⊙ *I now bring in $[number] over the course of the year. In return for this, I offer my best work advising college students in their academic thriving and career planning, and compassionately assisting them in their overall well-being.* [Note that Napoleon Hill writes in terms of naming dollar amounts to be collected over time. I personally leave out numbers, but many teachers are enamored of getting specific with amounts. Go with what you feel drawn to, and drop the numbers if they evoke a stress response.]

⊙ *I thrive physically, feeling graceful, strong, and confident in my body. I am youthful and well-rested.* [If you'd like an affirmation for a specific health issue, check out Louise Hay's *You Can Heal Your Life*. There, she correlates any number of ailments and diseases (and even body parts) with negative thought patterns, and gives a countering healing thought or affirmation to cultivate instead. I've found that when people go to this resource not treating it as definitive truth but simply following what resonates, they tend to locate something to contemplate; they see new possibilities to open to. You may want to look up her suggested affirmation for any ongoing or recurring condition or a physical weakness of yours and see if it inspires some phrasing to point you toward healing and wellness. The worth of including such statements here is to keep you from writing a negative statement about not having a certain ailment, or even from giving it focus as a problem by stating it's improving.]

⊙ *I, [Name], trust that I am being guided to the perfect work and perfect life. I feel harmonious, happy, inspired, and productive, and in turn I inspire those around me. I trust my intuition and am getting better and better at swift decision making. All the paths I've ever gone down have been worthwhile, and it only gets better as I keep choosing from the heart.* [I sent this statement to a client who had a long-held belief that she couldn't choose a particular career path and would forever flounder trying and discarding one option after another. You can use this sort of statement to counteract anything you've been learning about how you view life and move through it. Noticing how untrusting you are? Declare trust. Taking in that you act like you're moving through life all alone and separate? Declare connection to self, Source, and others. Just realized you don't believe you can ever get out of old stories and patterns? Declare new possibility, a belief in healing and transformation, a connection to guidance. And so on …]

Create a statement of your plan for sharing your money.
I give away X percent of my income to liberal political causes, to environmental causes, to groups that help people (especially women) across the globe, and to individuals.

[Note that Victor Boc, in *How to Solve All Your Money Problems Forever*, advocates choosing a percentage between 1 and 5. The accepted notion of a 10 percent tithe from the Judeo-Christian tradition is optional—unless it has some particular meaning for you. But the concept of giving away a cut of your income is presented by most teachers as nonnegotiable. Give with joy. Give as proof of your own expanding financial freedom: you have so much to spare you give it away! And you so appreciate all you've been given that you want to give back.]

Make a list of "I am" statements.
[An alternative to a separate section of "I am" statements is to use this phrase liberally in the statements above—and you can certainly do both.]

- *I am successful in my business.*
- *I am a great mama.*
- *I am full of life in body and soul.*
- *I am equanimity.*
- *I am love and joy and well-being.*

Add a closing statement calling forth your vision.
I live in awe and appreciation of my life. I keep stepping into what feels better and more true to who I am. I now call this vision into being—this or something better for the good of all concerned. So it is. [If you want to get Tosha Silveresque about it, you can add "in alignment with divine order" instead of or in addition to "for the good of all concerned."]

BASIC MANIFESTO BLUEPRINT
(just the scaffolding)

Write an overarching statement of what you're creating in the realms of life you wish to emphasize. You may wish to include something about your stance toward life or Higher Power.

Add specific statements of what your thriving will look like in each life realm you wish to expound on.

Create a statement of your plan for sharing your money.

Make a list of "I am" statements.

Add a closing statement calling forth your vision.

FOUR SQUARES OF LIFE MANIFESTO BLUEPRINT
(with examples and explanations)

Write an overarching statement of your stance toward life, or how you move through life.
I, [Name], live with my loved ones in safe, peaceful, beautiful places in a Universe conspiring in my favor. I am at peace and provide a peaceful presence for others. I live connected to self, Source, and others, in an effortless circle of giving and receiving.

Make a general declaration of your thriving in the Four Squares of Life (Health, Wealth, Love, and Perfect Self-Expression, in any order).
I thrive in all aspects of life: health, wealth, love, and perfect self-expression. I am deeply fulfilled as a lover/partner, entrepreneur, creator, Earth steward, friend to animals, human being in a healthy body, contributing member of my community.

Create at least four sentences or paragraphs, expounding in turn on each of the Four Squares of Life.

⊙ **Health:** *I am healthy and whole. I eat the optimum diet and exercise as a way of life, choosing biking and walking over driving.*

⊙ **Wealth:** *I, [Name], have a perfect work, in a perfect way; I give a perfect service, for perfect pay. More money comes in than goes out.* [The first sentence comes from Florence Scovel Shinn, who had a thing for rhyming affirmations because they're easy to remember and roll off the tongue!]

⊙ **Love:** *I thrive in a mutually beneficial relationship with my spouse. The communication lines are open and we have space to move together and apart, creating home together and venturing out into the world individually and as a couple. I hold a daily awareness of loving and appreciating this adorable being and give myself the care and honoring I need to be available to love well. We both mind the fires of romance and passion. In all realms of life, I connect to kindred spirits in friendship, goodwill, and good humor. I am at peace with all sentient beings I encounter.*

⊙ **Pefect Self-expression:** *I thrive in my feng-shui practice, entering homes of all kinds that welcome me, and leaving them with increased energy flow and greater beauty. I inspire confidence and put others at ease. I love my diverse clientele and enjoy offering services with a number of price points, including high-impact free programming. I have a genius for color, texture, spaciousness, and flow.*

Create a general closing statement to capture anything left unsaid or to reiterate something important.

My home, my work, my relationships—my entire world is a colorful place of peace and beauty that I move through lovingly, joyfully, competently, creatively. I reach effortlessly for the right supports, solutions, and choices in the moment.

Create a statement to call your vision into being.

I embrace my manifesto and its colorful vision of peace and clarity that I live into every day. I now call it into being in dynamic alignment with divine flow—this or something better for the good of all concerned. So it is.

FOUR SQUARES OF LIFE MANIFESTO BLUEPRINT
(just the scaffolding)

Write an overarching statement of your stance toward life, or how you move through life.

Make a general declaration of your thriving in the Four Squares of Life (Health, Wealth, Love, and Perfect Self-Expression, in any order).

Create at least four sentences or paragraphs, expounding in turn on each of the Four Squares of Life.

Create a general closing statement to capture anything left unsaid or to reiterate something important.

Create a statement to call your vision into being.

My Own Personal Manifesto
What follows is my personal manifesto as it stood entering the summer of 2016. It's an exercise in pure bold vulnerability to print this here in black-and-white. It simply occurred to me that this is the most powerful way I can make the idea of the manifesto accessible to readers.

My manifesto changes periodically. The first one I created, in 2009, followed the format of the basic manifesto blueprint, the first one presented above, and contained twenty-two bullet points and any number of details. As these particulars came to be in my life, or as I found that I didn't hold to them anymore, I dropped them. I do believe it was helpful to include more details about my business when I was just beginning to build it and to understand what it meant to me to be a life coach. Specifics seemed useful, too, where I had little clue what I was doing in a number of things related to finding myself single in my mid-forties—single-mothering, being self-sufficient financially, considering what dating and repartnering might mean. But over time, I dropped specifics more and more as I went, until I came to the form and content below, which is probably an amalgam of the two versions offered here as blueprints.

Note that I used a non-rhyming synthesis of Florence Scovel Shinn's affirmation in the phrase "I have the perfect work with the perfect pay." Following a statement of guidance, I also adopted her words "I make right decisions quickly" (already mentioned in the chapter "Accessing Guidance in the Moment"). Again, emphasis on alignment with divine order, represented twice in my manifesto, comes from Tosha Silver.

Finally, let me add that I dropped any reference to partnering or dating when a crisis in my family brought me to the awareness I was healing something bigger than I'd realized. I noticed inner discord every time I came to intentions around love relationship in my manifesto recitation, so I dropped the whole thing. Love, in all its forms, is all over my manifesto, and welcome in every corner of my life. At some point, I let the romantic thing in through a side door by introducing words about my relationship skills and the qualities I know myself to have that simply convey in terms I can believe that I'm actually a good candidate for repartnering—while still leaving off anything about an unknown other.

As will be true of every manifesto, however you choose to set it up, mine has all the scaffolding removed so that what remains is my expression of what I envision in any realm of life I've covered. Here's my manifesto:

I, Jaya, am deeply connected, and I live in alignment with divine order. I am guided. I follow inspiration and guidance. I follow magic and synchronicity. I make right decisions quickly.

I meet all that happens—I am willing. I meet every face as the face of God.

I, Jaya, love my life. I open into new possibility every day. I move through life with confidence, joy, and gratitude, watching all things come to me effortlessly. I am love, I am light. I live the prayer How can I serve?

I, Jaya, thrive in the four squares of life: health, wealth, love, and perfect self-expression.

I am a healer. My healing influence extends to my kids, to my self, and to all I encounter. I support my kids in being fully themselves and in living in connection and thriving. I point them inward to their own guidance systems.

I have the perfect work with the perfect pay. I have all the support I need to get my work out to those who benefit from it. I am a channel for love, light, healing, laughter, beauty, wisdom.

I know what to do. I have all the time I need to do all I need to do. I do all that I do with excellence. I'm always as prepared as I need to be.

I, Jaya, live free and clear financially—clear with individuals, institutions, and governments. Everything is paid for. I share my resources with others, including for the care of the Earth and her marvelous creatures.

I live free and clear with all beings in every way. I live in a state of ongoing and lavish forgiveness, including toward myself. I offer my gifts and benefit consciously from the gifts of others, with appreciation. I am connected in community.

I, Jaya, am good at relationship. I am loving and tender and passionate. I communicate well. I share space well. I'm good at life. I'm open to adventure. I daily cultivate beginner's mind. I am funny and fun. I appreciate the humor, wisdom, and gifts of others. I'm good at adoring those I love, at finding them adorable.

I am at ease in a body in balance. My body wants only to course-correct toward alignment and well-being. I take excellent care of my body and am in the care of gifted healers.

I'm so grateful for the peace and personal power I've come to know and the healing I've done. I take it all further and deeper. It's a privilege in turn to guide others in their healing and growth processes and to be part of the healing of the Earth and of keeping her waters clean.

I love my manifesto. I stand in it, I live it. I align it with divine order. I now call it into being—this or something better for the good of all concerned. So it is.

Invitation

In working with clients on the manifesto, I've found that it tends to challenge people. Let me remind you that this is just a tool, and it's not required for you to have a good life or even to keep scooching into more of what you want. The thing is, it's an excellent tool. One of the reasons it's a challenge is that it requires the flimsy mind to do daily calisthenics with constant repetition of unpracticed thoughts, certainly thoughts counter to those you've religiously repeated unconsciously and feel okay with just because they're familiar, even though they cause suffering and point you in the wrong direction. The manifesto requires you to look again every day at what you actually want and nudges you to take note of whether you're headed that way or not. It may actively bring up your fears and disappointments in yourself, in others, in life itself. Remember, all of this comes up to clear out—not to show you what you're stuck with. Mind the pain body and tend the mind whenever such things are activated.

Staying with this could actually change your life. It could build a self-trust and a sense of your own marvelous reliability and perseverance. Besides being a (great) way to hold a vision, it promotes all kinds of movement toward the vision. I invite you to try it. If you don't want to, or if you do for a while then decide to drop it, there's no problem. In that case, I invite you to find a clear way that works for you to hold any vision you want to cultivate. I invite you, even in casual conversation, to use the right language to cultivate that vision and to support its expression in your daily life.

chapter 37

Two Scooching Stories in Visioning and Creating

Yvonne: From tedium to FUN

My client Yvonne came to me for reasons that had nothing to do with career and ended up discovering, as she moved toward better honoring herself in every way, that she had no desire to stay with the tedious technical work she was doing, most of which happened in the company of her computer. She was bored and frustrated, and her many skills, talents, and passions weren't even beginning to be included and addressed in the many hours of each day she gave to her job. She had all kinds of reasons to stay with it—related to how far she'd gone down a certain track, the amount of money she'd gotten to in salary, the retirement plan that would be juiciest if she stayed put, and so on. None of these reasons addressed the care of her soul, her joy, her feeling fulfilled, reaching her potential, or offering her highest service to the world.

So after questioning her thinking about what constitutes being responsible with finances, she decided to explore radical possibilities. She made a sprawling list cataloguing the ingredients and ended up being kind of amazed by what lay before her. She was fascinated by seeing this collection as an ingredients list: what *could* be cooked up from all of these cherished, particular components?

Here's her brilliant and beautiful list that reveals numerous facets of her being—a far cry from the resume she might write after a history of IT work, which might at best include a brief, globalized mention of environmentally oriented community projects she's been a part of, probably tossed in at the end. How about this instead:

Passions/Naturally drawn to
- Natural beauty
- Wild critters
- Environmental concerns
- Green technology

- Innovation (already regularly support other people's efforts to help bring about positive change)
- Sustainability
- Finding/researching ways to repurpose items
- Spiritual dimensions—not religious rhetoric, but New-Agey answers to questions
- Puzzles (actual, or some problem-solving component)

Considered careers
- Paleontologist
- Nun, priest, or spiritual director
- Artist, art therapist
- Environmental engineer (or something in recycling)
- Anger management
- Psychologist
- CAD operator, animator
- Songwriter
- Graphologist
- Animal communicator
- Bike messenger business
- Poet
- Editor, journalist
- Veterinarian
- Librarian

Things I've tried
- Clerk, secretary
- Research demographic analyst
- Post-consumer artist
- Newsletter editor
- Programmer
- Rebirther
- Writing for a blog

Training/Education
- BA (magna cum laude) in History/Humanities from small liberal arts college in Detroit

- Additional coursework in computer programming
- Toastmasters International (most enjoyed mentoring others)
- Rebirther training
- Started shamanic training
- Master composter
- Nature photography workshops
- Sea kayaking symposium

Self-taught skills/Hobbies
- Photoshop
- Woodworking
- Graphology (handwriting analysis)
- Pyrography (decorating wood with burn marks)
- Herbal medicine as need arises
- Home renovation (painting, drywall and framing, minor plumbing and electrical, tilework, etc.)
- Computer-related skills: Oracle database administrator, data-enabled website programming (C# ASP.NET object-oriented programming using VS 2008, AJAX, JavaScript, Classic ASP, PHP, CSS, XML, DHTML), image manipulation, Visual Basic 6.0, and Visual Basic for Applications (MS Access 97 and 2003)
- Kayaking—enjoy beauty, solitude, sneaking up on nature
- Cooking, baking—drawn to figuring out dietary challenges (gluten-free, vegan, fruit-sweetened, etc.)
- Gardening with native plants
- Needle arts (knitting, embroidery, etc.)
- Wilderness foraging
- Cycling—living without a car (own ELF tricycle, solar- and pedal-powered)
- Yoga

Honors/Achievements
- Distinguished Toastmaster award
- Volunteer of the Year (four-way tie) for Mid-Michigan Environmental Action Council, 2012
- Recognized by the City of Lansing in 2007 for organizing

the Drawdown Cleanup
- Co-founded a "Green Team" in the Grand Tower that became a model for other buildings around the state
- Member, Red Cedar Friends Quaker Meeting (two-time Publications Editor, Convenor for Nominating Committee, Meeting Librarian)
- Editor-in-Chief and photographer for Marygrove College's *Mg News* (restarted publication)
- Initiator/coordinator of the annual talent show (scholarship fundraiser) 1983-1987, Marygrove College
- Chorale European Tour participant
- Jorge Castellanos Award (annual award for historical research, Marygrove College)
- National Dean's List, Marygrove College
- President's List, Lansing Community College
- Who's Who Among Students in American Universities & Colleges
- Distinguished Student Award
- Saint Catherine Medal (Christian leadership)
- DAR Good Citizen Award
- Century III Leaders Award
- Top 10 in college and high-school graduating classes
- Civil Air Patrol Cadet of the Year and Certificate of Appreciation recipient

Recent volunteer gigs
- Photography stints
- Stream monitoring (dislike that they kill water bugs to assess river health)
- Collating for League of Michigan Bicyclists
- Staffed booth selling calendars to raise funds to help kids heal from sexual assault
- Assisted local environmental group with Bicycle Valet Parking
- Administer several Facebook groups
- Kayaker for Adopt a River cleanup and flag setting between dragon boat races

Where I thrive
- Quieter environments
- Less-pressured situations, but with a mental component to the work
- Do well with critters
- Some creative element to task at hand
- Solo, one-on-one, or small groups (or way to tune out others)
- Better with 8-year-olds if kids are involved
- Folks who are more open-minded (folk or peace groups, artists, yoga studios, New-Age stores; Native American, Quaker, UU, or Buddhist groups)
- Happiest I can ever remember being is just after dumpster-diving and finding everything I needed (to make a shield for a spiritual workshop but just couldn't bring myself to use the leather provided)

What others say I'm good at
- Told I was a great mentor in Toastmasters
- Told I'm a good listener
- Described as a "calming presence"
- Organizing
- Photography

Ideal Work Conditions
- I want to make a difference (preferably for a local environmental or community group)
- Work at or create an environmentally sustainable business
- Job needs to have a creative component
- Nothing with tedium
- Something with spirit/depth
- Quiet environment
- Less-pressured situations, but with a mental component to the work
- Solo, one-on-one, or small groups (or ability to tune out others)
- Enough money to support myself and set something aside
- Working from home preferred
- Possibility of passive income so I can pursue other interests
- Natural beauty, wild critters, environmental concerns
- Innovation (already regularly support other people's efforts to help bring about positive change)

- Green technology, sustainability, reuse ideas
- Spiritual dimensions—not religious rhetoric, but New-Agey answers to questions
- Puzzles (actual, or some problem-solving component)

Note that Yvonne didn't isolate nonnegotiables, but when she did the last category on ideal work conditions, she repeated some prior list items, thus emphasizing what she held most dear.

Taking my instruction to ponder the list, or simply hold it in her awareness, Yvonne put her Quaker spin on it, watching for a "leading" as she listened and sensed for where it would take her. What came to her was the possibility of becoming a courier using her existing utility bicycle (yep, she just happened to have on hand a big, bad bike able to carry some 40 pounds in each super-sized pannier, with room for more on the rack above). Her mind flashed ahead to a crew of women, perhaps mostly in her age range so that she could employ and empower females in their forties and fifties (while inspiring all concerned and inviting younger women to a better view of aging).

As she contemplated and researched this possibility, it was clear that the clientele it would attract in her city, Lansing, Michigan, would consist mostly of politicians and attorneys (not a population she was drawn to serve and interact with). Further, the work would be fast-paced in a way that evoked stress for her. Since a good rule of thumb in decoding guidance is to perceive expansions, joy, and relief as on-course feedback from the Universe, while taking contractions, heaviness, and feelings of stress as the cue to move away from something—Yvonne was leaning toward *no*. In terms of logistics, imagining a small battery of couriers in her care, she also got concerned from cautions coming her way about liability and the attendant insurance costs. She did some research—a step toward the vision—to get more information on that. In the final analysis, the courier bicycle idea was pretty appealing—definitely contained a good number of her ingredients—but it wasn't yet the right thing. She stayed open.

Let me remind you again that once you've set an intention, the Universe will either send whatever resources and supports you need to bring it into being, or redirect you to the right intention. When Yvonne and I started working together, but before we got into this career-shifting process, I had directed her, too, to Tosha Silver's *Outrageous Openness*. (I routinely recommend this book to my clients. If you've gotten this far in mine, you'll devour Tosha's.) Yvonne referred back to it often during this process to keep in view that she wasn't toiling all alone trying to figure it all out.

Not a week went by after her exploring and rejecting the courier idea before some dude posted a link on Yvonne's Facebook wall with the "top 10 bicycle ideas of 2013." For some reason, he flagged #9 on the list: "More than 50% of city freight could shift from truck to bike." May I just gleefully throw in that this guy had no idea what Yvonne was currently up to? He simply knew about her love of biking and shared what he thought might be of passing interest!

Through this, she learned that a company called B-line (with the tagline "Sustainable Urban Delivery") out of Portland, Oregon, had already created her dream business—or at least a business that instantly captured her fancy and seemed made of the very ingredients laid out in her list. This enterprise tweaked her idea from courier to cargo and from bicycle to tricycle (larger, sturdier vehicles fueled by a combination of electricity and pedal-power—and she already owned an ELF!). These simple shifts opened a door to a very different clientele—anyone who had anything that needed transporting within greater Lansing. Yvonne later wrote, "It was like some cosmic comic-strip light bulb went off over my head."

Asking for guidance, she put in a request to the Universe for someone with business savvy to show up, since she wasn't yet convinced she was the sort to start a business. A few days later, someone sat next to her at a New Year's Eve party and dropped an innocent "What do you do?"—which led Yvonne to describe what she was thinking about doing and this stranger to deliver a bunch of priceless advice.

Two days later, she found herself playing with business names. This felt important to her. (At every turn, every step of the way, Yvonne kept moving to each new thing that got her attention as the next priority, whether it came up from inside her or appeared as a directive from the outside that resonated within. In short, she kept following her guidance system as she moved toward the vision.) She set the following criteria for the right name: it would be "memorable, something folks could rally behind"; it would "convey a bit about the business, and be available on the internet and through the State of Michigan business listing."

It took her three weeks to land on Go Green Trikes. She wrote me about it in an e-mail:

When I started thinking about what name might sell itself, it became obvious. MSU is the main university in these parts, and their school colors are green and white. Go Green Trikes will both show that it's a local business and hint at its zero-carbon philosophy. I am keeping the symbol [from her first logo, created with the last name she considered], just swapping out the words. Jaya, if this takes off like my mind now hints it can, it probably won't be a co-op. [Setting up the business as a cooperative was just one early idea among the many she toyed with.] But if I can employ students to do the bulk of the riding and office help, too, then I and my personal trike can go do the community-building runs that would most speak to me. [At this point Yvonne had some exciting ideas about how her business could serve the community—for example, delivering leftover foods from restaurants to the area food pantries and charitable kitchens.]

It was kind of amazing to watch this woman in action, supported by the friendly Universe that kept sending the right resources, allies, and opportunities her way. One domain purchase plus another week later, she happened to learn from *Capital Gains* ("an online magazine and website showcasing the growth and investments transforming the Lansing region") that its monthly competition for new business ideas called "the Hatching" was set for that evening. That evening! She felt compelled to dive in and send them her pitch—figuring she had a chance at next month's round. One of the organizers instantly contacted her to say that a spot was hers that very night if she could send them a Power Point within the hour. Guess where Yvonne was that night? Guess who won both the "glory vote" (audience pick for best idea) and the cash prize of $1000 plus legal help to form into an LLC (limited liability company)?

All along the way, I kept thinking Yvonne was the poster child for the visioning ideas I walk my clients through. She applied them fearlessly and to the hilt. It's not that doubts and worries didn't come up for her. She would get temporarily discouraged. But she kept following my directives to question her negative thoughts and to tap into an idea of the friendly

332

Universe supporting her unfailingly, whether she could see evidence of this or not, whether things were happening to her liking or not. When she felt she was losing track of the joy in her project, she came up with the acronym FUN for Friendly Universe Network. I'm not sure that she had more fun than I did watching her vague initial idea of more fulfilling work come to fruition in the gorgeously specific form that is now Go Green Trikes cargo delivery service. And the fun isn't over. (Look Yvonne up online at gogreentrikes-dot-com!)

Ian: Starting with low-level commitment

Ian was younger than my typical clients, though I've had the privilege (and pure delight) of working with other twenty-somethings. My work with him covered a number of topics from various realms of life—whatever was up at any given moment. From the start, though, we launched a process to help him clarify where to put his energies in terms of career. A visual artist, he had a perfectly practical degree in design but had done relatively little income-producing work in the field since graduating. He'd taken a few easy-to-come-by jobs on a contract basis and had so far avoided a 9-to-5 situation in an office (the thought of which made him want to rip off his clothes and go run with the wolves). An avid mountaineer and snow-boarder, a musician, an ecologist and environmentalist—Ian was seriously worried about spending his life as a Jack of all trades, leaving him in both proverbial and practical terms master of none. Ah, but he was no less concerned about feeling hopelessly trapped if he buckled down and chose a single pursuit. Which would that be? At what cost?

I was fascinated and gained a new understanding of the Six personality type when I heard Russ Hudson of the Enneagram Institute describe its deep existential fear of choosing badly: *What if I go down the wrong path and end up living with unrelenting regret?* That was Ian all over. He stood frozen in his beautiful mountain town, on the precipice of any number of possibilities, gazing uncomfortably at his vast potential.

During the summers of his childhood, Ian had returned year after year to an outdoor-adventure camp that gave him great joy. For a long time, he had dreamed of returning there as a counselor, both to experience it from the other side and to give back in a way he'd been so richly given to. So far he'd never made it. There were several reasons for this: he was bad at organizing himself and planning ahead; he had some fear of being responsible for the well-being (the very lives!) of younger kids; and he dreaded making commitments of most any kind. What if he got the job, then his buddies ended up performing all summer in the best gigs ever? Why would he leave the music scene during the longest days of the year—and the happiest nights?

The first year I worked with Ian, as summer came and went, the camp decision made itself through his unwillingness to decide or (a prior step) to even explore the options. The following spring, as we looked at the reality that not much had happened in the career realm (and he was toying with a new idea in yet another direction, kind of the way a bored cat flicks its tail around), I challenged him to apply for a camp counselor position.

There were so many good reasons to go this route. For starters, he'd be fulfilling a long-held dream, so that would allow him to feel he was showing up for himself and giving himself actual experiences he wanted. Quite simply, it would feel like *something was happening*. Because he'd be successfully completing a paid venture from start to finish, he would gain some self-esteem—confidence established for the next wave of job seeking. And the chances he'd complete it (barely three months to hang in there!) were high. He also just plain loved the camp thing, so it would be fun and fulfilling. He had the profile (athletic build, killer good looks, an easy, genuine smile, great sense of humor, guitar in hand) that made him an obvious shoe-in for gaining devoted adoration from younger guys. And as the terror of adhering long-term to a single path was (so far) perpetually in Ian's way in the job search, it seemed wise for him to answer to this thing that asked for such a low-level commitment (come on, three months!).

The process of getting himself to camp was an exercise in building self-trust all along the way. Ian was easily overwhelmed by thinking of the whole process to get through, so I emphasized a one-step-at-a-time approach: just do the one thing you see to do, the thing that next makes sense. For starters, get information about programs. Contact the camp you already know and love! Use good ole Google search to find what else looks good. Go for what you already know you enjoy: snow-boarding, survival skills in the mountains, anything sports-related.

It didn't take much checking-out-the-scene for Ian to learn he'd be a better candidate with EMT training. This happened to be something else he'd been curious about for some time. The thing that most got in his way with this one was fearing he'd be forced to use these skills if he had them—and what if he messed up? Could this cost someone's life? We looked at the fact it could, in fact, save someone's life. We looked at the reality of failed rescue ventures despite the best efforts—no reason not to have skills in place and do one's best in the moment; there was so much to gain among all there was to lose. Ian also acknowledged he wasn't obligated to get a camp job or even tell them about his EMT training if he got it, so he decided to go for it. It was another step to take in building self-trust and teaching himself he could make something important to him happen in a relatively short period of time. He found a ten-day program happening soon in a nearby town. He signed up, showed up, loved every minute of it. When he was done, he wanted the next tier of training!

Getting a position was a breeze. He ended up at a noncompetitive day camp located in the mountains, serving as head of mountain-boarding (well-known territory) and ropes-course instructor (a stretch). The obstacle course he learned to run turned out to be a highlight, something Ian looked forward to daily. It reminded him how much he loved the position of mentor, how well he embodied it, and how deeply he was moved not only by what he got to watch his charges learn about themselves, but also by the fact that he had a hand in that learning.

One noteworthy aspect of the camp adventure was that Ian organized and played in a musical fundraiser that took place at the summer's end. Besides getting to play music and join in the camaraderie of the band (which he can't get enough of, excellent extrovert that he is), he also created a well-received tee-shirt design, with a matching poster to promote the gig. The concert itself was actually free, so that the sales of the shirts constituted the sole (and a successful!) money-maker.

Here it is again, and I don't tire of pointing out how this so elegantly works: the Universe loves to place people where any number of their interests, talents, and skills intersect in the most unexpected ways. I thought Ian was getting a great summer experience trading one of his skills for money, thus gradually easing himself into a taste for meaningful, income-producing work in which he could succeed. Instead, he got that, yes, and he also got to mountainboard, teach, mentor, play music, craft a design (seriously, a design opportunity smack in the middle of summer-camp life?!), gain and use EMT skills, and then some. He also built some of the self-trust and confidence we were after. The experience couldn't have been more successful.

Come wintertime, Ian was again frustrated with a sense of not moving forward into so-called serious work. This did leave the door open for adventure, however, as was crystal clear when we had a session prior to his nearly three-week trip to Costa Rica. He was musing about how to set clear intentions for what to do during his trip, and I reminded him that the search he'd been on in his real life could carry on—perhaps even be heightened—in vacation land. It likely wouldn't be the time to research or apply for jobs, but he could certainly invite and have experiences that would reveal more about how he moved through the world and where he might best place himself.

At the tail-end of that pre–Costa Rica session, Ian suddenly remembered to fill me in on two design jobs that he'd completed since our last conversation (the only two he'd taken on since that summertime success). One of them, the easier one that he'd originally felt better about, involved designing a logo for a small business. The job had yielded a beautiful product, and he'd moved through the process smoothly but with little overall joy. The other, still in progress, was giving him any amount of frustration and kicking up all kinds of resistance and fear—yet he was somehow experiencing it as super satisfying.

That second job involved creating an album cover for a band. It was tough trying to please seven different personalities who'd commissioned him for the job. Ian felt pressure to create an excellent product because these guys were friends of his. They liked his style—and that cool tee-shirt that he'd brought back from summer camp evoked some kind of promise they could count on something good. Performance anxiety slowed him down. At some point, the drummer told him to quit sweating it and just "do Ian"—which is precisely what I'd told him. I had to whack him with my golden flyswatter over this point (across 1,000 miles—no bruises, no lawsuits), because he almost missed that this directive was coming in from different angles. (Little does it matter which face of God gets through loudest and clearest; do take in when a message is repeating!)

He then described to me this lovely, idiosyncratic process he got involved with to get the photo he wanted for the design. How could I not love that it meant going into the woods at sunrise to capture by Polaroid, in just the right light, a photo stuck to a tree? More important, how could he not love that? No small wonder this was the design job that felt better in the long run.

Do I also need to point out this one involved music—more specifically, guys in a band? I did need to point it out to Ian. There's nothing particularly dense about him (the guy's smart). In general, people fail to connect the dots in this way, because nothing in our culture teaches us to watch for the marvelous ways all the part of a life fit together. We compartmentalize everything in our thinking, not because the parts of our lives are actually separate (in actuality, a whole life is a whole life), but because it helps us to grasp things or make sense of them when we break them down into parts. This is not a problem in itself: it may simply slow down our understanding of what's happening and how life is assisting us in our journey when we believe the mashed potatoes don't touch the peas. (Life isn't a kid's dinner plate.) We miss the magic of the Universe and the ways life is truly constantly weaving together and giving back to us all aspects of who we are and what we're doing here.

Let me add that Ian almost forgot to tell me about the design jobs because he was so focused on what was happening here and now—namely the adventure in Costa Rica, which he suspected was a distraction from what he ought to be giving his attention to. They were never separate in the first place. Short-term design jobs, quest for long-term career track, trip to Costa Rica: all gorgeous, interconnected terrain where life could reveal to him whatever needed revealing.

In Costa Rica, Ian injured his knee and other things happened to set the stage for breaking up with his girlfriend when they got home. This was as close to a serious relationship as he'd gotten in some time, and here he was breaking it off when it seemed to be on the brink of going deeper. Was this a fear of commitment? He felt that he had chosen very well this time, but still, this woman wasn't who he wanted to be with long-term. The strangeness of the vacation in which he ended up lying on a couch in pain, feeling like he was missing out on adventures in the moment, jolted him into another perspective on his whole life, and a sense that it was time to make choices—clearly, consciously.

The relationship ended about as well as those things can, and he soon got clarity about wanting to move to a nearby city that was larger and offered more of what he wanted. He also knew some guys there he could play music with. As winter shifted to spring, Ian kept mentally revisiting the summer camp of his childhood and wondering if he needed to be a counselor at that specific place in order for the camp story to reach its right conclusion. He contacted the person in charge, already known to him, and was promised a place heading up the rock climbing if he could commit by a certain date. This felt good to Ian. If he didn't find something better in his new city or feel a strong draw to stay there for the summer, he'd say yes to camp by that deadline.

As he explored day camps locally, he got sidetracked checking out design opportunities. Go figure: he had no conscious intention of doing any such thing. What caught his eye and piqued his curiosity was a design internship—three months, unpaid. Where some might balk at a sense of low returns for high output, he saw this as a heap of possibility with low pressure! Here it was again, the Universe offering up an opportunity for him to explore something through a low-level commitment. Working in an office day in and day out for that much time, he could learn a lot about his own work preferences and potential in the field: Would he love it or hate it? Would they like his ideas and execution or find him lacking? Would he feel trapped or well-contained? Would he enjoy the vast creative playing field and the chance to show his stuff there—or feel overwhelmed by all he didn't know and all he habitually experienced as difficult?

When he opened the application, it sparked something almost impish in him. It asked for creative answers to six very open-ended questions unrelated to design. He dashed off whatever came to him, long or short—there was even a one-word answer in the mix (*What makes you so awesome?* Kombucha.) One of his responses used word play and managed to sneak in the way he planned to show up with integrity and do what was needed to get the job done; the rest were pure whimsy. He signed off, "Thanks for the creative release, hopefully we'll be talkin' more." They talked more. Ian said yes to the internship, perhaps permanently letting go of revisiting the camp of his childhood.

Showing up daily at the design firm, Ian felt strongly that he was right where he needed to be. Sometimes you know you're in the right place because there are almost equal measures of thriving and being challenged. He especially loved being mentored. Interesting that he had

338

thrived playing the role of mentor at summer camp the year before, and now he got to experience the gains from the flip side. (Love of the mentor thing needs to have a place on Ian's sprawling list. The guy's got some business with the Mentor archetype!) He noticed early on that things got tricky when he fell into being the seen and comparing himself to others. (You have to be the seen to be in a comparison, as it's about your ranking, not your experience.) He found that if he saw himself in terms of what he didn't know as compared to what others knew, he wanted to hide what he didn't know out of self-preservation. This led to avoiding, concealing, and pretending—in short, loss of power. He described to me a scene in which a slightly younger intern made a presentation in a meeting. He could feel the moment—that switch-being-pulled phenomenon—when he went from being engaged with her ideas and loving them, to suddenly seeing himself in comparative terms (why hadn't he come up with something this good?) and instantly feeling self-conscious and no longer wanting to meet her eyes.

When I told him to cheerfully be an idiot, his relief receiving this counsel was palpable. If he was free to know nothing, to err on the side of revealing too much about what he didn't know, then he was also free to gain knowledge and experience, stay wide-open, be curious about what he could receive during these precious three months. Because the possible outcome of a job offer had been explicitly stated, the end of the internship now loomed with both possibility and pressure. Now the low-level commitment was more clearly a threshold into greater commitment, and he suddenly couldn't imagine not wanting that! I invited him to detach. If they decided he was a total loser or even an ill-fitting team member during his brief internship, that would be good information to have about where he wasn't stopping for the long run. More important, he could learn from his own experience (not their idea of it) what he might next want to gravitate toward in order to secure his rightful place.

This story ends wherever it ends. As I put this book to bed, Ian's in the midst of year one in a full-time job that followed on the heels of the internship, but with a different company. No question he's on a beautiful journey, in a Universe conspiring in his favor. No question that's true for you too.

conclusion

Now What?

Of course it's never all about any one thing, but I've still given way to the temptation to conclude with these words: *It's all about presence.*

I recently attended a workshop that boldly offered the Key to healing, personal growth, and transformation: presence. Ah, but no definition of *presence* was ever stated. There were no tips given for catching yourself out of presence. A bit was said in passing on one aspect of getting present: breathe, ground yourself. More often, participants were simply told to get present. In the instructors' defense, I loved just about everything else about the workshop, whose topic was one facet of the Enneagram, not presence. On the evaluation form, I filled in the blanks with lots of admiring and appreciative feedback, all genuine. I did also mention that I don't think most people have a clue what it means to *get present*.

I suppose plenty of people do have a clue, but I want lots and lots of people—multitudes, masses, the majority—to be able to clearly define and discuss what it means to be present, to get present, to come back to presence. I want this to be common knowledge.

How to define *presence*? If you're present, you're right here, right now—meaning, you're aware of being right here, right now. You're probably not standing with the hedge clippers over the kitchen sink going, "Now why did I bring these in here?" because you were aware of the whole trip and kept track of its purpose. If you're present, you're not in your head, which is likely to take you to some other place and time, past or future, or to the theoretical or imaginary. These things aren't inherently evil by a long stretch, or even problematic, necessarily. It can be quite lovely and purposeful to ponder, to imagine, to time-travel mentally—especially when you step into such things consciously, by choice, instead of sliding in and finding yourself there when you meant to be doing something else, like driving, or listening to your kid tell you about something that matters.

There's something to be said for spending at least some of your time actively cultivating full engagement with being where you are and doing

341

what you're doing, even (or perhaps especially) if it's boring or provides you with no special identity.

Since presence occurs in the here and now, and more important, in your occupying the here and now consciously—it asks that you be embodied. You need to experience yourself in your body to be present. This includes connecting to breath, feet, posture, and senses.

The topic of the breath is all over this book. The work with the pain body discussed in these pages is useful (profoundly so) on so many levels, in part because it connects you to your body—and kind awareness of what's happening in the body right now. It also connects you to breath. When you mind the pain body (awareness and breath, awareness and breath), you're present, and you're embodied.

Add any modicum of grounding to that, and you're doing even better. At its most basic level, grounding involves feeling the bottom of your own feet. Feel where they connect to the ground. If you're seated, notice where your body connects with furniture or floor or earth and, while you're at it, appreciate what supports you. If you want to take it further, you might imagine, even for a moment, that roots are shooting down into the earth through the bottoms of your feet. Mind your connection to planet Earth. You are connected; know that you're connected. If you're playing with looking for all that supports you, this imaginary rooting moment could be a time to thank the Earth, to appreciate the miracle of gravity, how it just won't let you go.

No matter what you're doing—whatever's happening here and now— you can always return to the simple act of watching your breath go in and out (and experience the magic of the unforced expansion when that naturally happens—which is often). Watch your breath go in and out while you're experiencing your connection to your own feet and your feet's connection to the floor or ground that supports you. Notice through repeated practice whether this brings you more solidly into the here and now.

One gift of embodiment is the gorgeous privilege of experiencing consciousness through the five senses. These inherently promote presence when you tune in to them consciously. Ask yourself what you see, feel, hear, taste, smell in this moment. Even posing the question brings you closer to presence. Do stop and smell the roses, and pause a moment under the magnolia tree when it's in bloom (look up into colors and textures on the canvas of blue sky; sniff the air!). Take in the sky at various times of day, in various weathers, in different places; note that its colors and textures are innumerable. Taste your food and notice how much you're chewing it. Chew more. Feel the water on your skin when you're showering or doing dishes. Listen to music; turn it off to hear the rain, to take in the silence. Everyone should shave their head at least once to feel breeze against skull. Don't go to sleep without feeling your body from head to toe, experiencing how mattress and pillows support you, consciously minding your position, bringing consciousness to any muscles you're squeezing as if you must exert effort to lie there. Attune to your sensory experience here and now, again, again, again, now and now and now.

As with everything else, you won't stay in presence. Don't even say you'd like to stay present. Think in terms of getting present, or coming back to presence—not staying present. Catch yourself out of presence and come back. This means noticing you don't know where you are, coming to from a daydream and immediately checking in with what's actually happening here and now, connecting to this reality through the senses. See the colors in the vegetables you're chopping, feel the textures, pressure, and resistance as the knife slices through them. Feel your posture before the computer: locate your shoulders and mentally trace your spine upward, pull your chin back, consciously watch one breath go in and out.

I'm sure I was present the time I got a kindly admonishing call from Ithaca Carshare. I was walking with my daughter along Cayuga Street, laughing at one of her spontaneous stand-up tirades, noticing all the colors in her hair and how the summer sunlight played with this latest mermaid-medley of green, blue, and purple. But the call that came in told me I hadn't been present just moments before, in the harried maneuvering to get the car back on time and parked in its marked spot in front of the Moosewood restaurant (I'm pretty sure some lumbering beast trudges over from the kitchen and pees there to mark the spot). So it seems the person on duty at Carshare received a computer alert that the car I'd just vacated was parked and locked with the motor still running. Distracted, *moi?* Good thing I don't claim to stay present.

Beginner's mind, by the way, is a great support in cultivating presence. In the story I just told, I was watching my mermaid daughter with beginner's mind. It's a game I love to play with my various beloveds: I seek to take in what they look like right now, in detail, as if I'd never seen them

343

before. This is so much more fulfilling than believing I've memorized their faces. You can do this with the route you habitually take to work, various views of your world that you glimpse in a day, the familiar trees and birds, the fragrance of your forever-favorite lotion, the scent of the rice cooking. (My current love is brown Mekong Flower rice from Lotus Foods—crazy-fragrant!) Don't simply know *in theory* any people, places, or things you know: know them now; know your actual sensory experience of them right now.

To conclude, I'd like to briefly speak to what Eckhart Tolle has so wisely named *the power of now*. If you're consciously healing or growing yourself, now is the only time you can do any such thing. You must be present to the moment to invite and experience the healing it contains—or perhaps to respond to the invitation for healing this particular moment extends to you. Returning to the fabulous workshop I attended that (maybe) missed the mark with presence, I have one more gripe, which was the presenters' emphasis on what a looooooooong, slooooooooow process the healing is bound to involve. Wow. My younger self would have paired that concept of slow-going with whatever the workshop revealed to me about all I needed to clean up in myself—and that would've been my next nose-dive into total despair.

If you step out of linear time—which is just a concept and, some say, an illusion—then all you have is *now*. Experientially speaking, that's all you've got anyway. So if, *right now*, you step into your healing; if, *in this moment*, you're consciously course-correcting out of what you caught yourself in and toward what better matches your intention—then, right now, you're healing. No slow-going about it. Drop timelines and go for *now*: Is it happening now? Then it's happening.

That's really as good as it gets. Right now, you're on a lovely journey. Right now, the transformation is underway, and you're fully engaged with it. Anyone else find this more heartening than "This is going to take a long, long time"? And that, again, is what scooching is all about.

This is how you can work with and expand and even master everything contained in these pages: play with presence. Witness the breath; ground yourself with feet on earth; be embodied—feel your body; use and appreciate your marvelous senses. Don't try to stay present—you can't. Have an intention to be present, catch yourself out of presence, and come back to presence: right here, right now. If you feel confused or overwhelmed and can't flip the switch to presence, will you just pause and watch your breath go in and out? Now you're already more present. Is there one more thing you see to do to point yourself roughly in the right direction? Do that thing. Or, in a word, *scooch!*

bibliography

Boc, Victor. *How to Solve All Your Money Problems Forever: Creating a Positive Flow of Money into Your Life.* Third ed. New York: Berkley Publishing, 1996.

Chandler, Steve. *MindShift: The Steve Chandler Success Course.* Anna Maria, Fla.: Stephen Chandler Incorporated. Audio. (This can be downloaded online at stevechandler-dot-com.)

Chopra, Deepak. *Magical Mind, Magical Body: Mastering the Mind/Body Connection for Perfect Health and Total Well-Being.* Chicago: Nightingale-Conant, 1990. Audio.
————. *The Spontaneous Fulfillment of Desire: Harnessing the Infinite Power of Coincidence.* New York: Harmony Books, 2003.

De Beauvoir, Simone. *The Second Sex.* Trans. Constance Borde and Sheila Malovany Chevallier. New York: Vintage Books, 2011.

De Becker, Gavin. *Protecting the Gift: Keeping Children and Teenagers Safe (and Parents Sane).* New York: Dell Publishing, 1999.

Gallagher, B. J., and Steve Ventura. *Yes Lives in the Land of No: A Tale of Triumph over Negativity.* San Francisco: Berrett-Koehler, 2006.

Hay, Louise L. *You Can Heal Your Life.* Carlsbad, CA: Hay House, 1999.

Hicks, Esther, and Jerry Hicks. *Ask and It Is Given: Learning to Manifest Your Desires.* Carlsbad, CA: Hay House, 2004.

Hill, Napoleon. *Think and Grow Rich.* New York: Gildan Media, 2007. Audio.

Katie, Byron, with Stephen Mitchell. *Loving What Is: Four Questions That Can Change Your Life.* New York: Harmony Books, 2002.

————. *A Thousand Names for Joy: Living in Harmony with the Way Things Are*. New York: Harmony Books, 2007.

Kinkade, Amelia. *Straight from the Horse's Mouth: How to Talk to Animals and Get Answers*. Novato, CA: New World Library, 2001.

Michael Port. *Book Yourself Solid: The Fastest, Easiest, and Most Reliable System for Getting More Clients than You Can Handle Even if You Hate Marketing and Selling*. Hoboken, NJ: John Wiley & Sons, 2011.

Price, John Randolph. *The Abundance Book*. Rev. ed. Carlsbad, CA: Hay House, 1996.

Riso, Don Richard and Russ Hudson. *Understanding the Enneagram: The Practical Guide to Personality Types*. Rev. ed. Boston: Houghton Mifflin, 2000.

Ruiz, Don Miguel. *The Four Agreements: A Practical Guide to Personal Freedom*. 15th Anniversary ed. San Rafael, CA: Amber-Allen Publishing, 2012.

Shinn, Florence Scovel. *The Game of Life and How to Play It*. Camarillo, CA: DeVorss Publications, 1979.

Silver, Tosha. *Outrageous Openness: Letting the Divine Take the Lead*. New York: Atria Books, 2014.

Tolle, Eckhart. *The Power of Now*. Novato, CA: New World Library, 1999.

Whetten, Brian. *Yes Yes Hell No: The Little Book for Making Big Decisions*. Woodland Hills, CA: Spiritual Roar Publications, 2014.

Williamson, Marianne. *A Return to Love: Reflections on the Principles of A Course in Miracles*. New York: HarperCollins, 1992.

CPSIA information can be obtained
at www.ICGtesting.com
Printed in the USA
BVHW01s1834040118
504331BV00002B/177/P